T0166908

P.

AND HOW DO YOU FEEL ABOUT THAT?

Aruna Gopakumar is a psychotherapist, a CTA (Certified Transactional Analyst) and an MCC (Master Certified Coach). She is the current president of SAATA (South Asian Association of Transactional Analysts). As a Teaching and Supervising Transactional Analyst, Aruna is engaged in long-term training of aspiring Transactional Analysts. She has a Tedx Talk called 'Psychotherapy, the New Normal' and a psychotherapy supervision podcast called 'The Third Mind'.

She founded Navgati (navgati.in) in 1999. Today, Navgati is a market leader in the design and delivery of high-impact leadership-development interventions. She has an engineering degree from Anna University and an MBA degree from IIM-Bangalore.

Aruna lives in Bangalore with her husband, daughter, son, and two noisy black labradors.

Yashodhara Lal is a bestselling author, coach and therapist. An IIM-Bangalore graduate with almost two decades of corporate experience, she has a Diploma in Transactional Analysis and is certified in Solution Focussed Coaching.

She has a Tedx talk called 'Exploring Multiple Dimensions to Uncover Your Full Potential' and has founded Allsomeness (allsomeness.in), committed to working with people seeking to be the fullest versions of themselves.

A student of Yoga and Vedanta who enjoys music, dance, and fitness, she has published eight books and is always working on some writing project or the other.

Yashodhara lives in Goa, where she moved with her husband and three kids in her quest for a quieter life. Their newly acquired dog, Punter, has thwarted her plan.

Aruna and Yashodhara talk about what really happens in the therapy room on their Instagram page @inthetherapyroom. You can write to them at contactintherapyroom@gmail.com.

ADVANCE PRAISE

'The intrigue of therapy room processes is resolved in this fascinating collection of fifty stories. The blend of contextual narratives and conversations in each story render what actually transpires in the therapy room to the reader with remarkable evocativeness and simplicity.'—Dr Shekhar Seshadri, former Dean, Behavioral Sciences Division and former Director, NIMHANS

'You do not have to be looking for therapy, be in therapy or out of therapy to read this book. Irrespective, at least one adult in every family should read it. Someday or the other, it will make a difference to you. And by the way, I liked reading it. You will like it too.' —Subroto Bagchi, Co-founder, Mindtree

'Dr Oliver Sacks—I was so in awe of his work and his ability to communicate complex concepts using case studies and storytelling! Aruna Gopakumar and Yashodhara Lal follow a somewhat similar approach, recounting their clinical work and, in the process, deconstructing seemingly mystical concepts. They present the many dimensions of the human condition in an engaging manner, making it relatable to all. A must read for all those interested in mental health, life and emotions!'—Vandana Gopikumar, Co-founder, The Banyan & The Banyan Academy of Leadership in Mental Health (BALM)

'Accessible, relatable and informative, Aruna's and Yashodhara's stories illustrate that therapy is for anyone seeking clarity on everyday life—relationships, work and careers, family and more—and not just for those with a clinical diagnosis of a mental health issue. As someone who has been to therapists for years, I hope it will encourage many to seek and discover the many benefits and joys of professional therapy.'—Aparna Piramal Raje, author of *Chemical Khichdi*

And how do you feel about that?

BREAKDOWNS AND **BREAKTHROUGHS** IN THE THERAPY ROOM

ARUNA GOPAKUMAR
YASHODHARA LAL

PENGUIN BOOKS

An imprint of Penguin Random House

PENGUIN BOOKS

USA | Canada | UK | Ireland | Australia
New Zealand | India | South Africa | China

Penguin Books is part of the Penguin Random House group of companies
whose addresses can be found at global.penguinrandomhouse.com

Published by Penguin Random House India Pvt. Ltd
4th Floor, Capital Tower 1, MG Road,
Gurugram 122 002, Haryana, India

Penguin
Random House
India

First published in Penguin Books by Penguin Random House India 2022

Copyright © Yashodhara Lal and Aruna Gopakumar 2022

All rights reserved

10 9 8 7 6 5 4 3 2 1

The views and opinions expressed in this book are the authors' own and the facts
are as reported by them which have been verified to the extent possible, and the
publishers are not in any way liable for the same. Names and characters are either
the product of the authors' imagination or are used fictitiously, and any resemblance
to any actual person, living or dead, events or locales is entirely coincidental.

ISBN 9780143457428

Typeset in Bembo Std by Manipal Technologies Limited, Manipal
Printed at Thomson Press India Ltd, New Delhi

This book is sold subject to the condition that it shall not, by way of trade
or otherwise, be lent, resold, hired out, or otherwise circulated without the
publisher's prior consent in any form of binding or cover other than that in
which it is published and without a similar condition including this condition
being imposed on the subsequent purchaser.

www.penguin.co.in

MIX
Paper
FSC FSC® C010615

To those brave enough to look within

'When children were planning their lives they often followed the plot of a favourite story. The real surprise was that these plans persisted for twenty, forty or eighty years, and that in the long run they generally prevailed over common sense.'

Dr Eric Berne
Creator of Transactional Analysis

Contents

Foreword

What do you imagine happens in the therapy room? Do you picture a client sprawled on the couch talking into the air, and the therapist peering through her glasses, asking on loop, 'And how do you feel about that?' In case it isn't already clear, our use of this phrase as the title for this book is firmly tongue-in-cheek, because therapy is so much more!

TV and cinema have contributed to highly misguided notions of what goes on in the therapy room. Psychotherapists are often portrayed as know-it-alls who magically psych out what is going on with their clients. Or they get involved in ways that are harmful, like falling in love with their clients or shaming the clients into change through 'truth telling'. So, what makes for entertaining TV often contributes to keeping people out of the therapy room.

Several other myths about therapy abound—therapy is only for the weak, therapy is mostly just listening, therapists make you blame your parents, and so on . . .

While the pandemic saw an increased focus on the topic of mental health, it has also led to a surge of self-help advice online, in the form of inspiring-sounding quotes that are not always grounded in solid theory and practical experience. And crowd-sourced answers to anonymous questions continue to yield entertaining, black-and-white options (such as—Leave him right now!) that may harm more than help.

As two practising therapists, therefore, our main goal is to demystify therapy for you. Here, we tread a fine line— between oversimplifying what goes on in the therapy room and making this book unnecessarily complex. Luckily, we have found our balance, with the use of that simple, wonderful device called storytelling. In writing these stories based on our clinical practice, we have also enjoyed ourselves thoroughly!

These fifty brief, fictionalized stories will take you right into the therapy room where client and therapist engage with what goes on within themselves and between them. You can be a fly on the wall and sit in on these intimate conversations and journey along with us. We have deliberately selected stories of everyday challenges that people tend to bring to therapy, so that you, dear reader, will likely find yourself in a story or two and go 'That's me!' We hope to celebrate moments that may not be easily recognized as momentous—for instance, our attitudes to compliments may change, we may own our own sadness, or accept the imperfections in our loved ones.

You might find us enquiring about our client's histories in many stories, an act misunderstood as 'blaming the parents for everything'. Many of our deep-seated patterns do originate early in relation to the significant authority figures in our life (mostly parents!). As children, we were vulnerable emotionally. If a parent shouted at us, it may have felt like an all-powerful, all-knowing big person deciding that we were no good. Loud arguments between adults might have felt catastrophic. Even praise, if only limited to achievements like doing well in school, might have felt like pressure to always do well—or else! The impact of these is profoundly significant. We may develop patterns that repeat and strengthen over years or decades—we may stop trusting others, or avoid conflict like hell, or find even minor failures enough to crush our spirit. Exploring early experiences helps us to understand the context in which our patterns originated, to face painful feelings that were pushed away—and allows us to take responsibility for our lives going forward, rather than repeating what hurts us.

We practise a form of therapy called TA (Transactional Analysis), created in the twentieth century by Dr Eric Berne (famed for his international bestseller *Games People Play*). Berne had the vision of making the theory of human development and functioning more accessible to everyone. Transactional Analysis offers an approach not in the form of mystified theories understandable only to psychotherapists, but in the form of explanations understandable to the person who needs them, namely, the one in emotional difficulty.

Berne said it best by remarking that 'if something can't be understood by an intelligent eight-year-old, it isn't worth saying'. We can't be sure about eight-year-olds, but we have tried to live up to his vision by keeping this book as coherent and simple as possible. We have kept jargon to the minimum though you may have to forgive us if you find it peeking out through the text in a few places where necessary. Luckily, most terms such as *ego states*, *games*, *rackets*, *drivers* and so on were creatively chosen by Berne as a way to provide an easy understanding of complex internal processes. We have defined them in simple ways so that the focus stays on the story. We have also showcased a range of methods that can be used in therapy to highlight how creative and engaging the process can be.

The philosophy of TA trusts that people are fundamentally OK. The therapist trusts that clients are acting in ways that feel safe to them and explores their meaning-making to see if constructing alternate meanings can allow them to feel OK about who they are. The process of slowing down and writing this book has only deepened our respect for our clients, towards whom we feel renewed gratitude for allowing us to be part of their journey. Even though we emphasize that these stories feature fictional clients, there is no denying that much inspiration, richness, and depth in these stories has come from our actual work with real people.

Therapy is hard work. Both client and therapist bring all of themselves (yes, the therapist along with years of training, supervision, practice also brings their whole self, along with their vulnerabilities) into the present moment and co-create the meaning that emerges. You will therefore find not just our fictionalized clients in these pages but also catch a glimpse of our internal worlds as therapists. We hope that you are entertained, moved, disturbed, and, in some way, transformed.

And how do you feel about that?

1

Will You Fix Me?

Aruna

I did a little dance when I saw an email from a person named Kavan, saying he was looking for a therapist. I was a new therapist, ready to jump at any opportunity to work with clients.

Kavan came into my office smiling, looking eager. I smiled back, equally eager, and directed him to a chair. He sat down and continued to smile. I said 'hello' and waited for him to start. He said 'hello', the smile remaining intact.

'Yes, Kavan, what brought you here?' I asked, finally getting tired of the prolonged polite smiling.

'Oh,' he said, his smile fading and his round eyes becoming rounder. 'What happened?' I asked, a little alarmed at his shock.

'I didn't know I was supposed to start. I thought you would give me a questionnaire or something to assess me, then you would tell me what my problem was, and then you would also tell me how to fix it.'

I gazed at him. I realized that to him I was a fairy godmother, who could look deep into him, get straight to the root of the issue, and use fairy dust to make it vanish. No wonder he was smiling so much.

This was my first lesson—that I needed to explain clearly what psychotherapy was before taking in clients. I took a deep breath, and then went on to explain, 'Therapy begins with awareness. The first thing I propose we do is explore how things are for you and learn more about your patterns: patterns of how you think, act and feel, patterns in your relationships, and so on. We might look at the origin and purpose of patterns that are not working so well for you today, and what you could do. For my part, I will listen and support you, but also challenge you at times. Does this sound like the sort of thing that you are looking for?'

He had been listening intently to me, and I was relieved when he nodded thoughtfully. 'How are you feeling?' I asked.

'Scared,' he said, his smile fading.

'I understand,' I said kindly. 'Visiting painful memories and getting to know parts of us that we don't like too much can feel scary. Are you willing to sign up despite the fear?'

'Let's do this,' he said, smiling again bravely. I heaved a sigh of relief, and we began our work.

2

The Problem Is . . .

Yashodhara

'The problem is that,' Saurabh continued, 'knowing my inability to really stick with one thing, I don't know if I'll be able to continue with this healthy streak. I mean, it's been four days in a row, but . . .'

I nodded as I listened to the content of Saurabh's complaints about himself, but a part of me was beginning to feel a familiar mix of resignation and irritation. In so many months of working with him, I was by now well aware of Saurabh's self-critical pattern and his tendency to look at the negative side. His favourite phrase to discount any improvement seemed to be '*the problem is . . .*'

'Saurabh,' I said gently, 'you started by talking about how great it felt to work out this week, and even eat healthy. I noticed that you moved on very quickly to mention your inability to stick with things. Can we look at what happened right now?'

'Happened?' He blinked, looking a little confused. 'I wouldn't say anything happened . . . I just . . . I guess I don't believe I will sustain this habit, I usually just . . . fall off the wagon, like we've discussed. I'm afraid the same thing will happen right now.'

'Right.' I was thoughtful. I hesitated for a moment, wondering whether to say what was coming up for me, but decided to go ahead. 'Could I share my observation?'

He nodded, and I went ahead: 'I noticed that it was when I smiled and expressed pleasure when you talked about a good week that you shifted into saying you might not be able to stick with it. I wonder if there was something about my response that impacted you?'

He had a little frown on his face as he heard this, but then he bit his lip, reminding me of a little guilty child. After a few moments of silence, his face took on a half-smile, and then he nodded slowly. 'I think it might be. You did look happy, almost excited at my progress, and for a moment, I felt happy, but then maybe I realized I really don't want to let you down.'

'Let me down,' I repeated. I was curious.

'Well . . . yeah.' Saurabh said, a faraway expression coming onto his face. 'I feel like you've, you know . . . been there for me all these months. I was hoping by now I would have shown some progress. But I feel I always wind up at the same place. And I guess I feel that maybe I might be disappointing you.'

'Okay.' I said slowly. 'So, I'm trying to understand this— there is a part of you that feels like you're disappointing me with what you call "no progress", and then the part of you that doesn't want to raise my hopes adds quickly the caveat that "this progress won't last . . . "'

It took him a few moments to process this, but when he did, he returned with a hint of triumph. 'They may just be the same part, right? I don't want to disappoint you like I probably will; hence, I don't want to raise your expectations.'

He had just voiced in a pithy and more accurate way what I had been struggling to articulate. I felt a sense of admiration—in fact pride—for his intelligence, coupled with a momentary tinge of—what was it—shame for my having fumbled to put it well. Why would that be, I wondered for a split second. It's not like I was competing with my client. Or was I?

Putting the thought aside, while making a mental note that I should reflect on it by myself later, I asked him, 'What would disappointing me mean to you, Saurabh?'

This time the smile was twisted and wry. 'I guess it would be in line with how it's always been for me. I've always let everyone down—my parents, my teachers, my big brother . . .'

'And is there someone I probably remind you of, Saurabh, whom you believe you disappointed when you were growing up?'

'Dad,' he said after a moment's thought. 'He was always excited about my potential. But he kept pushing me towards things I didn't like. I mean, I didn't want to play cricket like the other kids in the colony, but he would go on and on about it, how it was good for me to get out and build muscle and connect with other boys. It was the same thing throughout, with subjects and extra-curricular activities I didn't even like. Like debating and elocution, of all things! Me! I hated science, and I hated talking on stage—and then he'd be disappointed in me, saying I had potential that I wasn't using.'

'I get that.' I knew Saurabh's pain at never having been allowed to do what he really wanted. I wondered how the internalized relationship with his father was now showing up in the relationship with me. Was that fleeting moment I had experienced as a mix of pride and competitiveness a clue in some way, or was that more to do with my own way of being? I decided to ask about it.

'Saurabh—do you feel pressured by me to change?'

He wrinkled his forehead at the question. 'Pressure . . . no. I mean, I don't think so. I'm the one who really wants to change but can't, right? I always wind up in this same place, feeling stuck.'

The speed of his response and his scanning of my face for approval told me that at that moment he was a little boy scared of hurting me.

I thought out aloud, 'Did you answer in a rush?'

'Maybe,' he admitted after a moment's thought.

'So, you *are* experiencing some pressure?' I asked.

'Yes—but I am wondering if it is from you, or me?' he said thoughtfully.

'Lovely question. And what is the answer?'

Once again, I saw the biting of the lip. For a second, he looked like a little boy about to cry. But the expression disappeared in a flash, replaced by his usual passive blank expression. I intuitively decided to not press for the answer.

'You know,' I said, teasingly, 'I know there is one thing you actually have sustained for months, so that's some evidence that you don't always drop things.'

'What?' He looked suspicious.

'These sessions!' I laughed as his expression relaxed, and he saw the truth in what I was saying. 'When you first came to me, you even said you were afraid you would drop out after the first few sessions. Well, it's been over twenty weeks, and you haven't missed a single appointment. What do you think about that?'

He took a couple of seconds before he spoke, the half-smile back again. 'I think you're right about that. I suppose I've also been surprised that I've stuck to these sessions for so long. And I know I'm feeling better about myself . . .' The half-smile disappeared, and the faraway look was back as he went on, '*The problem is . . .*'

And just like that, we were right back where we had started. But this time, I just sat back and listened, more relaxed than before. I could now see the little boy, carrying his enthusiastic but admonishing father in his head. What he needed to heal was not another parent who pressured him to do better but someone who would accept him *completely*. In that space, he would hopefully over time be able to contact who he was and separate it from who he thought others wanted him to be. I knew that this meant I would need to hold back a lot more from the urge to make suggestions, balancing these delicately with my role of confronting him from self-discounting and encouraging him to acknowledge his progress. But the most important thing I could do would be to let him know that I accepted him for who he was. As far as I was concerned, he didn't need to change a thing.

3

Bath Time Battles Fought Across Generations!

Aruna

'My son hates baths!' Ravi complained loudly. He was referring to his three-year-old. I smiled. I imagined for a moment that this was part of the first few minutes of banter, similar to 'Can you believe this traffic!' or 'It is getting so hot these days!' But no, this was his agenda for the session.

'Things are getting very stressful at home. Three adults are needed to get this tiny fellow ready for school. I have to hold a kicking and screaming child tight, while my mum pours water on him. My wife is ready outside with a story to calm him down. I find this a really stressful start to the day and the stress just carries forward.'

I must admit I was a little entertained by the description of the drama. However, I could see that it was a big deal for him. I wondered if I should say something empathetic like 'That sounds awful.' I chose my words carefully for

I was worried my feeling amused would leak into the conversation.

'How are you feeling as you share this with me?'

Ravi just looked at me expectantly, as if waiting for me to offer a solution. 'I feel confused. How do I deal with this?'

I nodded, recognizing the intensity of his stress.

'Asking him politely doesn't work and we don't want to punish him. We are doing all that we can to get him ready for school,' he insisted. I experienced him in that moment as a little, agitated child telling me that he was doing his best and imploring me to help him.

'You are doing *all* that you can?' I played back his words, wondering if he would recognize the grandiosity in his thinking. *Grandiosity* is an internal mechanism involving a maximization or minimization of some aspect of self, others, or the situation. Here, he was maximizing the problem and minimizing the options that he had.

'Yes,' his eyebrows came together in puzzlement. My question confused him. I asked more directly, 'Why does he need to have a bath in the morning?'

Ravi's eyes widened for a moment. He shook his head, 'I can't imagine it any other way.' A minute later he added, 'My mother would never agree.'

'Mother would never agree!'

'I mean I have not had that conversation with her. But I know that. In our family, we always start our day with baths.'

'And do you know why that is important?' I was curious.

'Yes, my mum would often talk about how a bath washed away her stresses and how she felt energized and clear- headed after a bath. She would love scrubbing my hair dry and often tell me how clean and fresh I was looking.'

So, the idea that 'We must start our day with a bath' was Ravi's conditioned response based on what he, as a little child, had seen his caregivers do. This was 'normal' life. He had never challenged or questioned it because he was not even aware that he was living his life with that assumption.

'And if I asked your mum how she got to love her baths, what would she say?' I asked.

'Ha ha ha,' he laughed at the unexpected question. 'You are asking how I got to be this way.' He became thoughtfully silent as he reflected upon it.

'You seem to have remembered something,' I said, observing him keenly.

'My grandfather woke up every morning at 5.00 a.m. and started his day with a bath. He would, in fact, say that baths must be had before sunrise. My grandmother woke up earlier than he did. She would wait for him to finish his bath before going for hers.'

I offered my imagination, 'And perhaps if I asked your grandfather, he would say that "My father would go early to the river for a bath before it got crowded."'

'Ha ha. You are right. Maybe that is how it started. Everyone went to the river before it got too hot or too crowded,' he said, playing along with me. I could see that the attachment to the idea that baths 'must' be had in the morning was weakening. He learnt that caregivers had also learnt from their caregivers. This unconscious learning, handed down across generations, had come into his awareness and now there was a way for him to evaluate if it was still relevant.

'What could happen if you sent your son to school without a bath?' I questioned.

'Mum will be upset the whole day,' he replied after pondering.

And that was another lesson that he had introjected—that he needed to be an obedient son, and not upset elders. *Introjection* is what we observe in our parent figures and make ours unconsciously, swallowing without digesting. It is like a microchip implanted in the head with all the values, expectations, attitudes, mannerisms, habits, coping mechanisms of our parental figures and the culture we grow up in.

'How do you feel if Mum is upset?'

'I don't like the idea. Because she will sulk. My wife will then get upset,' he reflected.

'Can you tolerate that?' I asked.

Ravi looked thoughtful. The idea that he could tolerate another being upset with him was new. In his current way of being, he took responsibility for the feelings of others. He attended to the needs of others over his own needs. Perhaps he had learnt it from his grandmother, who had modelled it to him, by never having a bath earlier than the grandfather even though she woke up earlier. 'Don't get authority figures upset' was implanted in the microchip in his head.

'I have never really thought about it. But I know I certainly don't want it. Mum is old. I don't want to upset her.'

'Are you seeing yourself as responsible for her getting upset?'

'Am I not?' he challenged me.

'Are you?' I persisted, inviting him to think for himself.

'Maybe,' he sighed. He sounded tentative. I was curious if he was appeasing me by not getting into an argument.

'I wonder if you feel safe to disagree with me,' I thought aloud. Since the client's patterns of relating to others play out with the therapist as well, I was watchful of whether Ravi was eager to be the 'good child' even in the therapy room.

He considered what I had said carefully. 'Maybe I am scared of upsetting you, just as I am scared of upsetting my mum,' he said contemplatively and then went on to add, 'Man, I never realized how pervasive this anxiety is.'

And we went on to explore his fear of authority figures.

Ravi had started the session with what in therapy we call a 'presenting issue'—'How do I make my son have a bath?' Often, the presenting issue is a symptom, and may not be where the work needs to happen. Therapy is about uncovering underlying causes of the symptom. Exploring the presenting issue of 'My son hates baths' led us to 'I am scared of upsetting others.' Ravi became aware of the 'musts' he had taken in without awareness. He got in touch with his fear of going against authority figures. We had begun important work.

4

The Smiling Saviour

Yashodhara

'The last couple of weeks have been much better at work,' said Vikas, with a huge smile on his face. 'I went ahead with what we had talked about last time—I pushed back on projects and didn't work on the weekend either!'

'Well, that's great!' I smiled back at him. 'You're taking time off! You are attending to your need for rest.'

'Yes, it is, isn't it?' He grinned widely. 'I even told the CEO . . .'

As he kept talking, I realized something odd. I felt my smile was false, and my face was hurting. I realized it was because of my unconscious mirroring of his smile. Vikas had started by saying that he had some progress to report—in fact, I was always surprised about the speed of his progress. Just over our first few sessions, he had already reported changes in his work-life—around his tendency to please others, to overwork himself, and so on. I had begun to wonder if perhaps there was something deeper that he was avoiding and had been waiting for an opportunity to discover it. But today, I was aware that there was something that felt out of place for me, and I couldn't quite put my finger on it. After a few more seconds, there was a pause in the conversation, and I decided to check if he felt it too.

'Vikas,' I enquired curiously, 'is your face hurting right now?'

'Hurting?' he paused. 'Why would my face hurt?'

'I don't know.' I confessed honestly. 'But I feel like I have been smiling too much.'

'Oh.' His smile widened even further. 'Well, I guess my face is used to that.'

'Yes,' I said slowly, 'I've actually seen you smile even when you're talking about someone's behaviour making you angry.'

His smile dropped a little now. 'Yes.' His tone had changed, his voice was softer.

'What is going on with you right now?' I asked gently, noting that he looked sad. It wasn't often that I had seen him this way.

'I think my face does hurt, actually.' He admitted. 'I didn't realize the effort that goes in to exercise all those muscles—actually, do you know the number of muscles it takes to smile? I used to be a quizzer, and . . .'

I noticed his smile was back and interrupted gently, 'I thought I saw you looking sad a moment ago. I wonder if you are distancing yourself from it by smiling?'

A few moments of silence passed. This was another first with Vikas, I noted. Usually, his cheerful conversation filled every pause quickly. I waited.

'My mother, I guess,' he said, so softly that I had to strain to make out his words. 'She always needed me to smile and be happy.'

Almost all my sessions so far with Vikas had been focused on his professional life, despite my attempts to enquire about his past. I knew he had lost his father when he was only eight, but he had brushed over my attempts to know more about that period in his life. I had waited though, and my patience was paying off today because he now continued of his own accord. 'After Dad died, especially. He had always been the cheerful one, getting her out of her low moods and taking care of her. She was just so shocked after he died—she kept falling sick after that. And then it was only her and me.'

'What about you?' I prodded. 'What happened to you when you learnt of your dad's death?'

'Ah.' He leaned back in his chair. 'Well, of course, I was shocked too—but Mom, she was . . . totally distraught. And my uncles came, and they all told me I had to be strong for her. So, you know . . .'

His voice trailed off and he shrugged. I nodded slowly.

As children, we're constantly looking to our parents for signs of validation. The behaviours that seem to get rewarded or noticed are the ones that become part of our survival strategy. Taibi Kahler named these coping mechanisms *drivers* because they seem to have a compulsive quality about them and identified five such drivers: Be Strong, Please

Others, Be Perfect, Try Hard, and Hurry Up. These are strengths when we are not under stress; otherwise, these are defence mechanisms to keep painful feelings at bay.

I could see that the constant pressure Vikas felt to smile came from his need to please others and to always show up as the strong one. I felt my heart going out to the little boy for whom grief at such a significant event as his own father's death had been denied. I waited for him to go on, and after a few moments, he spoke again.

'They all said at every family gathering for years "Vikas is our only hope!"—and Mom always agreed with it. I was always good at studies, but after Dad died, I became unbeatable. I studied and worked really hard, and I topped every subject all through school and college.'

I could see the little boy using his intelligence to do well in life and his cheerfulness to take care of his mother. 'You mentioned quizzing? Did well with that too?'

'Yes,' he said. 'I knew everything about everything! I knew quizzing would help me in my studies too. But I dropped all the other stuff that had no meaning.'

'Such as?'

'I used to read a lot of fiction, but I changed to books that increased my general knowledge. Science. Oh, I gave up the drums.'

'Drums!' I exclaimed. 'You used to play?'

'Yes, for a while. My cousin had passed on a set to me. But I gave it back after Dad died. It used to bother Mom anyway; she had her headaches and so much else to deal with . . .'

Our conversation led Vikas to gain several insights. He became aware of his difficulty with accessing and allowing himself to feel his sadness. His mother still lived with him, and while she had a separate floor to herself, he became aware of his unspoken resentment against her for often violating his personal space and not letting him have his privacy. She still demanded a lot of his time and attention, and her worries and insecurities about money, despite his doing well in his career, were a constant burden on him. He now recognized his outward, cheerful demeanour as forced—especially around her.

'Vikas,' I offered, 'it sounds like you haven't really been allowed to be a child?'

His smile came on automatically, but then, he seemed to allow himself to consciously drop it before saying, thoughtfully, 'Well, she still treats me like a child with all the worrying and questions like "What time will you come home?" But yes—I've been the "family hope", and especially hers, for the longest time.'

'That's a lot of burden to be placed on small, eight-year-old shoulders,' I commented, watching his face closely.

'Yes.' He nodded slowly.

Along with his sadness, I noted traces of something else. 'Are you feeling angry?'

After a pause, he said, 'Yes. Yes, I am.'

'You are angry that . . .'

'I had to parent my parent.'

Over the next few sessions, we spoke further about his relationship with his mother. He harboured a lot of guilt for blaming her in any way, given all that she had been through; it was difficult for him to consider confronting her for the current interference in his adult life 'after all that she had done for him'. But he was slowly beginning to see how her constant fragility and helplessness had denied him many things over the years—his own feelings, especially sadness, the ability to express his needs, and the right to be a playful child instead of a high performing, avuncularly cheerful, and overly responsible boy. He began to understand why he hadn't ever been able to fully relax.

He was back one day to report his progress again, but this time on the home front. 'I've set some boundaries with mom.' He announced seriously. 'I actually told her there is a lot of stuff that she and I need to work through that we haven't talked about for years, and that includes how things may need to change going forward too. To begin with, I've told her I need more space. She now spends a lot more time on her floor downstairs, and we meet once a day, usually for dinner. It's so much better.'

'I'm glad.' I smiled.

'Yes.' And his face took on a crafty smile. 'And I think it'll be even easier to get my space from her now—I just bought myself a new set of drums and I plan to start lessons! My rhythm needs work, but yesterday, I spent an hour just banging on those like a kid. I love it!'

This time when I mirrored his grin of pure child-like pride and pleasure, my face didn't hurt. I suspected his didn't either.

5

Do Me Something

Aruna

Rumeet looked up at me with wide eyes and a watery smile. 'I hate being helpless,' she said, crying. 'Why am I this helpless? Everybody else seems to know what to do.'

When I first started working with Rumeet, I was keen to help her change. I would invite her attention to what she was discounting—she was from a premier engineering college and was heading the India operations of an MNC, overseeing a 100-member team. She had made several bold decisions in her life. However, she was not able to admire herself for any of these. She could only see herself as helpless in relationships. She was unable to offer feedback or ask for what she needed. She felt one-down in all her relationships, even with people who reported to her. 'I hate how whiny I am,' she would often say in despair.

Though she looked at me starry-eyed, I recognized that many things I said or did had no effect on her. I found myself trying harder with her, getting frustrated at her discounting my interventions. I wondered what was going on between us. Why was I trying so hard?

Understanding her history gave me some answers.

Rumeet was the second daughter to her parents. With an always-sulking father and an overly anxious mother, little Rumeet did not have the experience of stable parents who could offer containment for her feelings. Very confused and overwhelmed with her own feelings, she would turn to her older sister, who would constantly rattle off advice and judge her for her 'stupidity'.

Our relational patterns are born out of our early experiences. We carry these patterns into adulthood. They are very likely to get repeated in the relationship with the therapist. When I looked at what was going on between Rumeet and me, I could see that our dynamics were the same as that between her and her sister. By staying helpless and looking up to me for advice, she had unconsciously extended a strong invitation to me to take on the role of the rescuing, judging sister. I had unconsciously responded to her invitation by trying hard to 'fix' her and feeling frustrated at her lack of responsiveness. This was a familiar relational pattern for her, and she felt safe in this dynamic.

With my awareness of this, I decided that I would shift my role and offer her a relationship that she hadn't experienced earlier. I began to simply listen to her, asking her about her meaning-making. I refrained from urging her to change in any way or even offering suggestions. I allowed myself to sit in silence in the therapy session, resisting any pressure I felt to jump in and take charge. Rumeet smiled awkwardly in the sessions. I could see that she was confused that I stayed with questions and refrained from expressing my views, even though she asked for mine. Both of us stayed with the tension of Rumeet's issues remaining unresolved. A couple of months went by and the tension in the room grew.

And then it happened. One day, as we sat in silence, she couldn't bear the tension anymore and smiled weakly and said, 'What are we doing here?'

'What makes you ask?' I said.

She paused a while, 'I mean, you are not taking charge of the sessions and are waiting for me to take the lead. You are not sharing your own views with me.'

I smiled, 'Yes, I am not taking the lead. How is that for you?'

I could see that my response caused a disturbance in Rumeet. She shook her head, looking downward, to the left, frowning, in response to some internal dialogue.

'What is going on?' I was extremely curious.

And the penny dropped. She sat back in her chair, throwing down her hands, 'What am I doing? I am waiting for you to take charge of my life, rather than trusting my own thinking. I have just forgotten to think on my own. I cannot survive without having someone rescue me all the time.'

At that moment she got in touch with a powerful, knowing part of her. We both celebrated the enormity of her insight and spent time getting her to savour her newfound power. As we made connections to the coping strategies she had developed as a little child, she contacted her fantasy that if she waited long enough, someone would come and take charge, and all would be well.

A weight seemed to fall off her chest. She started giggling and said, 'How difficult it must have been for you to sit patiently without doing anything!' That statement was a marker of change for me. She was relating to me differently, more as an equal, rather than putting me on a pedestal. That session was a starting point for a series of changes in her life as she began to trust her own thinking and started relating to others on a more equal footing rather than from a one-down position.

6

Get Up and Do SOMETHING

Yashodhara

'If only he would help me more!' Sanchita lamented. 'I don't know why he can't just see it! Marriage is supposed to be fifty–fifty, but this is . . . ugh! He just shuts his door on me and the kids!'

Sanchita had been coming to me for several months now. She was a mother of two kids, and I knew that she read constantly about good parenting and tried to apply those principles to her own parenting; she had a full-time job in finance in a large organization, which was demanding in itself; she also had an intense and draining relationship with her mother, whom she supported emotionally and financially and who constantly required time and attention from her; and last but not least, she was dealing with an acrimonious relationship with her husband, whom she often felt did nothing to pull his weight around the house, leaving her to do 'everything'.

'You said he is shutting the door "on you"?'

'Yes! He is shutting us out—me as well as the kids. It is just so . . . *selfish.*'

'Tell me more about what is selfish here?'

She thought for a while. 'Well . . . my parents never shut the door. In fact, no one in our house shut their doors during the daytime—except maybe if they were changing clothes or something. Mom would knock on my door when I was a teenager if I shut it, asking what I was doing, and if something was wrong . . . it became easier to just leave the door open. That way, she would know I wasn't hiding anything!'

'So do you think your husband is hiding something when he shuts the door?'

'No,' she spoke slowly. 'I mean, maybe. I don't know. I have sometimes opened it softly. He's actually doing nothing—either reading or sleeping.'

'And is that what you see as selfish?'

'Yes,' she said immediately, 'because he often does it even when the kids are awake. They are small and need our attention. As it is, we are busy with our jobs. So at least on weekends, we should be the ones looking after them, instead of the help. But it's always just me! I wish he would *do* something too!'

'Right.' I nodded and went with my intuition. 'So, when do you shut your door?'

'I can't!' she scoffed. 'The girls are always crying for me when we are home. What can our help do, beyond a point? So, I never get to shut the door!' She paused for a moment, and then said more slowly, 'Well, except for . . . when I'm sick, I suppose.'

'You have mentioned falling sick fairly often in the last few months,' I observed. 'It seems like once a month?'

'Once a month,' she said, her voice becoming flat. After a few moments she added, looking puzzled, 'Always on weekends only.'

'Hmm,' I said, and waited.

'Why do I fall sick only on weekends?' Her brow was furrowed. 'That's really strange.'

I nodded, maintaining a receptive silence. I sensed that she was piecing together something important for herself.

After a few moments, her brow cleared, and then a slightly embarrassed smile came over her face.

'What did you just get in touch with, Sanchita?' I asked curiously.

'The crazy thought that just came into my head was . . . it would be too inconvenient if I were to fall sick on a weekday. The work would pile up and get crazy. So maybe that is why it's only on some Friday evenings that the tiredness and feeling of sickness really hits me,' she sighed. 'I was telling myself that I only notice it when things slow down, but I think it's more than that . . . maybe . . . I just want a real break sometimes . . .' Her voice trailed off.

'And a real break is permitted only when you're sick?' I offered.

The sheepish smile was back as she nodded 'Yes'.

'You're looking embarrassed about this.' I smiled too. 'Why?'

'I'm feeling a little silly . . . it's like being sneaky somehow. Not too fair on my husband.'

'Sanchita, you remember we talked about games? And how they are unconsciously played?'

I had explained to her previously that *games* are unconscious patterns of relating that tend to play out habitually between people—not necessarily negative phenomena in themselves, they are usually old self-protective strategies that may originate from strong messages in childhood. Eric Berne had described several common games in his book *Games People Play*, and one that he had written about reminded me of what Sanchita was now describing for herself.

'Yes . . .'

'What you're saying reminds me of one called 'Harried'— imagine a woman who busies herself by constantly filling up her days with one activity after the other. If she has a dinner party that she is throwing in the evening, everything must be perfect, and yet, that morning, she fixes a dental appointment for the kids, and then chooses to do volunteer work in the afternoon—so by the time evening arrives, she cannot take it anymore, and then breaks down, blaming others for not helping her.'

'But this is me!' Sanchita gasped. After a moment, she added, 'Wow, this feels weird . . . in a way, it's good to know this is actually something that does happen, and it's *not* just me. But why do I do it?'

'Good question,' I said. 'How come you are unable to rest or relax?'

As we wondered about how she got to be this way, Sanchita recalled how she never saw her own mother relaxed, and how she hadn't been given permission to relax herself as a child.

'Anytime Mum saw me or my brother lazing around the house, she'd get really angry with us. She'd tell us loudly to "Just get up and do *something*."'

Sanchita realized that ever since high school, she had been working furiously towards something or the other—whether it was studies and later work, or some project at home, and now raising her kids—she had always been busy, through holidays as well. We hypothesized together that because she didn't feel like she could ever take a break—the only legitimate reason for that was sickness, which was also what had been modelled by her mother—she would periodically overwork herself to a breakdown. Then, she could, in a guilt-free manner, accept help and care from others around her—including her husband, who was then reminded, yet again, that this had happened only because he never did enough around the house.

'But then, maybe if he did more, I would be able to rest sometimes,' she sounded like she was getting annoyed with him again. 'Actually, it's *better* that he shuts the door when he is being lazy. At least that way I don't get to see him just lying there and doing nothing.'

'I wonder if you wish he would just get up and do *something*.'

Her eyes widened as she made the connection—and then she laughed, slapping her forehead lightly. 'Wow! I'm exactly like my mother! I can't stand to see him relaxed.'

'And do you think you could stand your own relaxation?'

The silence was longer this time. 'I am not sure. But I'd *like* to be able to relax.'

'What might you do differently then?'

Sanchita took a deep breath and exhaled. 'I think there are maybe more things I can say no to. I've taken on organizing this event for my kids' school . . . and I just volunteered for a new project at work, even though I'm barely able to manage my current responsibilities. Maybe I need to talk to my manager about it and pull back on that one, it's early enough . . . though I may look foolish.'

'Will you, really?' I asked gently.

'No, not really,' she said, and went on more confidently, 'in fact, he had said I should take a week to think about it— and I know there are others in the team who can handle it.'

'Right,' I nodded. 'So, you can choose to take on less stress at work and outside of work too.'

'Yes.' She was thoughtful. 'And I also think it's the same thing at home—my hubby *does* say often he can manage the girls for a couple of hours when we're at home so that I do my own thing. I just don't let him do it because I think they'll fuss and cry, and then he'll let them watch TV or something . . . but maybe I need to be less exacting about how he manages them and let him follow through properly on his offer, instead of blocking him from doing it or jumping in, and then blaming him for not helping me. It's hard for me to not come out when I hear them fussing, but . . . maybe, I can try just shutting the door on them all!'

'That's an interesting idea,' I smiled. 'And would it be okay for the kids to watch TV for a while too?'

She paused. 'I'm hearing my mother's voice saying "No, it's not okay" . . . but I'm thinking, "Why not? They're just small kids. If it boils down to it, why not let them watch it sometimes—what's the big deal! I certainly don't want to repeat the same thing with them, by telling them they need to always be busy and productive all the time!"'

'Right,' I nodded. 'So, could you model it by also getting rest yourself? Is it also okay for you to use your time behind the closed door to take a nap?'

She seemed to be considering this. When she finally spoke, it was to say, in all seriousness, 'I will need earplugs, you know.'

I fought to keep my own face straight as I nodded, 'Sounds like a worthwhile investment.'

Sanchita let out a long exhale as she considered the possibility of this new way of being, and a sense of quiet calm filled the space between us. I sensed intuitively that perhaps her relaxation was already beginning.

7

Leave My Parents Out of This, Please!

Aruna

'I am going to cry a lot' was Ibtisam's first sentence of our first session. Her eyes glistened. I noticed how her expression was in contrast to her name, a beautiful Arabic name that meant smiling and blooming.

She reminded me of a rabbit peeping out of its hole—small, shivering, and scared. It was making up its mind on whether it could come out of its hole and show up fully. Was it safe?

'It is okay. Tears are welcome in this space, as are all emotions. Cry as much as you would like,' I comforted her.

'Thank you,' she said gratefully.

We both paused. I held her in silence with a compassionate gaze. Her breathing relaxed.

'Tell me about your tears right now. What is going on?' The here-and-now is often a good place to begin.

'Oh, I feel teary all the time, and I don't even know why. I feel I am not good enough. I am uncomfortable in my own skin. If my boss asks me to make a presentation, I get very anxious. I am unable to sleep all night. I put in so much effort into my work, and then I think it isn't good enough. I feel so ashamed of my output that I don't show up for work at all. I don't think I am good at anything.'

The rabbit had stepped out of the hole. She was taking a risk by being vulnerable with me here.

I encouraged her to continue talking. I could see her relaxing as she gave me the context of her immediate family and her work. As we progressed, I asked her to share with me details of her childhood. Getting a sense of early history and connecting the client's pattern of meaning making in the here-and-now can help suss out patterns that they may be living out in an unconscious way. In Transactional Analysis, we call this unconscious narrative that we live out the *life script* or simply the *script*. This is the story we have told ourselves and others about who we are, what we deserve, how our relationships with important others will be, and how our life will turn out.

'I am the middle child. I have two sisters. My father was a technician in BEL and my mother was a schoolteacher,' she said. Ibtisam's sharing helped me understand the cultural context in which she had grown up and how that had shaped her script. In the world she grew up in, incomes were small, but life felt safe and predictable. As she described her home, I could picture the family of five in a two-bedroom apartment. I intuited that the girls would have received the following messages: 'Study hard, work hard, don't create any trouble, keep your needs in check, be obedient, don't answer back.'

By now, Ibtisam had stopped crying. She was quite involved with telling her own story.

'My father passed away when I was ten,' she said. I imagined that their life would have become very difficult after that. Ibtisam continued, 'My mother had to take the support of relatives. They would humiliate her. My mother would cry all the time.

Actually, I remember her crying constantly even when my father was alive. I have a memory of her crying in the bathroom for hours. I sat outside, urging her to come out. I comforted her as best as I could.'

'How old were you then?' I enquired.

'Around five, I think,' she said, narrowing her eyes trying to remember. 'How did you feel when your mother shut herself in the bathroom and cried?'

'I was worried for her. I wanted to know that she was OK.' I could see how early in life Ibtisam had learnt to be responsible.

'How did your father respond to your mother's crying?' I asked.

'He would just ignore her tears. He had his own challenges around money, and he wasn't able to do much to comfort her,' she said. 'He would tell us to work hard. He wanted us to study well. He believed that our education was the formula out of our financial difficulties. I remember when I was six and in Class 1, I scored poorly in a test.

He returned home late at night. When he heard about my marks, he became furious. I was terrified.'

She paused. Something about the pause filled me with dread. I felt a churn in the pit of my stomach.

'He took off his belt and gave me a few lashes,' Ibtisam continued in a matter-of-fact way.

She probably would have gone on without a pause had it not been for my clapping my hand over my mouth in shock. 'I am so sorry to hear this,' I said, deeply pained.

Her eyes welled up. She squirmed in her chair, mortified by my reaction. 'My father loved me!' Her eyes implored me not to judge him.

'I am sure he did. But parents are fallible beings. They make mistakes. This shouldn't have happened to you,' I said.

'This wasn't often. And I can understand his difficulties too. He had to educate three of us,' her face was flushed. I saw the rabbit scrambling back into the hole. I wondered if I had made a mistake by making my response so evident. But I told myself that I was human and what I offered her was a relationship with a real person. I breathed deeply to ground myself and come back to the present. Seeing how painful my response was for her and given that it was the first session, I didn't press further. I needed to build trust with her first. However, I sensed she had become guarded again. I wondered if the damage had already been done, and if she would come back.

My assessment from what I had heard in this session was that Ibtisam had no opportunity to be a child. She had taken care of her emotionally overwhelmed parents by understanding them, being grateful, and even comforting them in their distress. Fearing that her own feelings would add to their distress, she had pushed them away. She developed a coping strategy of pleasing them, believing that as long as she made them happy, she would be OK.

Ibtisam did come back. I was relieved. I wondered if she was angry with me for saying that her father's action was wrong.

'I was agitated after our session,' she said, 'and I spent the whole night crying. I sat up in the middle of the night and spoke to my dad in my mind. "Sorry, Papa, that I said mean things about you," I told him. I said to myself, "Are you happy, now that you have blamed your father for your problems?"'

I felt really sad to hear this. She was feeling guilty about her unwitting revelation. She had no permission at all to see him as limited. Again, I am all too familiar with the cultural expectation that children must be grateful to their parents for all their sacrifices. Any negative judgements of parental attitudes or actions is seen as 'ingratitude'.

'Is that what you believe? That you blamed your father?' I explored her meaning-making. She looked at me tearfully. 'I know that is not true, but it feels like that,' she said.

'So, what is true?' I asked.

She paused and then ventured, 'That I was sharing my story with you.'

'That is correct. You were sharing your story. You were not blaming him,' I reassured her.

I held back my urge to tell her that all parents have their own challenges and limitations and may sometimes act in ways that are harmful to children. I was afraid that the idea would dent her idealized image of her father. It can be psychologically too painful for a child to believe and fully confront the idea that someone they love may actually harm them. So as a defence, they may convince themselves that it is they who are bad and deserve the ill-treatment. This gave me a clue as to where her deep shame came from.

'You may not want to blame him, but you can grieve for what little Ibtisam went through,' I said, carefully scanning her face for emotions.

This time she didn't defend against the grief. Her face crumbled and her shoulders heaved as she cried. She seemed to know what the tears were for.

8

If I Can't See You, You Can't See Me

Yashodhara

'It's the same old, same old.' Pritika complained. 'Nothing's *changing!*'

Almost every session with Pritika began the same way. It had been about five months of working together, and I had been surprised that she was turning into a long-term client despite constantly reporting that she was exactly where she was when she had started.

'What happened, Pritika?' I asked gently, while being aware of a sinking feeling inside. I realized I had stopped looking forward to sessions with her, knowing that a familiar sense of stuckness would come up for both of us.

'I had another interview,' she said, looking off to the side, 'and it just went . . . meh.'

Pritika had talked in the initial months about a desire to change her job, and she had recently begun to apply outside her company. This was actually an indicator of movement and change that she was discounting. I recognized my own urge to contradict her but held back as I was curious about her interview.

'This really seems to be bothering you.' I observed her eyes darting around, looking everywhere but at me. Her face was impassive, but I got the sense of a sulking teenager. 'What happened during the interview?'

'I don't know!' She sounded irritated, almost snappy. 'I'm qualified for the role, and I was feeling pretty good about this one—I was all prepared and everything. But it just goes downhill from the moment the interview starts!'

She clammed up again and looked off to the side. I felt my own irritation rise. I reminded myself that my own urge to sharply judge her was a clue to what she may have experienced as a child. Our dynamics with significant others get re-created in the therapy room.

'Pritika,' I said, 'may I check something with you? It's a hunch that I have.'

'Sure,' she said, sounding a little surprised. She met my eyes only for a millisecond, and then averted her gaze again. 'Whatever.'

'I was wondering about this,' I said, weighing my words. 'I notice that it is only on very few occasions that you look at me directly—as in, maintain eye contact.'

This got her attention, and she was now looking at me, wide-eyed.

'Such as right now.' I smiled at her, and she mirrored it unconsciously. I went on, 'I notice you do look at me when you are smiling or have an insight you are excited to report—but mostly, you are looking anywhere but at my face when we speak. Are you aware of this?'

She kept her gaze on me, and I could tell it was deliberately so. She nodded slowly. 'I think so. No one's ever really told me this, but I have noticed. I do it sometimes—probably when I'm not comfortable. Which is a lot of times.' She gave a laugh. Her dry sense of humour was showing up.

'I wonder what you would feel if you said that without laughing,' I asked.

She lowered her gaze. I sensed that she was sad and wondered if she was ready to explore it. But then, she turned her gaze upward, biting her lip and looking thoughtful. After a long pause, she returned firmly. 'Yes! I definitely avoid eye contact. Right after the first hello.'

'Why do you think that is?' She hadn't answered my question, but I was letting her take the lead.

'I don't know.' The blocking and the darting eyes were back. 'I guess, I maybe never really thought about whether it's a big deal.'

'What are you feeling right now?'

'Just . . . a little . . . uncomfortable. Like maybe . . . you want me to say something, which I don't have the answer to.' She looked away. 'Wow, I think being watched *really* gets to me.'

'And do you imagine me watching you?'

'I imagine you judging me.' She turned her gaze back on me and I could see this took her effort. 'And when I'm not looking at you, you may feel I am not interested in what you have to say—that I'm . . . just not really listening, disengaged . . .' Her voice trailed off for a moment. 'And now that I think about it, an interviewer who doesn't know me at all may think the same. But it's not true. I am listening really carefully to the conversation. Maybe I just listen *better* when I'm not looking the person in the eye!'

'What do you remember about this?' I leaned forward with curiosity. 'Do you have any memories around eye contact?'

Pritika had always claimed to have close to zero memories from childhood. But this time, I saw her screw up her eyes and make a genuine effort to think about this question. After just a moment, her face cleared.

'Dad's questions about our studies.' She gave a hollow laugh. 'At the dining table. We all four siblings could get quizzed any time. I used to just keep my eyes on the food. Somehow, if you just looked at him, and he caught your eye, it was like a cue for him—I could see the wheels turning in his head, and then he would throw out questions: "What's the capital of Colombia?" or "What's seventeen squared?", or "Who's this or that country's Prime Minister?"'

'How do you remember feeling?'

'Caught off guard . . . and then judged!' She emphasized, 'You couldn't prepare for these random questions. He'd expect us to know everything! It felt unfair . . . and I was the eldest, so especially if I didn't know something, it would be like "*You* should know this. You're not studying or reading enough."'

'So, in all of this . . .' I was still looking for her to get in touch with her emotions, 'you felt?'

Her shoulders slumped visibly. 'Hopeless.'

'You are looking sad.'

'I am. I was never good enough for him.'

We made the connections together in the rest of that conversation. Her outward disengagement and lack of interest was a defence against a fear of being judged. Her experience, repeated at the dining table over years of growing up, was now reflected in her reluctance to maintain eye contact in work meetings and interview situations.

We also discovered that her assumption at the beginning of each interview was that the process would in some way be unfair—and her unconscious belief was, 'I don't know enough; I will be judged badly, and there is really no point since I won't come out of this well.' She understood her unconscious tendency to avoid eye contact as stemming from the fear of being judged.

Pritika was able to use her new awareness to see the flaws in this old strategy and was able to uncover and challenge her beliefs that she would be unfairly judged. She could also challenge the hopelessness rooted in the idea that things would never work out for her because she would never know 'enough'. I helped her to reimagine the dining table scenes: she practised visualizing comfortable dinner conversations, looking Dad in the eye, and even asking him to 'let us just eat together as a family!' I noticed that her engagement in our sessions was increasing.

After a few months, Pritika opened the session with a bright-eyed smile and informed me of a breakthrough—she had aced multiple rounds of interviews with a tech organization. 'And I've got a new job offer!' she said proudly. I rejoiced at the news and also at how she said it—looking me straight in the eye.

9

Secret Messages

Aruna

'How come we are here again?' asked a perplexed Ayesha. 'Akash and I fight so much. All about things to be done around the house. We were so excited about moving in together. Where has the joy gone? How come we end up feeling bad so often?'

'Tell me what happened.'

'We live in an old house that needs plenty of work. I have a list of things that need to be done. I keep asking him to help. Like yesterday, I asked him to trim the bougainvillea in the garden. He is taller, stronger, and better suited to do it than I am.'

'And then?'

'He said "okay". Then he did nothing for two days. I got angry and asked him how many times I should remind him. Then he got mad. "Stop nagging", he said and walked away from me.'

'Then?'

'Then, in anger I took the gardening shears and the ladder and did it myself. I was quite dramatic and noisy. It was hot and I was angry. I took my anger out on the plant and pruned it quite jaggedly. My arms hurt; I had a headache. I am sure Akash could hear me. But he never came out of the room or offered to help. I went to bed crying.'

'What were your thoughts as you went to bed?' I asked.

'I have to do it alone. It is all up to me. He doesn't care,' and then after a pause, she said, 'and he gets me to do the work. How clever is he!' She looked puzzled and angry at the same time.

I pulled out my notebook and drew three stacked circles. 'This is your personality. You have three parts to your personality that often function as three people inside you—A Parent, an Adult and a Child. So has Akash,' I said, drawing another set of stacked circles next to her and labelling them P, A and C. I was using the ego state model developed by Eric Berne to understand how our personalities were structured.

'So, when you go to him with a list of things to be done around the house, at an overt level you are asking him for help.' I drew an arrow using a solid line from her Adult to his Adult.

'And he says "okay", which looks like a response from his Adult to yours.' I went on, drawing another vector from his Adult to hers.

'Yes.' She peered curiously at the drawing.

'But there is something else happening at a covert level. When you go to him with a list of things to be done, do you think there may be a secret message that you may be communicating but not verbalizing?' I asked.

'Well, yes,' she said slowly, frowning, 'I am irritated, and I am saying "Come on, pick it up. Why aren't you noticing that there are so many things to be done? Why is it up to me to bring it up?"'

'Good awareness,' I said. 'The secret message is often delivered non-verbally. I am sure he picks up on the irritation.'

'Oh, yes.' She rolled her eyes.

'How do you think we would draw the arrows for the secret message?' I asked her, confident that she would arrive at it on her own.

'I think I am in my Parent ego state. I am scolding him for not doing enough,' she said immediately. 'So that makes him the Child!'

'Well done,' I said, drawing an arrow from her Parent circle to his Child circle. But this time, I drew the arrow with dotted lines to indicate that this was communicated non-verbally.

'And when he says "okay", is he really in his Adult?' I challenged her.

'Oh my God, he is being an evasive child. This is just like I would respond to my mom. Outwardly, I would say "okay", but inside, I would be saying "whatever".' Ayesha stared at the diagram in disbelief, 'O-M-G. That is the last thing I want to be, a nagging mother! But this is our pattern.'

'When you push, you are likely to get a push back!' I highlighted.

'Yes, I am impatient. I want things done today. I want him to understand my restlessness at the number of things to be done. We both have so much work to do. Unless we plan, it will not happen,' she said, agitated.

'But when you asked him for help, he said "okay", didn't he?' I enquired. 'Yes, but if I leave him to do it, he will only do it next season!' she said.

I smiled gently. 'There is a part of you that is anxious that he won't do it. That part of you believes that he will not do it till you force him.'

'I agree,' she said, holding her head in her hands. She was recognizing her own thought process and not liking what she saw.

'Why are you not letting him know what exactly you would like and giving him a chance to respond to that?' I inquired.

'Like asking him if he could do it by Sunday instead of waiting for him to plan it on his own?' she asked.

'Yes!'

'I don't know why I am not doing that. Seems so simple. Why am I not doing that?' She was puzzled.

'Could I share my intuition with you?' I offered.

'Please!' she said impatiently, eager to get to the bottom of it.

'Is there a part of you that expects to be disappointed and is inviting him to disappoint you?' I proposed, knowing that this could be an unusual, unexpected idea for her.

She took in what I said and sat in silence for a few moments.

'I do feel disappointed and hurt. Are you saying I *want* to feel disappointed and hurt?' She looked dismayed.

I allowed a pause as she processed her own question. She seemed to know the answer.

'You are not doing it consciously. This is what, in Transactional Analysis, we call a *game*. Games are a way to justify what we already feel and believe, and shift the responsibility to the other person,' I explained.

Ayesha was listening intently. I could see her taking in what I was saying. I continued, 'I heard you say "He gets me to do the work."'

'Yes, I heard myself say that too.'

'You are an adult. He didn't get you to do it. At what point do you think you *chose* to participate in the game?' I challenged.

Ayesha thought about it for a moment before responding, 'I think from the very beginning. I think when I went to him with the list, I already, at some level, believed that finally I would end up doing it. Outwardly, my hope was that I would get help, but at the core I believed that I would eventually have to do it alone. I have no one to help me.'

'So, at a deep level, you believe no one will help you.'

'Yes,' her lips curled downwards.

'I see your sadness.'

After a few moments of silence, she said, 'I can see how I am setting myself up to feel sad. My list is never-ending. If

Akash did the trimming of the bougainvillea immediately, I would have another few things for him to do.'

'So, he would eventually push back.'

'Yes. And then, I would be disappointed and hurt at how I had to do things alone,' she sighed.

'Good awareness,' I said encouragingly. She was bravely recognizing her own limiting patterns.

'So should I just wait for him to do it whenever he pleases?' she suddenly changed her tone, becoming impatient again.

'Oh dear! There we go again,' I smiled, playfully bringing her awareness to her moving back to a game role.

She smiled and sighed, 'I just had the epiphany and, in no time, I am back to my game.'

'Don't be hard on yourself. Stepping out of an entrenched pattern can take time,' I reassured her.

'I understand. How could I start?'

'Let us play out the possibilities. You ask him to trim the hedge, let's assume, within a week and he says "okay". Then what happens?'

'Then he doesn't do it for a month!' she said smugly.

'Ok, he hasn't done it for a month. How do you respond?' She was silent for a minute. I could see her eyes glinting. 'I let it be. The bougainvillea grows wild,' she grinned.

'And how do you feel about that?'

'Strangely, I am not irritated. I am wondering why I so badly want it trimmed. I want to be more loving, but I end up fighting with him all the time. I keep pushing him away with my demands.'

'I can see how puzzling this is for you. Have I shared with you what *strokes* are?'

'Yes—the ways in which we recognize or acknowledge or support or affirm each other.'

'Fantastic. And strokes can be positive or negative based on whether they feel good or bad. We need strokes for survival. When we can't obtain positive strokes, we may not just accept, we may even seek out negative strokes. A good way to understand it is that a hungry man may eat rotten food in extreme need, if fresh food is inaccessible.'

'So how do I make sense of what is going on for me? Akash and I seem to be exchanging only negative strokes. Like we are eating rotten food with a vengeance. So where is the fresh food?'

'Good question. We may have to explore at a deeper level what your relationship with positive strokes is. Even though you want them, perhaps they feel scary. Meanwhile, to survive, you can get strokes through games—they are painful, but they are predictable.'

Ayesha sighed. 'I feel a little messed up. I pick fights with Akash to get him to engage with me. I do that with everybody, I think. I go after them with lists—so they all give me negative strokes.'

'Oh okay, so you see a pattern here. You are also in touch with the belief that you will end up alone, underneath all of this.'

'So the solution seems to be to not look for reasons to believe that I will end up all alone. And not nag people so they avoid me. It is a big change for me, letting go.'

It was indeed a big change for her. She had recognized an unconscious pattern of finding a way to get angry with people. At an unconscious level, keeping people away from her protected her in some way. We would hopefully get to that as we worked longer together. Today, this insight was significant.

'Do you feel ready for this big change?' I asked.

'I am,' she looked straight at me. 'I don't want to set myself up for fights. I want a loving relationship with Akash. I can let some things go and enjoy myself more.'

'Could you describe this change to me?'

'I don't let the wild bougainvillea upset me. I don't want to be a nag with a long list of things to do.'

'And how are you, instead?'

'I let go of many things. I am more relaxed and loving,' Ayesha looked somewhere at a point beyond me. 'I see an overgrown, untidy bougainvillea bush, a sunset, and the silhouette of Akash and me sipping tea against that glorious backdrop.'

'Wow!' I cheered.

'I love the picture,' she said, with the most relaxed smile I had ever seen on her face.

10

Tell Me What to Do

Yashodhara

'So, what do I *do*, Yash?' pleaded Tina, leaning forward in her chair, eyes wide. 'Tell me what to do!'

I took in a deep breath, to make sure that my voice reflected the calm that I knew was so important for Tina whenever she reached this state of panic. She had been speaking for the last ten minutes, describing to me in detail the events of the last week—her teenage daughter was rebelling and performing poorly in school, her husband's business had taken a turn for the worse, and now, she felt that her own job was under threat because of murmurs about organizational changes.

'Tina,' I began gently, but I didn't get a chance to finish.

'I know!' she interrupted, her face screwing up in pain, 'I know you *won't* tell me what to do. But this is a real crisis, and I can't think! I just can't take the idea of going in to work tomorrow morning and hearing some bad news, on top of everything going on at home. I'm going to end up having a breakdown!'

Her shoulders started heaving and tears ran down her face. I wordlessly reached out and offered her a box of tissues, and she took two of them and wiped her tears. She blew her nose softly. I felt an urge to protect her. In our sessions, Tina was often like a helpless, lost little girl, and I knew it was just in this space and in very few personal relationships that she allowed this side of her to emerge. In fact, it was the pressure of keeping up the appearance of a strong, tough person who never needed to ask for help that caused her immense stress.

When her tears subsided enough for her to speak, I asked her, 'What do you think would help you most right now?'

'I don't *know*,' she sniffed and then went on, 'I mean, I do know but I won't get that because you've said before a therapist's role is not to advise—but I *need* someone to tell me what to do. I just can't think when things all come at me at once like this. This is one of those times.'

I smiled kindly. I heard her ulterior message, 'Please, please, see my suffering and give me advice,' but stayed grounded. I was not going to be hooked. 'Alright then,' I said, 'could I propose an experiment?'

'What?' She blinked at me a couple of times. 'Okay, I guess.' Her curiosity made her move out of her 'poor me' stance.

'There is a part of you that feels lost and needs advice.' I recognized this as the Child in Tina. It dominated her personality. I hoped to help her see and strengthen her Adult resources.

'Yes,' she said, listening keenly.

'You seem very blended with that part. And yet—you are so much more than that lost Tina.'

'I'd like to think so,' she said wistfully.

'Would you like to listen to the lost part of you? Perhaps creating a distance from it can be helpful.'

She nodded in agreement. I pointed to the second chair next to her. I stood up and walked around the table to help position the empty chair for her.

She looked unsure but complied, shifting chairs, and now facing the one that she had been sitting on previously.

'Tina,' I said, pointing to the first chair. 'Over there is the part of you that is feeling lost and worried right now. Can you see her?'

Tina crossed her arms over her chest as she heard me. I asked her to respond to that part. When she spoke, it wasn't the little girl's voice—it was a stern one that snapped, 'Of course, she's asking for help—to think! It's just another way to avoid taking responsibility for her own life and own messes. She should just get her act together and do what needs to be . . .' She stopped abruptly.

'What happened?' I noticed her stiffening up in the chair.

She exclaimed, 'I sound exactly like my mom. This is how she used to speak to me before the exams when I got scared.'

'So, Mom judged your helplessness?'

'Yes. I guess her idea was to lick me into shape. I was very nervous and anxious, but her sharpness made me go quiet. Inside, I'd feel even worse—like I was also weak and silly and useless for feeling scared.'

When we are young, we take in the voices and attitudes of parents and parental figures. These then become a part of our own psyche as our Parent ego state and show up as self-talk. I could see that Tina had a strong internal Critical Parent voice; she needed a more comforting, encouraging resource, that is, a Nurturing Parent voice.

'And was there anyone who nurtured you?'

She shrugged. 'My parents gave me what I *needed*. But I don't really remember kind or comforting words from them. Or anyone in my family, really—they were all the "tough-love" variety.'

'Would you be willing to offer yourself some nurturing now?'

'I don't know if I can do that.' She sounded dubious. 'Don't think I have it in me.'

'Let us give it a try,' I said encouragingly. 'Come, sit here instead, on this chair.' I stood up and wheeled my own chair around the table. The shift in energy that a physical change effected could be useful.

For a moment, she looked like she would protest. Tina wasn't used to this sort of exercise in our sessions, preferring instead to use our time to talk about her problems, pausing to see if I would offer some magic words of wisdom. I wasn't giving into the pressure I felt from her today though, and she stood up and took the third chair and faced the empty chair in front of her. I invited her to imagine that a lost, wounded Tina was sitting on that chair. To my surprise, her face softened immediately, and she said, 'You don't have to listen to her.' She said gently to lost Tina, pointing to the Mom chair she had just vacated. 'She means well, but she bullies you a lot. I know you don't look to avoid responsibility. In fact, I think the problem is the opposite, you take on *too much* responsibility. When you try to do so much, things can just pile up on top of you and it can be tough. I feel you right now.'

I hadn't actually heard this tone from Tina before and was both surprised and intrigued. 'What shall we call this part of you that just spoke so nurturingly?' I asked.

'The Kind Tina,' she said, smiling.

I intuitively decided to help strengthen the nurturing voice, 'So what do you think Tina needs to do? Can you tell her?'

Tina paused for only a moment, and then went on, sounding both self-assured and reassuring, 'You need to do *nothing*. You're doing just fine. If your daughter isn't studying hard enough, she's going to have to learn the consequences—you've done so much already and, in fact, if you pull back, maybe she'll step up. Same thing about Atul's business. Your worrying about it and interfering in his decisions isn't going to help matters. He's handled such times before; he'll do it again. You keep your own energies and focus on your job. And even there, you're doing fine. If you're concerned about these organizational changes, you can just go up and speak to your boss—you're senior enough to ask to be in the know on this sort of thing, and it's okay to voice your worries and get information. Just relax. You've been around for so long and you're extremely valuable to the organization. Don't worry, you've got this!'

I nodded, although she wasn't looking at me—she was still gazing at the first chair. 'Wow,' I said, 'this really is the kind *and* wise Tina.' That made her look at me, and she nodded in agreement.

I asked, 'Would you please move into the chair of Lost Tina now, and respond to what Kind Tina said?'

Tina obliged. When she spoke now, she seemed to be back in the Child, but nowhere near as scared. 'Thank you for that.' She said to the empty chair softly, 'It's just the money thing that scares me. If Sheetal does make it to a college abroad, it will be so expensive. I just don't know if we will be able to afford that; our savings aren't that great.' She gazed at the chair and repeated, 'So . . . it's the money thing.'

I indicated that she should go back onto the Nurturing Parent chair. After she shifted physically, her energy too did the same again. 'The money thing,' she responded without needing any further cue from me, 'is really another thing you needn't worry about. You do have enough savings; you've been planning for this for years. Even if Atul's had a setback, it will be just a while before you guys recover. And there's always the option of a loan, which I know you've avoided so far, but your track record indicates you'll be able to handle it. One thing I want you to remember— you guys will always have a roof over your head. You'll certainly never ever go hungry.' She had a twinkle in the eye. 'Remember—there's always the Langar at a nearby Gurudwara!'

I found myself smiling at that one as I invited her to shift chairs a final time. She went back into her original chair, and I marvelled at her relaxed energy as she burst out laughing, answering herself, 'I remember! I remember when I first had that thought—I was around ten and we had all gone to the Gurudwara and I felt so happy and grateful to think this thought, at least we'll *never* go hungry. It was a beautiful moment. I had forgotten about it till now!'

'You want to say anything to the Kind Tina voice now?' I asked.

'Just thank you,' she said simply, the gratitude evident on her face. I waited a few moments for her to take it in.

'Now you can shake all other voices off, Tina. Try this!' I stood up and shook my hands as if I was getting something to fall off.

She stood up and shook herself. She took her seat again and then looked up at me and said in a tone of wonder, 'Okay, wow. Did I just counsel myself?'

'I think you certainly counselled—and comforted—yourself,' I said, smiling, 'and a very wise voice it was too. Better than anything I—and maybe anyone else—could have said.'

She nodded slowly. We had just uncovered a very valuable, underleveraged resource for her—a new wise, nurturing, and kind Parent voice, with a light touch, that could help her to step outside of her frightened Child self and be the support to herself that she most needed—and that would help to lighten the pressure that she put on herself. I made a mental note to get her to practise accessing this voice often and to also get her to trust her own here-and-now, rational Adult thinking—years of using a harsh internal tone towards herself couldn't be undone in a day. And yet, today was an important day because a remarkably different voice had finally made itself heard.

11

Laddoos and Love

Aruna

'I behave like Dr Jekyll and Mr Hyde when it comes to food!' sighed Elmy. 'There are weeks when I can stop eating completely, and then suddenly I eat as if food was going to run out. I binge on sugary stuff.'

Elmy had an uncomfortable relationship with food. I could see the battle between her internal Controlling Parent (Don't eat too much) and Rebellious Child (I will not be controlled), each winning alternately. My task was to make this battle explicit and understand the origins of it.

I enquired into Elmy's history. She said her father had been a schoolteacher and didn't earn much. Her mother had been an air hostess who also did some modelling assignments on the side to earn an additional income.

'Mum believed Dad was useless, and it was up to her to earn for the family and raise our standard of living. Mum would travel a lot for work. Because she was a model, she really attended to her looks and weight. She planned her meals carefully and carried many small tiffin boxes to work. She never ate sugar. I was brought up by a nanny who was given strict instructions by Mum on what I should be fed. My food was measured. I was never to say no to fruits, vegetables, or nuts. If something was put on my plate, I was to finish it, no questions asked. We never kept sugar at home. In fact, I did not discover the existence of sugar till I was five years old, in a neighbour's house, where I was offered ice cream,' Elmy said.

'What flavour was it? How was it to taste ice cream for the first time?' I was curious.

'It was vanilla,' she said, smiling wistfully. 'I thought I had tasted something from heaven.'

'What happened then?' I asked.

'When I told my mum about it, she looked horrified and told me I had had "white poison". She said "You'll become fat. You won't be able to dance or even run fast. Fat people can't wear shorts or sleeveless tops. People make fun of fat people." I felt ashamed.'

'And you were only five!' I said in disbelief, unable to hide how appalled I was at the idea of a five-year-old having to hear these messages.

'Yes,' she said, as tears first pooled in her eyes before starting to flow down her cheeks.

'The only way for me to have food that I liked was in secret. I started stealing money from home. I bought ice cream and candy at school. I would eat a lot in other people's houses. I started begging my friends to smuggle in snacks for me.'

I nodded, listening with rapt attention.

'Once when my mum was travelling, my aunt sent a jar of homemade laddoos. I asked Dad if I could have one. He said "Just one, otherwise Mum will find out." I ate one and it was delicious. I decided one more wouldn't be missed, and I ate another. What I was doing felt dangerous, but I couldn't stop. I knew Mum would be furious and I would be punished. She might never give me any more laddoos. So, I ate another in fear. And then another one in anger. Then I ate another to teach her a lesson. Soon, I had eaten over twenty laddoos at a feverish pace, maybe in less than twenty minutes!'

'My father was shocked when he found out and scolded me, saying "Wait till your mum is home!" He reported it to my mom when she returned, and she punished me by saying that I would not be given any dinner and would have to eat boiled vegetables for lunch for a week. It was so harsh! I looked to my father for support. But he just smirked as if to say, "You little glutton, this should teach you a lesson."'

'You remember the smirk! How did you feel?'

'I hated him for that. I glared at him with rage. He glared right back. They shoved me into my room. I went hungry that night, and I knew they were eating dinner outside. I thought to myself "When I grow up, I won't let anyone control me. I will eat whatever I want, whenever I want."'

I repeated, 'When I grow up, I won't let anyone control me. I will eat whatever I want whenever I want.'

We both took in the significance of the statement. We had found the origin of the battle between the Controlling Parent and the Rebellious Child.

'So, you are eating today in protest of what they did to you as a child?' I asked.

'I probably am. I am!' she sighed.

I held the space for her in silence as she continued.

'Mum never loved me for who I was,' she said, tears flowing down her cheeks.

'And Dad?'

'He was around, but I don't remember him having his own opinion on anything. He would go along with whatever Mum said. She was the smarter one. She was earning more. She had a glamorous job. I think Dad was scared that she would leave him.'

I noted that there was plenty of material there to explore around gender roles, money, and careers. For another time. This session was about exploring her relationship with food.

'How *did* they show you their love?' I asked.

'I am not sure,' she said despondently. 'I don't think I was ever hugged or treated affectionately. I thought maybe my father too didn't love me because I was fat. They did all the basic things, but most of the focus was on controlling my diet. That was their way of taking care of me. All conversations were about food, fatness, and money.'

I could see Elmy's pain. As a child, she had never been hugged or touched enough. Food was often withheld, and she experienced her parents' love and approval as being conditional.

I knew she had never been allowed to be angry. I invited her to express her anger towards her mother in the therapy room, by imagining her sitting on an empty chair opposite her.

As she addressed her mother, her anger escalated, 'All you cared about was my weight. You made me feel ugly and unlovable. I hated the remarks you made about my being fat. I hate you. I wish you were dead.' She sobbed bitterly as she said that. I saw the battered child, beneath the anger.

'I never knew I was this angry,' she said to me after she finished the process. 'I don't really want her to die.'

'I know that,' I reassured her, 'but I am glad you were able to access and express the anger that you were never allowed to.'

'Yes,' she agreed. 'So am I.'

'This anger was present in you even though you may not have been in contact with it. I wonder in what unconscious ways this anger showed up?'

Elmy said, 'I see it so clearly now! She wanted me to be thin, stylish, and married to a rich man. I'm fat, sloppy, single, and independent. She wanted me to be a model; I am an accountant.'

'So, you, in your anger, decided to not give her what she wanted.'

'Yes. I wanted to *never* give her what she wanted. I would do the opposite of whatever she wanted. I hated her comments about my being fat, but I hated her delight when I lost weight even more. If someone said in front of her that I looked nice, she would take all the credit for it. She would gloat that it was because of her. My thinness belonged to her.'

'So, you decided that you would never be thin. You couldn't let her win.'

'I couldn't let her win. How could I?' she said, starting to cry.

'How do you make sense of the intense diets you put yourself through?'

'I guess I also believed all that she said about everybody laughing at fat people.'

'You believed that you would be loved if you were thin?'

'I still believe it. Whenever I feel intensely lonely, I go on these diets.'

'Complete this sentence for me: "If I were thin . . ."'

'Then I would never be lonely again.'

This was a momentous insight. I repeated it for her and waited for the significance of it to percolate.

'And yet every time you lose weight, you unconsciously believe that your mother has won,' I said.

'Yes. In fact, when people compliment me on my weight loss, I feel invaded and patronized, and then the reverse process starts. I start binging.'

'I wonder if you are angry with your father too.'

'Well, he was so indifferent to my suffering. I believed he also wanted me to be thin. I adopted a "who needs you, anyway" stance with my father.'

'And do you think that affects how you are with men today?'

'It does—I believe that I don't need them. My mother's belief that men are useless has somewhere become mine.'

Over the next few months, Elmy began to uncover more of her life script and allowed her repressed feelings to surface. She felt less need to stuff her feelings down with food. She made a decision to love herself for who she was, trusting that if she learnt to love herself unconditionally, she would be able to take in unconditional love from others.

I was delighted when she walked in with a confident smile in a sleeveless top one day. 'I do not have to wait till I am thin in order to do the things I enjoy or have the things I want,' she declared.

I agreed wholeheartedly.

12

Rock A-Bye, Baby

Yashodhara

'So, what would you like in today's session?'

'I don't know, really. Haven't had much time to think, been busy at work.' Renu's face was impassive, her arms folded defensively around her body, and her answer didn't surprise me one bit.

When Renu had first come in for therapy, she had said she felt stuck and just wanted to 'move' somehow— across all key areas of her life, including her job and her relationships. She'd had many insights at an intellectual level in the course of our sessions—especially about her fear of failure being the main reason for not taking action. I'd felt it hard to get close to her, and as more time passed, it felt as if it was becoming even tougher for me to connect with her. She seemed committed to being in therapy for the long term, but I wondered what she was actually getting out of our sessions. I decided to ask directly.

'Renu,' I began, 'I am curious about your motivation for continuing therapy. Could we talk about what you might be getting out of our work here?'

There was a flicker of uncertainty on her face, but it passed, and she said nonchalantly, beginning to rock her body back and forth on her chair, 'I don't know. I guess it's just one space where I can sort of speak without filtering. I've told you stuff I haven't really talked about to anyone else, childhood and all. It just helps to know you're—I mean, the space—is there.'

I noted the correction of 'you' to 'the space'—Renu often spoke in a way that depersonalized things. It was a sign of having difficulty with feeling. And yet, it was clear that this was precisely where our work was getting stuck. My attempts to get her to feel, acknowledge, and speak about her feelings were stonewalled. I tried yet again.

'Is it perhaps hard for you to talk about how you feel about me?' I ventured.

She looked a bit stricken, like a deer caught in headlights, but then burst out laughing. 'No! Why would that be hard? I mean—I . . . I like you, I guess, you . . . it helps to know if I'm in trouble, you'd probably help or something.'

'Probably help or something?' I said. 'Say more about that?'

'I mean, I don't know. I've had some *really* bad days in the last month and thought of calling you, but then figured I wouldn't want to disturb you and our sessions were scheduled anyway, so I just waited. And the bad days passed.'

'Ah.' I took this in. 'You didn't actually mention the bad days the last couple of times we have talked, though.'

She shrugged her shoulders dismissively, continuing to rock herself.

'Renu,' I decided to enquire about it, 'do you know that you're rocking yourself?'

'What? Oh!' She dropped her arms to the side and stopped rocking immediately.

'No, don't stop.' I wrapped my arms around my body and mirrored her back and forth movement. 'Do this.'

'Okay, now I feel silly.'

'Let's be a bit silly?'

Renu gave a sardonic grin. She wrapped her arms tight around herself and rocked her body back and forth.

'Could I invite you to close your eyes and keep doing it?' She obliged. 'That's right. Just keep rocking like that and be in touch with your felt experience of this rocking.'

She kept rocking herself, her eyes closed. After a few moments, when I saw her relaxing into the movement, I said, 'Okay, tell me how it feels?'

'It's . . . I don't know, comforting, I guess?'

'Okay,' I said gently, 'any thoughts coming up?'

I was half-expecting her to resist but there was now some curiosity on her face as she said 'huh'.

'What are you getting in touch with, Renu?'

'It's weird. I remembered something.' She opened her eyes.

'What did you remember?' I enquired.

'Well, I told you Mom had this miscarriage when I was small, right? I was pretty tiny, like two-and-a-half or something, so it's something that I learned about later.'

'Right,' I said. Renu had mentioned it, almost in passing, as an insignificant detail in an early session. 'And now?'

'Now, I just had this impression of being in the room with her, and I don't know, she's like, really upset or something . . . probably really silent, she wouldn't have cried or anything, not the type . . . And even though I'm not feeling good about something, I know I shouldn't trouble her.'

Just like she had not wanted to trouble me on her bad days, I thought. 'So, you're rocking yourself—to soothe yourself?'

'Yes,' she said, 'actually I think she used to rock me earlier, maybe. There's this old lullaby she used to sing, I don't remember, something silly she made up—it would always calm me down when I was upset.' She screwed up her face as if listening for the long-forgotten tune. After a few moments, she looked disappointed. 'I don't remember, but anyway, she stopped doing it afterwards.'

'After the miscarriage?' I asked. 'You must have missed her comforting you?'

'I guess.' She shrugged, but I noticed the fleeting glimpse of sadness pass over her face. 'But she's the strong type, even though she gets nervous sometimes. We all are a bit like that in the family. We don't like to think about what went wrong, it's about just . . . we just keep moving, I guess.'

Moving. I connected this to the original contract she had come in with. Renu had a coping strategy developed in childhood, of just comforting herself, not having or expressing her own needs, and by just diving into action. And yet, as it tended to happen, a stage had come in her adulthood where the suppression of her feelings and her lack of vulnerability were possibly the very things that were causing her to be stuck and unable to move. Her anxiety about taking any step out of her comfort zone was possibly the result of an important emotion—sadness—being disallowed and remaining unprocessed.

Indeed, further exploration revealed that while worry and fear were acceptable emotions and had been modelled by both her parents when she was growing up, sadness had never been expressed in the family. Some important shifts took place after this. Over a period of six months, we were able to explore Renu's underlying sadness and inability to open up to people. As she made herself more vulnerable with me, she also began to communicate in other key relationships, including the one with her mother—with whom the distance had grown over many years. She also realized that when it came to other aspects of her life where she felt stuck, it was more than the fear of failure—she was dealing with the fear of being hurt and disappointed, which felt like unbearable emotions to her. As she acknowledged this and allowed for further exploration by getting deeper into her memories around feeling hurt and alone, this fear loosened its grip on her. She began to explore the world of dating and managed to make a step change in her career by shifting out of her 'dead-end' role to a new company.

She was moving again, and this time, it wasn't about just pushing down sadness and being alone. She was learning to trust and count on other people as well. I knew this first hand, because her bad days were no longer kept a secret from me.

13

Cash for Sympathy

Aruna

'Here is the therapy fee in cash,' Keerti said, handing over a big bundle.

'You are paying for twenty-four sessions upfront!' I exclaimed in surprise as she mentioned the amount. 'You don't have to. Most clients pay for six sessions at a time.'

'No, no, no, take it from me,' she said, pushing the money towards me, turning her head away as if she did not even want to look at it.

'If I keep it with me, I will spend it,' she explained. 'I have saved this for over one year. Every time someone paid me for therapy (she was a therapist herself), I would take the money and immediately put it into a piggy bank. If I saw it, I would get tempted to have an occasional ice cream or take an auto somewhere instead of the bus. I can't tell you how thrilled I am to have saved this up.'

I felt confused. A part of me was admiring, 'Wow! She is so committed to her therapy.' Another part of me felt guilty. I wondered, 'Should I return the money to her? Or I could reduce the fee? She seems to be struggling.'

'I am feeling sad that you are depriving yourself of ice cream,' I said to her, the bundle of cash still in my hands.

'No, no, no, don't feel sad,' Keerti came in strongly, fighting her tears. 'I made a choice. I wanted to ensure that I paid you for the full year before I started. I was worried I would run into trouble halfway and then ask you for a favour.' At that moment, I felt powerless against her determination. I accepted the money even though I was significantly uncomfortable.

There were other patterns in my work with Keerti that increased my discomfort. For instance, I noticed that she brought a new issue into therapy every session. In one session, she spoke about being jealous of a friend, and the next session, she spoke about her mother-in-law.

'I am curious about how things shifted with your friend after the last session. You were going to meet her and were very stressed about it. How did it go?'

'Oh, that went just fine!' she said, brushing off the issue with a dismissive wave of her hand.

'What made it fine?' I was curious.

'Well, because of all that we discussed,' she frowned impatiently. 'I want to talk about what happened with my mother-in-law.'

I found the progress she claimed magical and improbable, yet I found myself unable to challenge her. I realized that she was putting up a defence against going deeper and accessing her vulnerability. I repeatedly experienced a loss of power against her strength. She would at times unexpectedly change the topic in our sessions and very firmly stay in control over what issues we actually discussed in the room.

I took the powerlessness that I experienced for supervision. As an ethical practice that is part of continued self-development, we as therapists often take our work into supervision with senior practitioners. For this issue, I needed a safe space to reflect and receive some guidance. The unconscious dynamic between Keerti and me became clearer to me in the supervision session. I recognized that I felt 'bought' with the fee and the story that came along with it.

Her secret message to me was, 'Don't take me where I don't want to go.' And I responded with, 'Yes, I will not, because you have really struggled to make this work. I feel guilty for charging you.' I recognized how, through her actions, she was zealously defending herself from feeling vulnerable. I was able to drop my guilt once I recognized the pattern. I decided that I would invite Keerti into feelings that were scary for her and help her explore and contain them.

In the next session, Keerti shared with me how difficult her marriage was and how she felt unseen and humiliated by her husband.

'I wonder how this narrative is serving you. What is your investment in sustaining this dynamic between you and your husband?' I gently challenged her. I was aware, present, and grounded.

She went silent and looked ashamed momentarily and then responded with, 'I am not asking for too much from him. Just a little love and understanding. Is that too much to ask?' This was a tangential response—an unconscious avoidance of my question.

'Did you hear my question?' I asked, deliberately not letting the conversation go off on the tangent.

'Yes,' she said sheepishly. 'You are asking what advantage I have in feeling sad for myself.'

'That's right. What might it be?' I asked. I noticed her hesitation to answer. She looked down in silence.

'What are you feeling?' She continued to be silent.

'I sense shame,' I said, naming the emotion. Naming an emotion is an act of acknowledging and facing it, and that can bring relief. It can be the start of the process of change.

She nodded, with her head still down.

'Tell me more about it,' I asked gently.

'I am a therapist. I should know better,' she whispered.

That answer of hers explained a lot of her behaviour to me. The moment we began to examine her process, she would experience shame at her own inadequacy and quickly change the topic so that we wouldn't explore the area any further.

'I wonder what you think of me,' she said.

'What is your fantasy? What do you imagine me thinking about you?' I asked.

'I imagine you are disgusted. I am such a mess. You might be thinking—how could she even be a therapist?'

'What is your belief about how a therapist should be?'

'I should be able to manage my own issues. I can't be this troubled,' she said.

I nodded slowly. I was only too familiar with this myth that therapists must be all sorted for them to help clients. We worked through this belief of hers. While it is true that regular self-work and self-care are responsibilities of a therapist so that their own issues do not interfere with their ability to make contact with clients, we all need to accept our humanness and limitations.

My empathetic reception of Keerti's sharing invited her to gradually let her guard down in sessions. We spoke about how she protected herself from feeling her feelings by staying in control. She recognized her Be Strong driver, an unconscious script decision to protect herself from pain by being invulnerable at all times.

'I now understand why I have often been called aggressive in relationships. It is a manifestation of my wanting to stay in control,' she said.

As she became more reflective about her own internal world, I pushed in more boldly. 'I wondered what could have been going on for you when you paid me for twenty-four sessions and shared that you had given up ice cream to accumulate this amount,' I wondered with her.

'Oh, I was just sharing that,' she said, getting defensive. 'I wasn't manipulating you.'

'I am curious if there was an unconscious process at work,' I said. There was a pause.

'Perhaps I wanted your sympathy,' she responded reflectively.

'I wonder if you wanted me to be sympathetic so that I wouldn't challenge you.'

'Yes, there were many times I wanted you to change direction and not press me to go further down some paths.'

'Which is what I did too. It was an unconscious process for me as well,' I revealed. 'I felt anxious about challenging you; I felt an urge to take care.'

My statement left her a little open-mouthed, 'You were anxious?'

'How does my saying that impact you?' I was very curious.

'You said it so easily. It felt very natural and the right thing to do.'

'Are you attracted to being this way?' I asked.

'Yes, I am. But I can never be like that,' she said dolefully, shaking her head from side to side. 'Why not?'

Her eyes welled up. 'I am beyond repair.' 'What does that mean?' I asked kindly.

'I haven't been able to make a single relationship work in my life. I push people away. I am ugly, selfish, and mean.'

I was struck by the harshness of the words she used. I wondered about the harshness she had experienced as a child for her to see herself in this way. To accept and love herself, it would be important for her to have consistent acceptance and validation from another.

'Let us make *our* relationship work!' I offered.

She smiled.

As I listened to her compassionately over several sessions, she transformed from this stoic, in-control woman to a wounded, disorderly child, inconsolable at times. She shared her life story in a faltering voice, stopping only to take in raspy gulps of air. 'Our family was shamed often for not having enough money. I have been shamed by my parents for wanting things for myself. I don't want anyone to point a finger at me or have pity for me or do me any favours with regard to money.' She shared with me that her mother had been mentally ill and had attempted to take her own life numerous times. My heart ached as she described this, how her father had a drinking problem, and how he would come home drunk and become violent with both her and her mother. His drinking meant he couldn't hold on to any job.

'I felt everyone in the neighbourhood either laughed at us or looked at us with pity. I wanted to hide, sometimes even from myself. And run far away, where nobody knew who my parents were, and I could start life afresh.'

Shame was the theme of Keerti's life. She felt fundamentally flawed and unworthy of love and belonging.

In our work, she recognized that she was running away from shame by staying in control. I drew her back into feeling it and making meaning of it, regulating her shame with a deep steady compassion and unwavering acceptance of her. I was 'being *with*', rather than '*doing to*' her.

Over several months, she allowed herself to experience my warmth and presence. 'You are listening to more than my words,' she said. My seeing and accepting the parts of her that she had disowned created a bridge for her to connect with those parts of herself. As she became less defensive, her narrative changed. She no longer felt humiliated by her husband. Her guilt around her needs reduced. She showed up more authentically in our conversations.

'I have transformed in the last one year through our conversations. People who don't understand therapy would think we were just chatting,' she said incredulously.

'Just chatting!' I repeated, smiling. Often people expect the therapist to visibly 'do' something. But significant therapeutic work is often not dramatic, and therefore not easily recognized or understood. Subtle shifts add up over time.

'Many times, to me too, it felt like I was only talking all the time. Yet, I have changed so much. What is it about our conversations that shifted things?' she asked reflectively.

'What do you think it was?' I smiled.

'I felt seen,' she said, 'I could show you parts of me that I was ashamed of. And then I didn't feel as ashamed because you didn't judge them.'

I nodded sagely.

She continued, fascinated, 'And I saw *you*. I saw my impact on you. You were human.'

'So, while we were chatting, a lot was going on at an unconscious level!'

'I know. I learnt to make a relationship work.'

'So did I,' I added, accounting for how I had grown while working with her, marvelling at the transformative power of authentic relating.

14

Be the Biscuit!

Yashodhara

'I don't know how to control it,' Rahul said, a serious frown on his face. 'It's not good for my diabetes. But I can't stop.'

Rahul was a relatively new client, and not always forthcoming about his personal life. He had come in saying that he felt confused and stuck about his career, but as it often happened, the conversation in therapy moved across different areas. He came across as the responsible, staid provider for his family. He had described his childhood as an only child, living in a house with his parents and aged grandmother, and having learned early on to be a self-reliant kid who 'never caused any trouble'. So today I was seeing a new side to him, and I repeated, 'So, you're saying it's with *biscuits* in particular that you have no self-control?'

'Not just *any* biscuit,' he said emphatically, 'those damn *Bourbon* biscuits.'

I was familiar with the rectangular chocolate biscuits he was referring to. They'd been around a long time. My own relationship with Bourbon prompted my next question.

'Has this been a long-standing thing for you, with Bourbon?'

'Not really,' he screwed up his face, as if trying to remember. 'I've been good with my diet overall, ever since I was diagnosed five years ago. Last month, my wife got these biscuits home for the kids, and I saw them lying on the table, and—well, that was it.'

'So, what is it that happened when you saw them?'

'I just felt like trying one, and so I did. And it just tasted so good. Maybe also that I don't usually eat sweet things. No one was around, and before I knew it, I'd finished the packet! My wife would be so angry if she knew.'

'And since then?'

'Since then, I have been buying them on the way back from work, maybe three times a week! And when I get some time alone in my room, after dinner, when my wife is putting the kids to bed, I just eat the whole packet.'

'Even though you know it's bad for you.'

'Yes. I tell my wife I'm just doing a little puja for some time and lock the door . . . then I polish off the Bourbons! I do pray after that, feeling really guilty. And ever since this started happening, the other things, like my portion control, are going out the window too—I've gained 3 kgs in about as many weeks! I am not taking care of my health the same way anymore . . . I know I need to think more about the family . . .' He looked despairingly at me. 'Why do you think this is happening?'

'I really don't know,' I said honestly. 'But would you be willing to try something unusual?'

'Sure.'

'Can you become Bourbon?'

He looked blankly at me. 'Become—how?'

'Just imagine you're the pack of Bourbon biscuits. And speak to me as that pack.'

He looked doubtful, but his interest in uncovering what lay beneath this strange pattern seemed to override.

'Just stand up, walk around the chair, and sit down again. When you sit down, embody the biscuit pack.'

He played along with me and walked around the chair and sat down. 'Okay. I'm the biscuit pack, I guess.'

'Hi, Bourbon!' I said cheerily.

'Hello,' he replied, looking amused.

'Can you describe yourself to me?'

He started to speak, haltingly, 'Well . . . I'm rectangular and brown. Kind of like the biscuits I contain. They are really tasty, full of chocolate in the middle, and have little sugar crystals on top too.'

'Ah,' I said. 'You sound like a real treat for Rahul.'

'I am,' he said, smiling. 'He is very fond of me.' I could see that he had moved into the role.

'Why is he so fond of you?'

He suddenly looked thoughtful. 'I'm more than a treat. I'm his friend.'

'His friend, huh?' I said. 'Tell me more about that?'

'I was his favourite biscuit when he was a kid. But his mom always hid me in the storeroom. His Dadi always said not to feed him sweet things, because he was chubby.'

'How are you feeling right now, Bourbon, as you remember this?'

'I'm a little angry with him.' Rahul said after a pause, 'He forgot his only friend!'

'You were his only friend?'

'He was lonely. He was the only kid at home, and he didn't have many friends either. After school, he would often come and pick me up from the storeroom. It was when Mom was out, and Grandma was sleeping.'

'Yes? He came often to the kitchen to do this?'

'He told his grandma he was praying; there was a little puja area in the storeroom, but he would come and sneak me out, and take a couple of biscuits at a time. Never more than one or two, or the adults would know.'

'How do you think he felt when he did that?'

'He felt happy!' Rahul was really getting into the role now. 'He was doing something that he liked. He thought he deserved a treat now and then! But of course, he then also felt guilty and then studied and worked extra-hard. He wouldn't want to let his family down in any way. They all depended on him.'

'So, you were his secret friend who knew all this?'

'Yes,' affirmed the Rahul-Bourbon. 'I was his special secret—but secrets are not good.'

'It's not okay to have secrets?' I asked gently.

'No' was the immediate reply. 'Secrets mean you're doing something really bad and that you will pay.'

'Where did this message come from, Bourbon?'

'Rahul's dadi always said this. Her stories were full of people who paid dearly for the lies they told.'

'I see.' I could see the lonely little overly responsible boy who had felt so much guilt, fear, and pressure. 'So, Bourbon, if you had one thing to tell Rahul right now, what would it be?'

Rahul closed his eyes for a moment, and then opened them again. 'I'd tell him—You're not a child. And I'm really not good for you now, you've got diabetes. You've got to think about your family.'

'That doesn't sound like you, Bourbon.' I wondered if this was the voice of Dadi. I went on, 'You're telling him not to be a child, and that he's got to think about his family? Do you think that is what your friend needs to hear?'

'No,' Rahul said thoughtfully. 'He needs to hear something else.'

'So, what would you like to say to him, Bourbon?'

'He need not keep the relationship with me a secret. He can allow himself to be a child. Enough of being responsible!' After a pause, Rahul spoke in a slower, softer voice. 'He wasn't allowed to be a child when he was a child. But now, he needn't keep eating me and keeping it a secret! He can find other ways to be a kid and have fun.'

'What might some ways be, Bourbon, since you know him so well?'

A smile came over Rahul's face. 'Well, he loved going to the park and tossing Frisbees around by himself. And now he's got kids to play with too. He can do stuff like that with them.'

'That's a nice suggestion, Bourbon.' I mirrored Rahul's smile. He looked peaceful, if a little wistful.

After a few moments, I gently asked, 'Okay to end this exercise?' He nodded at me.

'Perhaps you can just shake off your Bourbon energy and come back to being Rahul?' I suggested.

He did that and for the rest of the session, we processed what had happened. Rahul was surprised at the insights he had gained and the connections he had made in just a short conversation by taking on the perspective of the biscuit pack.

Sometimes, an action method like this can help us get to the heart of the issue in unexpected ways. Having understood what might actually underlie his obsession with the biscuits—a deep-seated yearning to be allowed to be a child instead of the constantly guilt-ridden, responsible man of the family—Rahul was able to stop gorging in secret. Bourbon biscuits were no longer a temptation; instead, he began to give expression to his hidden desire through play and experimentation in different areas of his life.

And over the next few months, it wasn't merely physically that he became a far lighter version of himself.

15

A Thumbs Up from Hanuman

Aruna

'I feel guilty so easily,' said Purvi. 'I want to relax about it. I want to stop making myself small and anxious.'

'You recognize that you *make* yourself small and anxious,' I said admiringly. The admiration was for her recognizing her own role in the feelings she experienced. I saw that she was keen to take charge of herself, instead of blaming another or waiting for another to change. This shift of locus of control from outside to inside self is a significant marker of readiness for change.

Guilt and anxiety were Purvi's 'go to' feelings. In childhood, children observe that certain feelings are treated with outright disapproval by the family, while some are acceptable. These are feelings that children were 'allowed' to have, while other feelings were invalidated.

So, children learn how they are supposed to react; for instance, a child may conclude, 'In my family, when the going gets rough, we feel hurt.' This favoured feeling becomes a sort of conditioned reflex. That becomes the feeling that is experienced in all stressful situations, even though it doesn't help to resolve the issue. In Transactional Analysis, we call these 'racket feelings'. To the person experiencing them, racket feelings seem the natural, universal, and inevitable response to stress.

I had been working with Purvi for one year and knew some of her history. She was the third girl child. She described herself as 'saawali, not gori' (wheatish, not fair). The moment I heard this from her, I knew that our culture had imposed on her a heavy burden of not-OK-ness. Her mother had affirmed the cultural expectations by saying 'even though all of you were girls, your father distributed sweets when you were born', implying that the father had demonstrated a largeness of heart uncharacteristic of men, and that they ought to be grateful that their existence was accepted.

Purvi would often say 'I don't want to burden anyone with my troubles'. When describing her father to me earlier, she said, 'He was big built. He felt life had given him a very raw deal. He was unfulfilled in his career and had three girls to raise. He looked morose all the time. I felt guilty about speaking up in front of him because I thought it might trouble him further.'

The racket feeling is often a reference point that we use to uncover memories from the past where the coping patterns may have originated. I invited Purvi to think about her earliest memory of feeling guilty and anxious.

'I felt these almost every day in my childhood,' she said, 'when Papa came home from work.' I asked her to narrate any one scene as if it were happening in the moment.

She thought for a couple of minutes and began, 'I am seven years old; they call me Chutki at home. My sisters and I are playing carrom in the living room. Mama is next to us.'

'Can we explore this scene with some action right now?' I invited. Action methods bring the past into the present and invite clients to re-experience feelings instead of just remembering them. This allows for rich and creative processing of our internal worlds.

We set up four chairs, one each for her, her mother, and her sisters. We placed a cushion in the centre to represent the carrom board. Once again, I asked her to become a seven-year-old and imagine the scene as though it were happening in the present.

'Hello, Chutki, are you enjoying yourself with this game?' I asked her, using her pet name to invite her to get deeper into the role.

'Oh, very much,' she smiled, but then her face darkened, 'but I know it won't last long because Papa will be back home soon . . . We can now hear my father's car pull up. My mother's face turns anxious.'

'Can you move into your mother's chair?' I asked.

Purvi moved into her mother's chair and said anxiously and hurriedly, 'Time's up for playing. Pack up and go to your room and do something useful. Otherwise, Papa will be upset.'

'Okay, back into Chutki's chair please?' I said and Purvi moved back into her own chair. 'How are you feeling, Chutki?' I asked.

'Very scared and confused. My heart is pounding. I don't want to stop playing. But Mama is very anxious. She wants me to go to my room and be quiet. I am too scared of making Papa more sad than he already is.'

'Do you want to go to your room?' I asked.

'No,' she said, 'but I am scared. I don't think I have a choice.'

'What do you need right now?' I asked.

'I want somebody to hold my hand and tell me it is OK,' she said.

'Good idea. Who would you like right now to hold your hand?' I asked.

She was quiet for a while. My intuition told me that she was accessing sadness at not having a loving partner or close friends who could be of support to her.

I offered 'It can be anybody—a real person, a fictitious person from a movie or novel, someone who has passed on, a guru, or even God. Anybody who could offer the support you need at this moment.' Imagination is a powerful resource and allows us to construct our internal worlds. My statement opened up options for Purvi and her energy shifted.

'I am thinking of Hanuman,' she said, looking sheepishly at me, almost seeking permission from me. Hanuman is a popular Indian monkey God, known for his loyalty and devotion to Lord Rama. It was an unusual and creative choice. I was excited about how the process would unfold.

'Sure,' I smiled, 'can we use something to represent him?' She looked around and selected a green cushion to represent him. She reached out with her hand and held on to it.

'Feel the energy of Hanuman holding your hand,' I said. I could see her holding the cushion tight, drawing strength from it.

'Well, Chutki,' I went on, 'Mama is asking you to pack up and move to your room. How would you like to respond?'

'Can I respond as Hanuman?' she said.

'Of course!' I said.

She shifted to Hanuman's chair, looked at Mother, and said challengingly, 'Why does she need to pack up?'

'Be your mother now,' I said, and Purvi moved to her mother's chair.

'Why does she need to pack up, Mama?' I repeated Hanuman's question.

'Papa will be upset,' Purvi said from her mother's chair.

'Hanuman's chair, please,' I directed Purvi.

Purvi moved to Hanuman's chair and said, 'He will be alright. She doesn't have to stop playing.' Spontaneously, she gestured a thumbs up.

'Who is that for?' I asked.

'For Purvi,' she smiled. I directed her to move back to Purvi's chair. As a supporting actor, I moved into Hanuman's chair and gestured a thumbs up.

Purvi smiled. I mentally noted the smile as a marker of the transformation of the fear. 'What happens now?' I asked her.

'Papa comes in. We are all still there in the drawing room,' she said.

'You haven't packed up,' I emphasized the difference.

She nodded.

'Be your father now,' I invited.

She got into her father's role and walked in looking glum. She slumped on a chair, shoulders drooping, head hanging down.

'Papa,' I addressed him, 'your girls are playing carrom. Do you want to say anything?'

Purvi shook her head from left to right, still looking down. She turned to look at me and said, 'Papa never spoke much.'

'Can you move back into Hanuman's role?'

She then moved into Hanuman's role and smiled at the father and said a cheery 'Hello!' I noted that she brought in a very light and confident energy in the role of Hanuman.

'So, Hanuman, you aren't scared of Purvi's father!' I observed.

'No, I am bigger than her father, can't you see!' she said in Hanuman's role, smiling. In embodying the role, she accessed her spontaneity. She bodily experienced being tremendously confident.

'Back to Dad's role!' I said.

Purvi shifted to father's role and smiled weakly.

I asked her, 'Papa, is there anything you want to express?' 'I am very tired. I just want to have my tea,' said Purvi.

Purvi moved back to Hanuman's chair, turned to Purvi's, and said, 'Continue playing, it is your turn.'

Purvi came back to her own chair and said to me, 'Mama has gone to the kitchen; Papa is drinking his tea, looking sad. But my sisters and I continue playing. I pocket the queen and win the game!'

'Move to Hanuman's role,' I said. She moved to the role and clapped and gestured a thumbs up to little Purvi as Hanuman.

This was a very significant therapeutic shift. She disentangled emotionally from her father and did not take responsibility for his sadness. Her story had a new outcome. She was smiling. 'I loved how I felt as Hanuman,' she said excitedly. Her eyes were shining. The thinking, feeling, and behaviour seemed congruent. It was the beginning of her being able to access the feeling of joy instead of the persistent anxiety and guilt.

This was an experiential way of bringing about change. Purvi re-experienced an early scene where her autonomous expression was invalidated. Bringing in an external supporter helps the child find the resources to retain their autonomy. In choosing Hanuman, she used her imagination to bring in a nurturing, supportive energy. She bodily experienced a shift in feeling in relation to her father as she experienced herself as Hanuman.

After this session, Purvi decided to travel home to meet her parents. This time, she shared with her parents some of the difficulties she was facing in her personal life and at work. She later told me with delight that she found her father 'surprisingly supportive' of her decisions and choices, and he expressed to her that he was very confident that she would sail through all her challenges. He didn't seem as sad as she had usually experienced him.

When we change internally, the world around us changes.

16

Come Out and Talk, Demon

Yashodhara

'I've managed to drive him away too,' Shruti said morosely. 'And I thought this one might be the one.'

'I can see you're really sad,' I said gently.

'Yes.' A tear ran down her cheek and she wiped it away. 'It somehow feels worse this time. It's actually the third guy over the last year and a half—but this one was special. But I can't understand my own behaviour with him—it was pretty terrible.'

'What was terrible?' I invited her to explore this.

Her sadness was momentarily replaced by a flash of anger. 'I mean, I knew he was just really busy at work, but I kept picking fights with him over the tiniest things—like when he didn't take my calls, or return them quickly enough . . . I guess I can't really blame him for losing patience—I kept threatening him about walking out, over and over, saying "This won't work." And then, finally, he said "Okay, let's just end it." And then I was like, "Yeah, see? You gave up! *This* is why it would never have worked!"'

'Sounds like a part of you feels validated by his saying "Let's end it,"' I observed, 'like you *knew* it wouldn't work.'

'Well . . . yes,' she said. 'But you know what? I actually hate that part of me. It comes up and sabotages each relationship. How long is it going to keep me from having what I want? I'm thirty-three and have never been with a guy for more than a year!'

Her description of that part of her, which she said was the saboteur, reminded me of the Demon—the seemingly self-sabotaging 'mischievous trickster' inside us that shows up at key moments, often when we're on the threshold of something important, like being intimate. What is usually less understood about this paradoxical part of us is that when it first originated, it had a positive intent.

'How do you feel about actually getting to know that part better—and understand it, develop a relationship with it?'

'Ugh.' She wrinkled her nose. 'I don't want a relationship with it. I want it to let *me* have a *real* relationship.'

I could see she wanted to disown this part, treating it as an external entity controlling her actions.

'Is it okay to just have a conversation with it and then see where that goes?'

She thought for a moment and grinned. 'Yes. Okay. Let's talk to the little devil.'

'It's interesting you use that term. Sometimes there is a part of us that causes us to behave in ways we don't understand, taking us by surprise and creating trouble. It's called the Demon.'

'The Demon,' she said emphatically. 'That's how I think of her.'

'Her?' I leaned forward to find a pen and loose sheet of paper and pushed both towards her. 'Do you think you could draw her?'

'I'm not great at drawing,' Shruti murmured. But the pen was already moving across the paper, and her strokes were furious and sharp. In a few moments, she pushed it back toward me. 'Here.'

I looked at her drawing and was fascinated. Shruti herself was an immaculately dressed, pretty woman, not a hair out of place—and she had drawn her Demon as what looked like a snotty little girl in patchy tattered clothing, hair sticking out—were those flies she had drawn around her head? There was an unmistakably taunting smirk on the little girl's face, and one hand was on the hip, while the other held what looked like a stick. I became aware of a sense of discomfort, like I was going out of my depth suddenly. I took a breath to centre myself.

'I would like to get to know this part of you, Shruti—can you become her, and I'll ask you a few questions?'

This time, Shruti didn't seem to resist the idea. She nodded and leaned back. In fact, there was something in her face that was already changing, an expression taking over that was actually taunting, just like her drawing.

'Hello there,' I said calmly. 'How old are you?'

'I am ten years old.' Her tone was defiant.

'What are these things around your head?'

'These are flies. They hang around me because my head is full of garbage.'

'Your head is full of garbage? Who said that?'

'My father.'

'Your father said that?' I said gently. 'Did that hurt you?'

'No,' she said shortly. 'I don't get hurt!'

'I see,' I nodded. 'And what's that in your hand?'

She looked proud. 'That's my poking stick. I use it to poke people who come too close.'

'Who tries to come too close?'

'Some people try,' she said, a little evasively. 'But I don't let them. Then they go away.'

'What might happen if they come too close?'

'That's when they will hurt Shruti, *na*,' she snapped at me impatiently.

'You seem angry about something,' I said. 'What are you angry about?'

'I'm angry with Shruti.'

'Why?'

'Shruti is always whining. She's weak . . . and now she's blaming me for it!'

'Could you tell me more about yourself?' I asked curiously. 'What are the things you like?'

'I don't like *anything* at all. There's no point to it. Oh, I like only one thing,' she corrected herself. 'I like to complain!'

'And you said that Shruti is always whining?'

'Whining is *different* from complaining,' snapped the Demon again, and I got the impression she wanted to stamp her feet. 'Whining is weak and kiddish; I know how to be angry and grown-up.'

'So, if you are angry and you complain, you are a grown-up?'

'Yes.'

'How do you know this?'

'Because Daddy is angry all the time, and everyone is afraid of him.'

'What about Mom?'

There was the slightest of pauses and she said, 'Mom is the most scared of him!'

'What do you feel about that?'

Her tone was derisive, but I thought I saw a flash of tenderness on her face as she said, 'Mom is a big softie. She doesn't earn any money and so she has to listen to Dad all the time. And she wants me to do that too, but I won't!'

'So, what do you do instead?'

'I can argue with Dad,' she said proudly. 'Even if he is mean to me and says he will hit me.'

'Does he hit you?'

'Sometimes,' she said, narrowing her eyes. 'But not much. I can make my voice big and loud, and I will act big even if I am scared.'

'So, you do feel scared sometimes?'

'No,' she corrected herself, 'Shruti is scared.'

'Got it,' I paused and asked, 'so you want to protect Shruti?'

There was a pause. The Demon seemed to be caught unaware by this. Then she shrugged and said, 'Yeah. Maybe. I want to protect her. And Mom.'

'Are you, maybe, trying to protect Shruti these days also?' I ventured.

A conspiratorial grin came over her face, and she said with the air of someone letting me in on a secret, 'Yes. From the boys.'

'How do you do that?'

'With my poking stick!' she said, looking quite pleased with herself. 'Boys are mean! And Shruti is a softie, and she can't see that they don't *really* want to be around—so I keep poking them and poking them and checking how much they mean what they say. And see? They don't mean any of it!'

I said softly, 'So, you really try very hard to protect Shruti from being hurt. That is a very caring thing to do.'

This time when the Demon spoke, her tone was softer. She admitted in a murmur, 'Maybe.'

I invited Shruti to come out of the role of the Demon, she stayed quiet for several moments before expressing her surprise at what had just emerged. She was able to make the connections between Dad's own fear of intimacy and overuse of anger as something that she had taken in, as well as Mom's yearning, anxiety, and desire to please. She also saw that she had been associating anger with power and had an archaic idea about the roles of men and women in relationships—she was afraid of being bullied like her mother had been, and this was what showed up in the behaviours that sabotaged her relationships.

As we worked together, she was able to feel a new sense of gratitude and understanding for the part of her that showed up as a prickly testing force when relationships became serious. As she got to know the Demon, she understood how it meant to protect her. She could recognize her own Child fears of intimacy. She began to challenge her fear of intimacy by practising more vulnerability in her relationships, including the one with me.

As she explored more genuine and authentic ways of being, including communicating her vulnerability, she was able to find and nurture a steady, trusting romantic relationship. Her Demon continues to show up sometimes with its prickly, distrusting behaviour but she is increasingly better at recognizing, soothing, containing, and working with it. Perhaps it will never go away, but that's okay— Shruti seems to be developing an increasingly steady, trusting relationship with her Demon as well.

17

Heroic Slaying of the 'Don'ts'

Aruna

'I have to deal with the strangest problems.' Anoura came into the session visibly agitated. 'My father-in-law stays with us. He used to drink heavily when he was younger. Now of course, because of several health complications, he has given it up. Of late I find that when we are at the breakfast table, Vikrant, my husband, regales the children with the misadventures of their grandfather's drinking. For example, he shared with them stories of when he tried to resuscitate a tree trunk on the road by giving it CPR, or how he came home on a stranger's cycle while his car was found in a ditch a few roads away. And my father-in-law sits there smiling as he listens to these stories.'

'How are you impacted by this?'

She took a few minutes to explain in an elaborate way that stories create images in the minds of children of what is acceptable and what is not. She concluded with, 'Children at this age are impressionable. You know that! If you call a child a clown several times, the child will believe he is a clown.'

I could see how much she wanted me to understand her. The anxious over-explanation made me imagine that perhaps, as a child, she had not had the experience of being easily understood.

'I am worried that the children will think it is fun or cool to get drunk. Vikrant is romanticizing drinking, and I wish he could just see that for himself. But I can't do anything about it.'

'Why can't you do anything about it?' I was curious about the powerlessness she experienced.

'Because it has taken so long for me to work on my relationship with Vikrant. We now have some intimacy in the relationship, and I really don't want to rock the boat at this point. And I am confused about this as well. Everyone is laughing at the table. So, should I really stop this? And now my father-in-law is old. He doesn't drink any more,' she paused. 'But I have an urge to say to Vikrant that all the stories about his father's drinking are not funny. In fact, most are disgusting and terrifying. He would run after his children with a knife. But should I share this? Will it spoil the relationship that the children have with their grandfather today?

As I say this, I am feeling very angry with my father-in-law. Why is he not stopping Vikrant? Why is he not saying "Children, you must never drink like I did." But I am wondering how this anger is helping me? Why am I holding on to it? Am I overthinking this? Should I just let it pass?' Anoura was now gasping for breath.

'Woah!' I exclaimed, realizing that I needed to invite Anoura to slow down. 'That's a lot. Why don't we pause a bit, breathe, and think about this?' She let out a big sigh and sat back in the chair.

In the fifteen minutes that we had spent together, I could see how she had trouble being focused. She jumped from one thought to another, second-guessed her own conclusions, and worked herself up to be confused.

'Let us start with what you want right now,' I suggested, extending an invitation to come to the present.

'I am confused. Should I work on what is happening at the dinner table? Or should I focus on the anger that I experience with my father-in-law?'

She was asking me to think for her. I said with awareness, 'What do you choose?'

She looked further agitated. It would have been easier for her if I had given her an answer.

'I am not sure. I think I want to let go of this anger for myself. Yes, I think that is it. Maybe I am worrying too much about the children. Maybe they won't be affected. Maybe I am overthinking this. This could be a non-issue.'

'Are you aware that you started with how impacted you are by this and now you are saying it is a non-issue?' I brought the incongruence to her attention.

'I am aware,' she said, slumping, sighing.

'What was the sigh about?'

'I always do this. Second-guess my own thinking.'

This was an important insight for her. She needed to start trusting her thinking again.

In what Anoura had shared with me, we could have worked with many things. There was the immediate issue of the stories that were shared. We could have discussed some problem-solving options. I also saw that the idea of confronting her husband never occurred to her.

She had fantasies that the confrontation would impair the relationship, and perhaps she could explore her beliefs around this and even build some skills in expressing her concern authentically. Further, she could also make meaning of her anger towards her father-in-law.

However, right now, I was drawn to work with her on how she gave up her own power by getting confused.

I started by validating her thinking. 'I can see that you are thinking ethically—you want to protect your children and are aware of your responsibility as a parent. You are aware of how stories that are shared with children create maps for them about what is acceptable and what is not. However, I am surprised that you discounted your own thinking. And you seem familiar with this pattern.'

'Yes,' she said, looking sad.

'You look sad. What are you experiencing?'

Our conversation went on to how both parents had been unavailable to her emotionally, too busy with their own lives. The little child had to do all the thinking for herself. Without anyone to validate her thinking, she had no basis of knowing what was right and what was wrong. Her thoughts would spiral in all directions. She would feel exhausted just thinking. Her speech patterns reflected her internal battles. She would go back and forth, contradicting herself multiple times.

In addition, her mother would find Anoura's questions and chatter 'irritating' and often invalidate her, saying she was 'stupid'. Being put down repeatedly had a deep and unconscious effect on Anoura's life. She took on the attribution and believed she was stupid. It showed up in her adult life as a constant confusion about issues. She would struggle with options in her head, unable to make decisions.

I reminded her of the sentence she had said earlier to me in the session, 'If you call a child a clown several times, the child will believe he is a clown.'

She nodded, and I went on, 'What do you think you concluded when your mother called you "stupid" repeatedly?' Her eyes welled up as she contacted her sadness at being invalidated.

Over several sessions, Anoura grieved for the losses she had had as a child. This grieving is an important part of the healing in the psychotherapy process. Little Anoura had not been seen or affirmed by her parents. Left to fend for herself, she had felt unprotected. The adult Anoura grieved for little Anoura's lost opportunities for joy, validation, and safety in her childhood. She became aware of her magical thinking that if she stayed helpless and confused, her parents would transform in some way and step in to offer her structure and support. Our work allowed her to come to terms with her reality and to give up waiting for her parents to change. She could now leave her past behind and learn to take charge of her life.

Over the next few months, Anoura gave herself permission to think and make mistakes. She also decided that she was important and therefore what she thought and felt was important. To put these new beliefs into action, Anoura made several decisions intuitively. She took up more space in all the groups that she was part of and expressed herself spontaneously. Over time, her confidence grew. The next time Vikrant brought up a funny drinking story at the dinner table, she said spontaneously, 'How come you find these stories funny? I feel sad when we talk about their grandpa like that. I want to share stories that make us proud.'

'How do you feel about what you said?' I had been marvelling at her transformation as I listened to her recount this.

'I felt very proud,' she said, raising her chin and looking into my eyes. 'He got the message. He stopped. And what I said didn't cause any tension.'

'You trusted your thinking and shared it,' I applauded, sharing in her delight.

Two months later, she proudly brought a certificate of hers into therapy and showed it to me, 'This is an exam I had almost finished last year. But I hadn't submitted it, because submitting it would have meant going against my belief that I was stupid. I have sabotaged myself in so many ways because I didn't trust my own intelligence or thinking. But I did it!'

As a psychotherapist, I have the privilege of witnessing some of the deepest struggles of my clients. She had just won a battle. I imagined her on a horse with a sword, dramatically slaying three of the strong 'Don'ts' (also called *injunctions*) that she had believed as a child—'Don't Think', 'Don't Be Important', and 'Don't Make It'. She was a hero. And the rest of the world would have thought it was just some random exam that she passed!

18

I Can Explain

Yashodhara

'Okay, I know you're mad at me, but I can explain.'

'So, you are imagining me being angry with you right now?' I said with careful composure.

'Yes . . . about the last missed session . . .'

A few days ago, Urmi had messaged me: *So, so sorry I forgot about our session—the house help came in late so the morning was chaotic and a work deadline came up, my head's been a mess . . .*

I had resisted my initial urge to respond to her with reassurance, and had replied with a simple:

Can we discuss this face to face in our next session, please?

I was aware that my message to her wasn't comforting, but it was a deliberate decision on my part. She had missed several sessions like this by now, and I could experience myself getting irritated and developing a narrative in my own head that I was being taken for granted. We had unconsciously moved into a game. Both our scripts were at play. I knew it would be useful to explore what was really going on between us.

There had been four instances in the last two months when I had booked my time and ended up waiting for her; I had a clear clause in my contract that said that no-shows were chargeable at full rate, and yet, for some reason, I hadn't enforced this particular clause with Urmi. I realized in supervision that there was something pulling me into being sympathetic, understanding her situation, and not holding her accountable. In all the instances, she had seemed to have some unavoidable crisis going on—someone falling ill, a last-minute visa appointment, a delay at the dentist. She had always been so profuse with her apologies, and so insistent with her detailed explanations that I had given in and let it go.

But not this time. I knew we stood to gain some insight by exploring the issue of her missing sessions, so I replied to her now.

'Actually, this is the fourth time it has happened. I am wondering what may be going on for you?'

'Fourth?' She screwed up her face. 'I think it's the . . . third, maybe. And the other times, you know what had happened. There was the visa thing that really couldn't be avoided, and . . .'

'Yes, it is the fourth,' I interrupted gently, yet firmly. From experience, I knew if Urmi launched into a story, it would take several minutes of session time away. 'In all these cases, you forgot to message me, and I ended up waiting. What might be behind that?'

She was a little sullen. When she spoke, it was in a petulant tone, 'See, I knew you were mad at me.'

I spoke mindfully, 'I am curious about what is going with you, and I notice you didn't answer my question, Urmi.'

'What question?'

'What might be behind your forgetting to message me?'

'Why would there be anything behind it! I can just be a little scatterbrained sometimes. I am always messing things up. Even at work, when it comes to deadlines, I tend to miss them. And my husband is always scolding me for forgetting to pay some bill or the other. The thing is, with the kids being so small, and time after work being limited . . .'

'Do you believe, Urmi, that it's just a coincidence this happened four times?'

'What else could it be? Why would I deliberately forget to inform you? It's not like I want this to happen!'

I could see her being defensive, and I explained, 'It's not a deliberate thing, Urmi. Often, there are unconscious patterns playing out. And what happens between us is a pattern of relating, which may represent how you relate with people in general. Does what is going on between us right now feel familiar to you?'

The invitation to think worked. Urmi had an intelligent mind, and I sensed that her tendency to say 'silly me' masked something. She went into deep thought for a few moments and then said, 'Well, there are times at work when I miss a deadline and in the heat of the moment with all the stress, I forget to inform the stakeholders involved—my boss often gets angry that I didn't tell him about it.'

'I see,' I nodded. 'So, what ends up happening then?'

'Well, I try to explain the reasons for the delay, and when I do submit the work, I make sure it's high quality . . . so I guess most of the time, I'm just able to explain it away.'

'And how do you feel during the process?'

'I'm relieved when I've gotten away without getting yelled at. A little surprised as well.'

'It's surprising because you're expecting the other person to be mad?'

'Yes. I also think . . .' Her voice trailed off. I waited.

She went on, 'I think maybe a part of me feels that I should communicate a miss on my part only when I'm able to explain things properly . . .'

'So, are you afraid of the other person being angry? You said you expect it.'

'Yes, I do. But yes, now I'm thinking, maybe when I forget, it's not exactly on purpose but in a way, maybe . . . it seems safer to just delay the conversation.'

'Safer?'

'Yes. It seems unsafe to face anger without being able to tell my side of the story properly.'

'So, are you feeling safe right now?' I wondered.

Urmi took a deep breath. 'Not really.'

It took me some effort to stay grounded. Her sharing challenged the ideal I held for myself about being a compassionate therapist. However, I was aware it was my process and I needed to deal with it outside the therapy room. Here I was in her service. I asked tentatively, 'Would you be okay to tell me more about what's going on for you right now?'

'Well,' she said, beginning to tear up, 'when I tried to explain over message that day, you said it would be better to just hold on and talk about it today. I've been stressed for days about it, not knowing what might happen. And even right now, you've cut me off multiple times when I was telling you my side of things.'

'You think I've cut you off multiple times?'

'Yes—when I tried to explain my side of the story to you.'

'And what meaning did you make of my action?'

'I thought you're losing patience with me.' She paused for a moment. 'But I do know I speak in long sentences and repeat myself . . . especially when I'm nervous. I tend to use long-winded explanations that maybe just make the other person fed up.'

'Was that a useful strategy when you were growing up, perhaps?'

The light of recognition dawned in her eyes. 'Yes. Especially with Dad. I was always scared of a scolding from him. I found that as long as I could provide him with a good explanation, I'd get away with things.'

'A good explanation? Say more?'

'Okay, actually, it was a long explanation.' She gave a short ironic laugh. 'I remember, late nights after he came home, Mom would complain about something I had done, but as long as I kept talking, he wouldn't say anything—he just seemed tired and once I'd finished my story, he'd say something like "Okay, just don't do that again" and then would tell me to go to bed.'

'How do you feel as you remember this?'

'Well,' she paused. 'I feel a little sad. I was scared of my dad a lot. Maybe I didn't need to be, he wasn't unreasonable, or even that angry. But Mom often used the whole "Wait till your dad comes home" threat. Maybe half my fear was just imagined.' She waited a few more seconds. 'I feel annoyed with Mom for that.'

I knew anger wasn't an easily accessible or 'permitted' emotion for Urmi. So, it was a good sign that she was recognizing her annoyance with Mom. 'It's okay to be angry—do you feel sad that you missed out on something because of your fear of Dad?'

'Yes. Closeness with him.' She was silent for a few moments and looked sad and vulnerable. It was unusual for her to be so quiet. I stayed silent as well. After a couple of minutes, she sighed.

'What did you just get in touch with?' I enquired gently.

'I don't want to be so scared of everything.'

'And how are you feeling right now about this space?'

'Actually,' she looked at me confidently, 'I feel pretty safe.' She took a deep breath. 'And I'm sorry about the missed sessions. I should have messaged. It won't happen again.'

'Thank you,' I nodded. After a moment, I reflected out loud, 'I experienced your apology as sincere and powerful.'

Her brow was furrowed. 'Yes. I really meant it. And I'm thinking—if I mess up, I can just own up and apologize and make a new commitment. Maybe I don't need to hide behind long explanations.'

Urmi decided to practice owning up to her mistakes, despite her fear of displeasing others, especially authority figures. As we processed further what had happened with her missed sessions, we also got in touch with other unconscious processes at play: her guilt about investing in therapy and prioritizing herself when a key part of her own narrative was 'I'm small and not important', as well as her unconscious fear of taking accountability and uncovering the need for changes that might be necessitated with the deep work of therapy.

All of this came from our decision to have an honest conversation about the missed sessions. I marvelled yet again as to how powerful it was to process what was happening in the therapeutic relationship, including something as seemingly simple as the contract to show up for sessions. After all, this space was often a highly reliable microcosm of how the client related in the real world—we could always learn from whatever was happening right here, right now, in the therapy room.

19

Not My Circus, Not My Monkeys

Aruna

'I missed the application deadline for the new role,' said Rahil flatly. 'I had three months to do it, yet I missed it.'

'How are you feeling about this?' I asked.

'I don't know,' he said.

In my work as a therapist, I often receive '*I don't knows*' in response to my questions. They can mean anything, including 'I am ashamed of what I feel; I don't want to acknowledge it' or 'don't ask me to think' or 'feelings are painful and confusing, I have numbed myself'.

In Rahil's case, my intuition was that he was almost relieved to have not applied and therefore to not have been promoted. I was curious about his internal process and how it served him.

'You don't know?'

'I know what I am *not* feeling—I am not angry with myself or sad at the loss. But why am I not? That is puzzling me.'

'And you had three months to do this?'

'Yes, and I was a strong candidate. If I had applied, the position would have been mine. Hmm,' he said. He was talking to himself now, gazing upwards, thinking deeply.

Though Rahil had missed applying for this role, he had had a meteoric rise in his career, with three significant promotions in ten years catapulting him from a fresh graduate to a senior leader in an MNC. Despite now being a senior leader, he had the personality of a schoolboy. He tended to play down his own accomplishments. He also dressed shabbily, not attending to his own appearance. The only thing that revealed his material success to me was that he spent large sums of money on drones.

'I wonder if you feel like an imposter,' I asked him, trusting my intuition.

'Oh God, yes!' he said with a start. 'It has all come too easy. I have been incredibly lucky with my promotions so far. I feel like a fraud.'

'Is that why, perhaps, without awareness, you dragged your feet on this application?' I enquired.

'Interesting,' he said thoughtfully.

'How far back does this feeling of being a fraud go?' I asked. He closed his eyes, trying to remember.

'Well, I felt it in school as well,' he said. 'I did not have to study to top the class.'

'And how do you feel about things coming easy to you?' I asked.

'I don't know,' he said. 'You don't know,' I repeated with a smile.

'I am not hiding it from you on purpose,' he protested.

'I know,' I reassured him. 'Do you have an early memory of feeling like a fraud?'

'Yes, plenty,' he said.

'Shall we draw any one scene that comes to your mind?' I proposed.

'Draw? But I am no artist!' he protested, even as his eyes glinted with curiosity.

'Stick figures will do, like a comic strip,' I encouraged, sliding a paper and sketch pens towards him.

He quickly drew some squiggles. After a few moments, he pushed the sheet towards me. 'Can you title this?' I asked.

'Fooling Mum and Dad!' he said.

'Brilliant,' I clapped. I can't stop being amazed at how these experiential processes can get to the heart of the issue quickly.

'What is going on here?' I asked.

'I'm sitting here. I have my physics book outside, and my comic book inside. My mum and elder brother are looking at me. Mum doesn't see the comic, but my brother does. Dad is sitting on the balcony with his drink,' he explained.

'Can you draw speech balloons for what each person is actually saying?' I instructed. He drew a balloon only for mom. She was saying, 'Hard work pays off.'

'Now draw balloons for what you imagine them thinking. And below it, write down the emotion that accompanies that.'

He wrote the following

Brother: 'You will get caught'—Angry and jealous.

Mother: 'Rahil will redeem us'—*Desperation.*

Father: 'I have enough troubles in life already to be bothered with anything'—*Sullen.*

Self: 'Let me look serious'—*Afraid that I would be caught.*

Rahil found this exercise fascinating. The pieces of the jigsaw began to fall into place. 'What are you getting in touch with about your script?' I asked.

'I had to *show* my mum that I was working hard,' he said. 'Why was that?' I asked.

'She said that was the only thing that gave her hope,' he replied.

'So, you needed to take care of her. In order to relieve her of her anxiety, you had to give up being yourself,' I offered a possible meaning he could have made.

'Yes,' he agreed, 'and my brother resented that she pinned all her hopes on me.'

He straightened up, and I could see he was getting in touch with something significant. 'Actually, he was the one who called me a fraud all the time. He believed that I got our parents' love and attention easily. He was very jealous.'

'But he never told Mum about your reading the comic?' I was curious.

'No. Now that I think of it, I guess it was because of my father. My father had to struggle a lot in his life. He would keep saying that he had no tolerance for any drama. He rarely displayed emotion. Even when I scored a 100 per cent, he was unmoved,' he said.

'So, your brother didn't rat you out because he was protecting your father from being further burdened?'

'Yes'.

'How did you feel when Dad was unmoved by your achievements?' I asked.

'I don't know,' he said, and then sighed. 'Oh God, I sound like a broken record.'

'When you say your father appeared unmoved, what do you think was going on for him?'

Rahil's face wrinkled up as he thought deeply. Then, he shook his head as if he were disagreeing with someone.

'Looks like a battle is going on inside your head?' I enquired. 'Yes, and I don't like the thoughts that are emerging.'

'What are they?'

'That he didn't want me to get 100 per cent!' Rahil blurted. This was really significant. We paused for a bit.

'What would it mean for him if you did well?'

'That I was rubbing my achievement in his face. He felt he hadn't achieved much because life had been very unfair to him. And it had been.'

'So, he was envious of you?' I offered. Rahil squirmed and shuddered.

'Your body is reacting strongly,' I observed.

'I don't want to think that he was envious. He was just very sad about his own life. I wanted to be sensitive.' Rahil became silent. He was getting in touch with an inner truth.

'Tell me what is going on,' I encouraged him to verbalize his internal process. 'I feel guilty,' he said with his head down.

I made a mental note that he hadn't said 'I don't know' and had acknowledged his feelings instead.

Out loud, I asked, 'Guilty about?'

'Doing well easily,' he said.

'Because it would make your father envious and even more sad about his own life?' I ventured.

'Yes.' He didn't protest this time.

'Does he know about your fancy drones?' I was curious.

'No,' he said, 'I have made some fantastic films with my drones but haven't shown them to him.'

'So, he has no idea of your success,' I said.

'No. In fact, I feel guilty about the money I make,' he said. 'Does he know about the kind of money you make?'

'No.'

'Does anyone?' I wondered.

'No. I hide it.'

Many things fell into place for Rahil that day. As a child, he had concluded that sharing success with his father was being insensitive to his father's sadness. And therefore, he experienced guilt at his success and, without awareness, decided to underplay it and even cap it in some way. In our work over many sessions, he would slowly disentangle from his father's and mother's emotions and learn that he did not have to take responsibility for them. He would begin to see his parents as fallible human beings with their own struggles, which he could separate from his own.

Right now, I asked him how it would be to draw the scene again with the new decisions that he was making. He readily drew the new one.

In the new drawing, he was reading the comic openly. His brother was playing too. Mum was angry with both. Dad was still sitting on the balcony with the drink, feeling sad.

I was curious, 'What has changed here?'

'I am not letting my mother's anxiety and being upset come in the way of my having fun. I trust that she will take care of herself, and so will Dad! They will find their own ways of dealing with their feelings.'

'What is the title of this work of art?' I asked, thrilled.

'*Not my circus, not my monkeys*!' he smiled, quoting the Polish proverb, letting me know that the penny had dropped. He was taking responsibility for his feelings and trusting that others would take care of theirs. I spontaneously applauded.

20

Of Grief and Goodbyes

Yashodhara

'I would like to hear from Arya,' said Shruti, breaking the silence.

I had just suggested to the members in the Grief Support Group, which I had been running, that they should feel free to just interact today and go with the flow. It was a closed group of eight people who had suffered losses during the pandemic, and now that it had been a month, I felt the group would benefit with some unstructured interactions with each other around their time together.

'Go ahead,' I nodded. 'Talk to her directly.' A ground rule that we had was that we would talk using I-and-You language with each other.

'Arya, I would like to hear how you are doing,' Shruti said, turning to face Arya, who sat on the chair right next to her. Arya had been the quietest in the group, maintaining an impassive face even through the most difficult moments we had shared over the last few weeks—all the group members had suffered the death of loved ones during the pandemic.

Arya looked a little taken aback for a moment, but her stone-faced expression came back almost immediately. 'I . . . am not sure what you want me to say,' she said, adding a little defensively, 'I have been listening.'

'You've certainly listened with great attention,' I said gently. 'Would you like to also share what is going on with you? How do you feel about Shruti's question?'

She hesitated for a few moments, and then said, 'I feel a little . . . guilty, actually.'

'Tell us about your guilt.'

'I . . . feel like I haven't been contributing much to the group. I see you all so open and vulnerable about your sharing. I lost my father-in-law while some people here have lost parents and siblings.' She began to speak faster. 'I don't find it easy to cry even when I'm alone, so crying in a group is very brave, which you guys have done. I'm just more . . . numb, I guess.'

'Do you believe the grief of losing an in-law is less than that of losing a parent?' This was a gentle confrontation on my part.

She paused and then said, 'Probably.'

'Are you able to see that this isn't necessarily true? Your father-in-law is also part of your family. Your grief cannot be compared to anyone else's.'

She nodded, and her face softened for just a moment before becoming impassive again. I intuited from Arya's stoic expression and trouble with vulnerability that she had perhaps learned early on to be strong, so much so that her own feelings were difficult for her to feel.

'Are you feeling anything else, Arya?'

She paused for a moment and then said in a quieter tone, lowering her eyes, 'There is anger.'

'What are you feeling angry about, Arya?'

'I'm feeling angry that my father-in-law was careless,' she said, cheeks flushing. 'He insisted on going for his morning walks, even when the pandemic was at its worst and we kept warning him not to do it. And he never wore his mask properly. We were all scared something would happen, and it did. And it's left my husband so broken—he was so attached to his father.' Her voice broke off, and she went silent, looking down at her hands.

'Are you ashamed about feeling angry with your father-in-law, Arya?' I ventured. She nodded, managing to look up at me for a second.

'When we lose someone, it is normal to have multiple conflicting emotions—anger is also a part of the grieving process, and we *can* be angry at the one we lost too. All emotions are meant to be acknowledged and processed.' I paused and then looked around the group. 'Would anyone like to share any resonance with Arya about what she has said?'

Malvika spoke up, 'Arya, I'm glad you said this, because you know what—I think I'm really angry with my dad. He's left a huge mess behind for my mom and me to clean up.'

Arya nodded gratefully. It looked like a weight was lifting off her.

Shruti, who had first invited her to speak, now pitched in, 'I also relate with what you said, Arya, about feeling guilty. I often tell myself I shouldn't feel this way or that way.' Her eyes became bright with tears. 'My mom is so devastated about my brother that I've been putting my own feelings aside for her sake . . . but I miss him terribly every day.'

I hadn't expected she might, but Arya reached out spontaneously and took Shruti's hand. Another group member sitting on Shruti's other side put a hand on her shoulder. After a few moments, Shruti smiled through her tears.

'What did Shruti's sharing open up for you just now, Arya?' I sensed the shift in Arya's own energy—her body language was more open, and she looked touched.

'I think . . . I've been mostly trying to be supportive towards my husband as he is grieving. But . . . I also had a really great relationship with my dad-in-law.' She laughed in a hollow way. 'I joined this group so I could figure out how to support my husband better—as if *I* didn't really have a right to miss his dad the way that I do. That seems silly to me now.'

'What was your relationship with your dad-in-law like?'

'He was . . . really nice and funny. He was open and welcoming of me, from the time that we got married. He often told Mummy to leave me alone and not expect me to do a lot of housework as I have a job. He was very supportive of what I did.' She had a wistful look on her face. 'It's like I've lost my biggest ally in our home.'

I nodded, saying, 'I can see the fondness that you had for him. It sounds like you really loved him.'

Arya suddenly looked sad and vulnerable as she took in my words. It was as if this was the first time that she was giving herself the permission to really feel the loss of her father-in-law. She swallowed, and spoke in almost a whisper, 'I was closer to him than I am to even my own dad. He was the one person who . . . just *loved* me the way I am. I don't know why.' She took a deep shuddering breath and then looked around the group again. 'I still can't cry.'

I had to smile at this. 'Arya, it's okay to cry—and it's also okay not to cry.' Crying can be a healthy process and a release of emotions that may be stuck in the body, but it needn't be thought of as the only way to express sadness. It also sometimes took much more work in personal therapy to investigate what long-standing beliefs a person might hold about crying. 'It is enough to know for yourself your real feelings—you are sad and will really miss him.'

She nodded, and then smiled as though she had just remembered something.

'What did you just get in touch with?'

She looked a little embarrassed, 'He used to call me Champion. Every time I brought home some good news about an accomplishment at work, a promotion or whatever, he would say "*Hamari* Champion *ka kamaal dekho*."'

I laughed, as did the rest of the group. Arya's voice had become deeper in a spontaneous imitation of her father-in-law's hearty voice. She added, 'But he also always told me to rest, to take care of myself, to not keep doing so much for others. I really liked that he said that though I rarely listened to him. I'm as stubborn as he is about doing my own thing.'

'So, what might he say to you right now, Arya, if he could see you?'

She thought for a moment, and then said in the same deep voice, 'Champion, *ab toh meri baat maan ja—apna dhyan rakh*.'

'So, he'd call you 'Champion' and say "At least now, listen to me and take care of yourself."' I replayed with a smile, adding instinctively, 'You are important, and your feelings are important.'

Arya nodded, her eyes bright.

'Want to say anything to him in response?' I asked.

'Thanks, Papa,' she said simply. 'I will take care and rest more.' She then added spontaneously, 'And *you* rest too, wherever you are.'

It felt to me like we had reached a place of closure for her—when we grieve for a loved one, it can be highly therapeutic to have a ritual of goodbye, imagining a dialogue with the person we have lost.

I invited the group to share what her process had opened up for them. Many group members also mentioned getting in touch with a favourite catchphrase that their loved ones had for them and what they might say right now. These fond memories coupled with imagination were becoming internal resources for each individual to cope and move forward. This was just one example of what a fluid group process could lead to. When one person is vulnerable, the entire group benefits by getting in touch with how they feel, and this is one of the biggest advantages of working in a group. Members connect and open up to one other, offering permissions and solidarity, mirroring and resonance. Group therapy reminds us that no matter what we may feel, we are not alone. And that itself is healing.

21

When Disillusionment Is Healing

Aruna

John towered over me. Six-foot tall and muscular, he sported a man-bun, a beard, and a snake tattoo along the length of his arm. It was easy for me to imagine that other people could be scared of him.

'My sister wants to re-establish contact . . . and I am scared,' he began the session with this. That wasn't the start I expected, but I knew that even big and strong people could be scared.

'What are you scared of?' I enquired.

'Of losing her. I am feeling fearful. I better not say anything she doesn't like. I walk on eggshells around her,' he said. 'Tell me more,' I said, sensing a heavy sadness around him.

'Michelle has not been talking to me for almost fifteen years now. I have tried maintaining contact with her even though she hasn't maintained contact with me. I wish her on her birthday and exchange some factual information occasionally. She responds briefly, but there are no signals from her that she would like to engage with me more. But last week, she reached out, saying we should meet. She is doing it for the sake of her daughter. She wants her daughter to know and get along with my son.'

'So, what is your fear about?'

'I cannot bear to see how she lives her life. She lives with an abusive husband. She harms herself by injuring herself off and on. I suspect she even takes drugs. What she is doing is really distressing . . . I try to not say anything because I don't want to upset her, but I eventually can't help expressing myself.'

'What do you say?'

'I tell her I cannot bear it. I say it as calmly as I can, but she knows my tone.'

'What is it about your tone?'

'I sound panicky, disgusted, angry.'

'So right now, you are scared that you will judge her, and she will withdraw from you again?'

'Exactly.'

'You really care for her.' I was moved.

'I do.' His face softened.

'How would you like to be with her?'

'I want to show up as a person who cares for her, and not as a person who judges her. I don't want to bring up what upsets me. But inside, I am deeply upset about her situation. So, I don't know if I can stay quiet about it.' He looked very confused.

'What is her response when you tell her you can't bear it?' I asked.

'She says "Fuck you. It's my life—I will harm myself as much as I want." And then she harms herself further.'

'To get back at you?'

'Yes. And then I back off. I send her gifts. I hope she recognizes that I am telling her, "I will never leave. I care about you. I am open to talking about this."'

'But she does not respond?' I guessed. 'No, she doesn't.' He looked sad. 'What could be going on for her?'

John sighed deeply. 'She is very angry with me and with life in general. I am the older one. I was the biological child to my parents. They adopted Michelle when I was six because Mum was keen to adopt a girl child. Michelle was an infant then. Then, five years later, my mother died. My father remarried, and the step-mother wasn't very kind to us. She would physically hit both of us. As I became larger and stronger, I could stop her from hitting me. I was also able to protect Michelle from being hit while I was around. I was furious with Dad for not stepping in to protect us. When I was sixteen, I left home in anger. I have made my own life. I worked part time and managed to study on my own and I have really made a decent life for myself.'

'What happened to Michelle after you left?' I asked.

'After I left, I had no way of contacting her. She did not have a phone then. When I called on the house landline, my step-mum would pick up the phone—she even told me that every time I called, Michelle would be beaten. So, I was not to contact her anymore. Michelle didn't respond to my emails either.'

'What did you make of that?' I asked, moved to tears by his story.

John turned pale, slumped, and said with quivering lips, 'She hated me. I had abandoned her. I left her in that house, alone with that horrible woman. She has never forgiven me for that.'

'Let it flow,' I said, seeing that he was holding back tears. 'You have held this sadness in for too long. I see your pain—and hers too. She has lost mothers twice before.'

'Why did I not remember that?' he said, his voice cracking.

'You were a child yourself,' I reminded him.

John gathered himself.

'It has been years of cold treatment from her now. I don't mind that. But I don't want to lose contact. And I don't want to get angry with her. Yet, I know I will. She loves me, yet she pushes against me. She is really angry.'

'And deeply wounded and sad and scared too,' I said. John silently considered what I said.

'Perhaps she is pushing you away because to her it may feel too risky to be close again?' I suggested, helping him see her actions differently.

'I think so. She is protecting herself from another abandonment perhaps,' he said thoughtfully.

I waited.

'But I wish she would not harm herself in the process. I can't bear to see her going to waste like this,' he protested.

'What do you mean she is going to waste?'

'It is very visible to me that she is hurting herself and also being hurt by her husband,' he said.

'Yet, she is choosing not to leave him,' I reminded him, deliberate in my words. 'I am very puzzled. I can't understand why she continues to be with this man.'

'We all accept the love that we think we deserve. Familiarity is safe. There is something that is working for her in this,' I said tentatively, wondering how he would receive what I said.

He sighed as he thought about this. 'Maybe. I suppose . . . I wish I could tell her she deserves better. But she doesn't trust me. Perhaps I should trust her. She *is* an adult. Her life is her life, even if it is self-destructive. My job is to calm myself around that—but it is really painful.'

'I know it is. I can see that you care very much. I am touched by your desire to change things, as well as your wisdom that says that it's not in your hands. It is not easy to see your loved ones suffer.'

John sighed.

'She has reached out,' I reminded him encouragingly. 'Hold on to the little light that is shining through the cracks.'

'And hope that it will grow,' he said, brightening up a little.

'Yes. But here is your test. It may or may not grow. She has been through repeated trauma.'

'You are right,' he said thoughtfully. 'I may never fully know what she is really going through.'

'So, your test is to love her anyway—even if she pushes against you, and even if she harms herself,' I challenged tentatively, scanning his face keenly for his response. 'I have read somewhere that those who need love the most ask in the most unloving ways.'

John smiled a sad smile. He was calm, yet full of feeling—what in therapy we call a *feelingful calm*, which comes from accepting one's pain.

'What is behind that smile?' I enquired gently.

'I remembered a cartoon I had seen called Disillusionment Cafe. The caption read "Your order isn't ready and never will be."'

I felt sad. 'You want to give up waiting for a perfect, loving relationship with Michelle.'

'Exactly. I have lost something precious, and I feel I will never get it back. I often wonder if I did something wrong by leaving home. Could I have waited a few years and taken her with me? Would it have been better then?'

'And what answer do you get when you ask yourself this?'

'Maybe, it would have been better. But I didn't do it. So, what is the point of wondering about how I could have made it better?'

'Good awareness. I wonder if you are taking full responsibility for how things are today?'

'I am. But I suppose my dad and step-mum are to blame too.'

'Michelle too has played a part in where things are today, through the choices she made. She has chosen to not forgive you despite your remorse and efforts.'

'I see that,' he said thoughtfully.

'How are you feeling?'

'I somehow feel . . . settled. Even though I know nothing has changed.'

'I think a lot has changed. You are trusting Michelle to know what works for her right now. You have made peace with letting her be who she is.'

Psychotherapy is often about grieving, grieving the loss of illusions about the perfection or perfectibility of our own self or the other. It is about the paradise lost and never regained. It is to do with transforming the need for others to be better than who they are into the capacity to accept them as they are. And accepting that sadness is an integral part of human experience.

'I agree. I have given up hoping that she or our relationship will get "fixed",' John smiled. I noticed that the smile wasn't as sad this time. The disillusionment was healing.

22

The Bedroom Game

Yashodhara

'Is it . . .' Ashka hesitated, '*normal* to not have . . . you know, *intimacy* . . . after a few years of marriage?'

'By intimacy, do you mean sex?' I sensed her discomfort in using this term, and hence offered it directly. Ashka nodded vigorously and seemed relieved that we had named what we were going to talk about.

'I don't know what "normal" might mean here,' I said, 'but this isn't about averages, right? Can we talk about what *you* are experiencing?'

'I want it,' she blurted out. 'And I think I want it more than he does.'

She sat back, and I noticed her cheeks had turned red. I nodded, 'It can happen often—that one partner's libido may be higher than the other's.'

She visibly relaxed; I could tell this topic was both difficult and important for her to discuss. 'It's been driving us crazy for the last few months,' she said. 'I mean, ever since the baby was born, it's been worse. But it's not like we didn't have problems before either.'

'What happens that drives you crazy?'

She blew out her cheeks. 'Well, he . . . first of all, hardly ever initiates it anymore. That makes me really mad; it is so frustrating for me to hint at and suggest that we do it.'

'Have you talked about this?'

'Yeah,' she gave a sharp sardonic laugh. 'And he says it is because of my temper that he doesn't feel like initiating! But he doesn't seem to get that this is what I am angry about. It's this strange cycle that we are on.'

'How does the cycle usually play out?'

'Well, I suggest that it's been a long time since we've had sex, so we should that night . . . we kind of have to plan it, you know, make sure the baby's asleep and all that.'

'Right,' I nodded. 'So then?'

'Well, the thing is, sometimes the baby does take a long time to fall asleep and by then, we're too tired . . . and even if we do make the time and space, he does some little thing that really annoys me—like, I don't know, make a dumb joke or a thoughtless comment or something like that—and I get angry with him, and I say "Fine, let's just not do it tonight." Then he gets upset and says "See, this is why it's so difficult to do it these days", and we end up having a huge fight, after which he just withdraws, maybe taking two days to recover and start talking properly again.'

'Right.' I nodded sympathetically. 'And how do you feel after the fight?'

'Very irritated and frustrated.'

'You said that he hardly ever initiates it anymore?'

'Yes!' She thought about it. 'Well, maybe that isn't right,' she admitted. 'Maybe he does *try*. But I somehow have trouble responding to it. I end up snapping at him, saying something like "Don't pretend you want to do it just to make me happy". Then he withdraws . . .'

'And in this case, you feel . . . what?' I prompted.

'Irritated and frustrated!' The light of recognition dawned in her eyes. 'Ugh. Always the same! In the end, I'm annoyed and angry, and he is withdrawn and hurt.'

'And that's the case no matter who initiates it,' I said. 'What do you think might really be going on between you two?'

'Beats me!' Her expression changed to one of puzzlement. 'I do see that while I've been blaming him, I am the one who behaves in a way each time that results in a fight . . . it's like he can do absolutely nothing right as far as I'm concerned.'

'So, it is perhaps as if you are waiting to catch him doing something wrong?'

'Yes.' She chewed on her lower lip. 'I'm almost looking for a reason to be angry.'

'You know, we've talked about this idea of games that we play—remember, we don't engage in them on purpose, but because there is some sort of payoff we get, which may be what we are used to getting, and not be what we truly want,' I said. 'There is one where a person is constantly looking out for the other to make a mistake so that they can express their anger with full force. It's called "Now I've Got You, You Sonofabitch."'

She laughed out loud. 'That's me completely! He even says he feels like he's being set up for a yelling on those nights; he's begun to expect it.' She looked confused. 'But I don't get it. I *do* want us to have sex. I don't think I *like* being angry with him.'

'Try getting in touch with what might be underneath your anger?' I suggested. 'What else might you be feeling about this?'

She bit her lip and looked off into space for a few moments. 'Well, I'm sad. I miss the connection that we had before the baby. I miss *him*.' Her eyes welled up. 'Also, I think I'm . . . a little scared.'

'I see you're hurt,' I said gently. 'Can you tell me what you are scared of?'

'That he might not want me anymore.' A tear rolled down her cheek. 'The C-section scar is there, and I haven't lost all the pregnancy weight. Even though I've tried so hard for months, I don't think my body will ever be the same.' She started to weep. 'I don't feel attractive at all anymore.'

It wasn't often that Ashka cried; she usually put up a strong front and had a sharp, no-nonsense way of being and her easily triggered temper was one of the key reasons for her coming into therapy. I could see that underneath the prickly façade was a hurting, scared Child. I held the space for her silently.

We were able to process together that a part of her was sabotaging the sex nights because she wasn't feeling confident and attractive in her own body. She was surprised to realize that all this while, she had blamed her husband for not desiring sexual intimacy, but in reality, her own fear of intimacy was causing her to push him away. As we spoke further, she experienced the relief of being able to talk about it, and also of discovering that this was a common phenomenon, and that there were ways out of it.

While games have a protective function and are used as ways of being that keep us in familiar, safe patterns, they are often at the cost of something valuable: the true authentic relating that we yearn for at a deep human level, that is, closeness to another. Intimacy often requires the kind of vulnerability that can feel unbearably risky when we haven't had enough childhood experiences of unconditional acceptance. Ashka's own experience with her family was of having to always perform well in school to feel accepted—while she had yearned for affection and hugs, which were rarely forthcoming from her parents. She was able to understand her own fear of rejection and her old story about being unworthy and unwanted and was eventually able to communicate with her husband about her need to feel wanted and desirable. They were able to revive their sexual relationship again, with its occasional hiccups. She reported that even on the nights when she did begin to get angry, he would manage to break the tension by informing her, 'Yes, yes, Madam, relax, you've already got the Sonofabitch!'—they would have a good laugh and get on with their planned business.

I was impressed that she had put all her cards on the table, using the language of Transactional Analysis at home to communicate what was going on inside her. By naming the game, she had empowered her husband to defuse it with humour. Ashka was learning that being authentic and vulnerable in relationships carried the risk of being hurt, but the upside was this kind of intimacy—and that made it more than worth it.

23

Say Something Nice!

Aruna

'My husband never appreciates me,' said Tanisha, scowling. 'You sound angry,' I mirrored her scowl.

'My son is applying to colleges, and I have been sitting with him and filling out all the forms. It has been taking hours. I don't mind doing it. In fact, I enjoy doing it. But I would like my husband to see and appreciate it. And when I shared how much I was doing yesterday, instead of appreciating it, he started giving me advice. It ended with both of us sulking.'

'You wanted appreciation, and he gave you advice?' 'Yes, he always does that,' she complained.

'Could you share what you said to him?' My hunch was that she might not have asked him directly.

'I said that I have spent seven hours a day in the last week, sitting with Amay and helping him fill out his college application forms.'

'I see. And?'

'He said "Why is it taking so long? So much material can be reused."'

'How did you interpret that?'

'I thought—*it is so easy for him to say it. He has not lifted a finger, and he has the cheek to criticize me.*'

'How did you respond?'

'I said that I know material can be reused. If you sat with him, you would know how much time these things take. And he replied "I know better than to spend time with him at all. He is old enough to do it by himself."'

'And then both of you sulked?'

'Yes.'

'Does this sort of thing happen over and over?' I was asking her to check for a pattern here. 'Oh yes,' she said, rolling her eyes and nodding her head vigorously.

'From what you shared with me, I didn't see you asking for appreciation explicitly. You stated what you had done and hoped he would say something nice. What do you feel about asking for appreciation directly?'

'Like what? Saying "Please appreciate me?" Eww.' She shuddered in disgust.

'Why not? What is so wrong about it?' I was curious about her bodily rejection of the idea. 'I believe that appreciation that is obtained by asking is not worth having,' she said firmly. 'So, unless it comes on its own, it has no value?'

'Yes.' She was firm.

'Is that really true?'

'It is true for me,' she said, staring defiantly back at me.

I paused, wondering how I could invite curiosity around her strong beliefs about asking for appreciation, or what in TA we would call asking for strokes.

'Do you think you might have strokes for people that you haven't shared with them?' I ventured in another direction.

'I do.'

'For whom?'

'For my husband,' she said sheepishly.

'Why haven't you shared them yet?'

'Because I believe that if I give strokes too easily, they will not have any value,' she declared confidently.

'Is that true?' I challenged her again.

'It is true for me,' she repeated, frowning.

'Are you aware that your body has tightened?' I asked. She nodded silently.

'I wonder if there was something that just happened between us that caused the tension?'

'You sounded impatient with me,' she said.

'And when I sound impatient, what happens to you?' I asked, becoming aware that I had possibly taken on the role of somebody from her past recreating a familiar dynamic.

'I begin to shrink. I want to disappear.'

'You are shrinking, and you want to disappear,' I repeated the words. They had tremendous clinical significance.

After a few moments, I ventured, 'I wonder if you wanted to shrink from someone as a child?'

'My mother.'

'Tell me more.'

'My mother was a working woman and extremely busy. She was strong. Nothing ever shocked her. She rarely showed emotions though I knew that she cried in private. She never needed any help and would reject any help that was offered, including mine.'

'So, she modelled being strong and stoic. How did that impact you?'

'I felt my mother was already overburdened and that I should not add to her tasks by having needs for myself. And she was impatient with me. It was safer to not get in her way,' she said.

'And how did you get your own needs met?'

'I believed they would never be met. Even on the rare occasions that I asked for support, my mother was not there.'

'Like when?'

'Like when I had my first period. Or when I was teased by my friends for being ugly. Or when I had my heart broken as a teen. It didn't matter to her,' she said, overcome by her sadness.

'You felt *you* didn't matter,' I changed the words, mirroring her tone and expression.

She sighed in agreement.

'I wonder if you feel you matter to me.'

She was silent for a while and then said, 'In our relationship, I have experienced that I matter. Right now, as you listen to me, I know I matter.'

'Yet, when you experienced me not understanding, you felt you didn't matter.'

'Exactly. It takes me very little to feel that I don't matter.' She paused for a while and said, 'Perhaps the same thing happens with my husband.'

'In what way?'

'He doesn't understand me. I feel I don't matter to him. So, there is no point asking for strokes.'

'Actually,' I said gently, 'you are already asking. But you are not asking directly, which may be confusing for him.'

'I didn't ask,' she said, looking puzzled.

'Why did you say to your husband "I have spent seven hours a day helping Amay fill application forms?"'

She thought for a bit and then said sheepishly, 'Okay, okay. So, I am actually asking . . . but my ask is not clear. And when my ask is not clear, he doesn't understand. And then, I shrink and believe I don't matter.'

'You are really quick at making these connections,' I admired.

'But I don't know how to ask differently. I have never asked.'

'And you just missed a stroke that I gave you!'

'Oh yes. Thank you. See, that is me. Chasing after strokes while ignoring the ones coming my way.'

'Well done again. You are really beginning to recognize your own patterns.'

'Thank you,' she said with a smile, gesturing with her hand and bowing her head as if she was curtsying. She added, 'And I also want to learn how to ask for strokes directly.'

'You are doing that right now, by directly asking me for what you need,' I highlighted.

'Oh!' She looked surprised. 'I see. Strokes are more than appreciation. If I ask for what I need, I am asking for a stroke?'

'Yes. Why don't we play around a bit and see how you can ask. What could you say to him?'

'I have worked very hard with Amay on his application forms.'

'Ask directly!' I prodded.

'Say something nice!' she said brightly. She looked amused with her option, and I could see her almost dismissing it as outlandish.

'Well done!' I clapped for her.

'I actually want to say "Don't give me advice; say something nice!"'

'Say it and see how it feels?'

'Maybe I can say "Don't give me advice", only if he gives me advice. Let me trust that he will respond to my ask directly.'

'Well done again! Are there other requests you can make more directly?'

'Now I am wondering why I am doing Amay's forms by myself. I could say "Could you help him with these two applications?"'

'Good awareness. You are recognizing how the little girl, who got strokes only by being responsible, shows up in your present relationships. And you can change that.'

'Right.' She paused, and then said suddenly, 'Can I ask you something?'

'Yes.'

'Say something nice!' she said, looking naughty.

'This is a twist I didn't expect!' I beamed, and she beamed right back triumphantly.

24

All About the Money

Yashodhara

'You got my message about the payment for this session, yes?' Lalita started the session with that.

'Yes,' I answered. 'You sent it just a few minutes ago perhaps? I did see it.'

'Okay, good.' She seemed to relax a little. 'I was just a little worried when you didn't acknowledge it.'

'I wonder,' I said curiously, 'what you were imagining when I didn't respond.'

'I guess I just want to make sure you know I've paid . . . you know, that you're comfortable.'

I took this in and got in touch with the part of me that actually didn't feel very comfortable. We had an agreement that she would pay two days in advance, but she invariably made the transfer just before each session, sometimes only minutes in advance. 'Actually, maybe we can spend some time talking about this today, Lalita?'

'Talk about what?' She looked cornered. 'Our pay–per–session deal? I really can't pay in advance. You know how it is with running the household on my salary—Rahul's got his start-up and no steady income, and we have two kids to put through college . . .'

Her voice trailed off. I resisted the urge to set her at ease and continued calmly, 'Could you slow down? Tell me what you are feeling as I raise the topic of money.'

'I don't know . . . panic?'

'I can see that in your eyes and breathing. Just be aware of your panic for a minute and tell me about it.'

'Well, okay.' She sighed. 'Actually, I have been feeling very worried about finances and wondering about whether I will get that raise this year. I thought maybe you'll tell me to start paying for several sessions in advance.'

Lalita had been a regular client with me and had requested that she pay before each session. I usually preferred contracting for six to eight sessions in advance, but I had agreed to her request as an exception. Yet, I needed to talk to her about honouring boundaries.

'Our arrangement was that you pay two days before the session.'

'Yes, I know,' she acknowledged, looking guilty.

'So, I wonder about your process of paying just a few minutes before each session and sending me a text message about it or bringing it up as the opening.'

There was a long silence, and I could see that she was thinking deeply about what I had said.

Finally, she nodded saying, 'You know, I know I've said I forget, but I was just thinking that I could put a reminder on my phone and just do it but somehow haven't . . .'

'Right.' I decided to invite her to use her Adult thinking. 'What do you think might be going on for you here?'

She bit her lip for a moment, and then ventured slowly, 'I may be just delaying parting with my money. I tend to do that sometimes, put payments that are due off to the last possible minute. And . . .' she looked a little uncomfortable but went ahead, 'I'm also perhaps reminding us that since money is tight for me, we should really get the most out of each session?'

'So, *each* session . . . we should be getting *the most* out of it?' I felt a sense of relief at being able to understand my own discomfort better. 'Does this pressure get in the way of our work together?'

'I am not sure . . .' She gazed at me for a while, 'Maybe it does, though I don't want it to.'

'Here's a hypothesis,' I offered. 'We've discussed that being close to people and trusting them is hard for you; I wonder, does something about this arrangement perhaps help keep a distance between us?'

'I don't know.' Her eyes widened, 'I mean . . . I never thought of it that way. I do have a lot of anxiety around money and trusting people, and trusting people when money is involved has always been the most difficult. That's why I can't even trust my boss to actually give me that raise despite how well I've performed this year.'

'Tell me about the messages around money you grew up with?' I invited.

'Okay.' She sat back. 'I remember Mom saying all the time that "We are very middle-class people. We are not rich like those people . . . "—the neighbours, usually.'

'Right,' I said. 'What else?'

'I was always confused about how much we had. They would say "This is not for children to know." In fact, I once had to fill in a form for something and it said to provide a salary range for your father's earnings, and when I asked Dad, he said "Why do they want to know?" and he refused to answer me!'

'Got it.' I encouraged her, 'Keep going.'

'Mom would say "Money doesn't grow on trees." I would get really annoyed; she said it all the time whenever we asked for money for the simplest things. Eventually we stopped asking only! She would maintain the accounts, scrutinize the bills, and question our maids, the vegetable vendor, shopkeepers—she would get angry if she thought we were being cheated . . . and she thought that a lot.'

'Right.' I looked carefully at her face. 'You're looking quite angry yourself right now.'

'Yes.' Her face darkened further. 'I was just remembering how I had only one skirt. Most of the other girls had at least three or four, but I had to keep mending my torn skirt and it was all patchy. I felt really ashamed. I don't think I even asked Mum about it though. Maybe I just didn't want a lecture about how money doesn't grow on trees or thought she would say no and remind me about how we don't have enough. The other kids laughed at me. I ignored them, but I hated it.' Her expression changed and she looked down.

'It must have been difficult,' I said gently. 'I see your sadness. What's going on for you now?'

She took a deep breath. 'I'm just getting in touch with . . . I don't know, all those worries about money. It's always felt like such a burden. And I think, even as a kid, I vowed to myself, I will have my own money, and no one will tell me what to buy or not. But even today, despite all these years of working so hard, I never feel I'll have enough!'

'Is that true', I challenged, 'that you don't have enough?'

'Well, it is actually *enough*,' she admitted. 'I don't have a lot of savings though. I spend so much money on clothes and bags, and it's expensive to maintain the home I have as well.'

'This version of you today,' I observed, 'is very different from that little girl with the patched-up skirt.'

'Oh, that's right.' She laughed sharply. 'Now I'm all about new outfits for each important occasion, matching accessories always. I think that's some sort of rebellion. My mom is horrified to this day at how much I spend on clothes. But it's my money!'

'We do tend to rebel sometimes against our parents and parental messages,' I reminded her, 'but if it's done compulsively and unconsciously—it's still a programmed response.'

'True,' she mused. 'It is compulsive.'

'How else might those childhood messages be affecting you today?'

She leaned back in her chair. 'I mean . . . I still find it difficult to *ask* when it comes to money. My colleagues keep on getting raises, and I'm maybe at 60–70 per cent of what I should be getting paid. But I still believe I shouldn't ask for a raise! And trust, yes, trusting people . . . or trusting, I don't know, *life,* when it comes to money . . . it's like money is *meant* to be a struggle.'

'That's very good awareness,' I said, 'and you can also question and challenge these beliefs—starting to practise asking for what is due, trusting that you do have and will always have enough, and, especially, believing that money may not have to be a struggle.'

'Yes. My parents had their financial struggles, especially when they were kids,' she said thoughtfully, and added with more confidence, 'but I'm in a different position, better off today than we ever were collectively.'

'It can be helpful to write down our old Parent or Child beliefs, which tend to operate unconsciously,' I offered, 'and then, for each, write out the updated Adult belief that is functional, conscious, and informed by today's reality. For example "I shouldn't ask for a raise"—what would you like to change that to?'

She thought for a moment, and then raised her chin, 'I'd like it to be "I can ask for what I deserve, and I definitely deserve a raise!"'

'Great!' I smiled, 'Will you write and reframe the others like this?'

'I'll do that,' she said determinedly. Then, with a twinkle in her eye, she added, 'After all, our phones get a software update every now and then. Why shouldn't we?'

I smiled at her. The shift in her energy was palpable, and I could sense a new relaxation in her—she had arrived at a much deeper understanding of where her worries and issues around money had come from, and she could work on changing her limiting beliefs. I also sensed that by talking openly about our own money-related issue today, we had been able to bridge the gap between us. We can effectively use what's going on in the present moment in service of the client. I felt intuitively that our relationship would deepen and become less transactional. It did, over time, and while we went on to explore many facets of her life, delayed payments were not required as a subject for conversation again.

25

Choosing to See

Aruna

'Should I go back to Shayan?' asked a distraught Samyukta, holding her head in her hands.

The eight years that Samyukta was married to Shayan had been full of stress. Last year, she decided to move to Bangalore from Pune to give herself some space to think about what was going on for her. She left her five-year old daughter, Laya, with Shayan. That was when she had reached out to me. We worked together on whether she should separate from him or go back, but our discussions offered her no clarity. I saw her justifying his actions and blaming herself, almost seeking permission from me to go back to a bad marriage.

'I sense that you would like to go back,' I voiced my intuition.

'I think so,' she said, relieved. 'I miss my daughter. She needs both parents. And Shayan is a very good father. I am the emotional wreck.'

'Emotional wreck' was one of the many labels Shayan had for her that she believed to be the truth. I explored her history to get to the origin of the pattern of easily believing the worst about herself. Samyukta had often been belittled as a child by her bullying father. She had no memories of feeling important or cherished. Her father had been violent towards her mother occasionally. She had internalized this power difference between men and women and couldn't imagine a different way of being. She carried into adulthood this feeling of being powerless and one-down in her relationships. She had what, in Transactional Analysis, we call an *existential position* or fundamental conviction of the belief 'I'm not OK-You are OK.'

She made a decision to go back to what I suspected was an abusive relationship. She missed her daughter, no doubt. But she wasn't able to recognize her husband's discount of her.

I contracted with her to continue therapy with me online, after she moved back to Pune. I saw my role as walking steadily alongside her as she navigated the difficult relationship again, helping her appraise situations realistically and recognize her resources as she dealt with the challenges.

The first month after she went back was tense for all. But soon things began to thaw. Even though Samyukta and Shayan slept in separate rooms, they started having meals together as a family. Samyukta was filled with the hope that things would get better.

During this period, she got a promotion and a hefty raise. At the same time, Shayan decided to quit because he was disillusioned with the 'meaningless corporate world'. Samyukta didn't mind—she believed he was free to choose his options. She was earning enough for all.

He would cook all meals. 'I feel very lucky, but also very guilty about that,' she told me.

'Do you want to cook?'

'I hate it and am not good at it.'

'Then why the guilt?'

'Because he is cooking *all* meals. I wish he would let me hire a cook.'

'Let you?!!' I was aghast.

She cowered in response.

I internally cringed at my judgement of her as I saw her draw herself in. I recognized my own unconscious expectation that as an IIM graduate leading a team of 500 people, she 'should' recognize her own agency.

I softened and explained, 'He has chosen to cook all meals. You don't have to take responsibility for his choice. How would it be for you to just enjoy the meals? Just as he can be who he is, you can be who you are.'

'It is not just my guilt that bothers me. I have practical challenges too. Last week he got into a bad mood, and he locked himself in his room and did not come out for two days. I had to figure out food for me and Laya. Swiggy *zindabad*,' she said, laughing.

I did not laugh with her. She stopped smiling too when she saw my expression.

'I know it is not funny,' she said sadly.

'What made him shut down?'

'I suggested that he set up something on his own. He was beginning to get depressed and was not going out and interacting with others.'

'How did he respond to your idea?'

'He asked me to not spout "corporate shit". And that I should reserve my "*gyan*" (lecturing) for my workplace. I began to cry when he said that. Then he called me a cry-baby. He asked me what I was learning in my sessions with you. "*Paagal log jate hain* counsellors *ke pas, paise barbaad karne*" (Only mad people go to counsellors and waste their money). He said I was crying with you, crying at home, crying at work, crying everywhere. I was a "*rondu*" (cry baby).'

I felt sad when I heard this, 'How do you feel about what he said?'

'He is right. I cry easily. I am needy, clingy, and need constant validation,' she said. I wondered how I could help her discern the strokes that belittled her, and not make them the truth.

As I paused, wondering about the next step, she added, 'I have made mistakes.'

'Like what?' I was curious.

'I need to talk endlessly. And Shayan is not good at listening. He has his moods. Many years ago, early in our marriage, I became close to Anil, a friend of ours from college. We would talk for long, sometimes for hours. That was when I realized that what I missed in our marriage was Shayan listening to me. One day, in a moment of weakness, I told Anil that Shayan and I weren't having sex. A couple of months later, Anil, in a conversation with Shayan, said "You are a fool to have a wife as beautiful as Sam and not satisfy her." I was aghast. How could a person I trusted betray me like this? Shayan was already cold to me. He turned rock hard after the incident and did not speak to me for a whole year. I am grateful he didn't throw me out.'

There was a lot to unpack in that story. Samyukta continued, 'I was gifted a lovely marriage. I ruined it. Had I not spoken to Anil, things wouldn't have become this bad. I have been apologizing to Shayan for years now, but he has never forgiven me for this.'

'Is it true that if you hadn't spoken to Anil, your marriage would have been fine?' I challenged.

'I betrayed Shayan by speaking to another about our sex life.'

'Perhaps you did. But that is one part of the story. Do you think Shayan and Anil also contributed to the outcome?'

She was quiet for a few minutes.

'He was cold and uncaring. This is why I sought a friend outside marriage in the first place. My dream has always been to have a best friend in my husband. But that didn't happen.'

'You are also very remorseful of your act and have apologized. But Shayan hasn't been able to forgive or let go.'

She dissolved into tears. 'God only knows the penances I have done to get him to forgive me. No one will believe how much I have apologized for this. I gave up being myself. I tried to be everything he wanted me to be.'

'And he didn't see this!' I said, feeling sad. In our culture, women are often punished harshly for their mistakes.

'So, you were not the only one who was gifted a lovely marriage. He was too. He too contributed to it going bad,' I said.

'Yes,' she said, beginning to see his role in the dynamics.

As our conversations progressed, she recognized Shayan's contribution to the breakdown of the marriage. As her internal critic relaxed, she gave herself a few permissions. 'I have done enough to beg for his forgiveness. If he cannot see how much I care, I could let it go and start being myself again.'

I rejoiced at this pivotal development in our sessions.

Over the next few months, Samyukta reached out to her friends, activating her dormant network. She joined an aerobics class. Slowly, she began to regain her confidence.

To help her be autonomous in her relationship with Shayan, I asked her to keep a journal of their exchanges. She was shocked at the data that emerged. 'Almost everything he says is a put-down. He judges me, my work, my looks, my decisions. And he has these intense mood swings where he just stops talking to me. Sometimes he walks out of the house and comes back after three days. I die worrying.'

'So, the journaling helped you see what you were discounting,' I highlighted. She looked grim.

'Are you aware that not talking to someone is a form of emotional abuse?' I named it for her, as she seemed ready to acknowledge it.

'But he has not raised a finger on me,' she protested. 'He is not like my father.'

'Physical violence is not the only form of violence,' I explained. 'Shayan shows his anger by shutting you out. Not talking is a form of manipulation, where you don't understand what is going on and have no opportunity to dialogue and fix things. His labels wear you down. He shames you for having opinions, being successful. When you have needs and he calls you needy, you begin to doubt whether you should have needs at all.'

Samyukta went silent.

After a few moments she said, 'He twists events to make it my fault. I am apologizing all the time, believing that I cannot do anything right. I have begun to believe all that he says. I have lost my identity in this relationship.'

She argued with herself as she continued, 'But it wasn't always like this. We were truly in love once. And we have some good moments even now.'

'Is that preventing you from seeing and accepting that things are not okay?'

'Looks like it. I cannot come to terms with what is happening in my marriage. We were in college when we fell in love. He would praise me for qualities no other person had ever appreciated before. I was smart, beautiful, and had foresight. Somehow, after the wedding, I became a cry-baby, needy, clingy and whiny.'

However, as we explored more stories, she recognized his put-downs even when they were courting.

'Why was I this blind?' Samyukta was puzzled.

I explained to her how we unconsciously recreate the dynamics of our dysfunctional childhood even though we are consciously trying to escape it. Given that she had a violent and critical father, she was drawn to an emotionally unavailable man who would put her down. Our unconscious mind has the uncanny intuitive ability to choose people with whom we can experience the same relational patterns that we had in our childhood.

'At an unconscious level, I chose not to see even though it was so evident!' she said incredulously.

I reiterated that familiarity offered stability. Being alone was scarier than being in an abusive relationship. That is why she never saw her abuse as abuse. Her unconscious mind protected her by allowing her to discount information that would make her face her fears.

As Samyukta 'chose to see' what was going on between her and Shayan, she initiated changes. She separated their bank accounts to signal that he would not have free access to what she earned. She hired a cook even though he refused to eat what the cook made. She stopped seeking his opinion. She tolerated his sulking. But what thrilled her the most was that she learnt to swear back at him when he swore at her.

'This is the first time in my life that I am actually swearing! I am not crying. It is fucking amazing,' she said, her eyes shining. She shared that her learning to fight actually de-escalated their conflict and made their relationship more equal.

'No shit!' I laughed, marvelling at the transformation.

26

The Dinner Time Drama

Yashodhara

'I do have something today.'

'Sure, Preeti.' I smiled. She was one of the quieter members in this therapy group and I was happy she wanted to participate today. I had just asked the group to attend to their inner worlds and see what was alive for them, and if they would like to process it in the group setting. 'Tell us what you have in mind?'

'Well,' she hesitated, 'it's just a little thing.'

'*Just* a *little* thing?' I smiled and repeated. It took time and practice for group members to become aware of their self-discounting language.

'Okay,' she smiled, 'it is something that has been bothering me quite a lot. At dinner last night, we were having a nice time, but then my son made fun of something I said—some silly goof-up. I asked him to get something from the refrigerator, and I said "flidge" instead of "fridge", and he said "Sure mom, I'll bling it" . . . and my daughter and husband also started laughing and they went on making jokes about me. I just went totally quiet and switched off, and then it became awkward for everyone. They were all trying to get me to talk again, but I just couldn't. It ended up in a mess.'

'How do you feel as you share this?'

She thought about it. 'Hurt. I tend to mess up what I'm saying when I speak fast, but it just really hurts when someone calls it out. Especially with the three of them, I can't take any jokes they make at my expense. I try not to take things so seriously . . . they keep telling me they wish I would lighten up, but I can't.'

'What would you like for yourself, Preeti?'

'I wish I wouldn't be so easily hurt. I wish I could laugh it off.'

'Would it be useful if we recreated the scene and you practised a different response?' I wondered aloud. In that moment, I felt that an exercise, where she accessed the energy of different ego states, might open up options for her.

She agreed, looking curiously excited.

I asked, 'Could you choose a space and set the scene?'

Preeti dragged a few chairs to the centre and placed them in a circle.

'This is the family sitting around the dining table.' I went on, 'Preeti, could you please pick three people to play your husband, son, and daughter?'

Preeti looked around the room. 'I choose Srini to play my husband, Abhay as my son, and Ritu as my daughter.'

The three group members she had named occupied the chairs that Preeti had set out so that they all sat in a circle. The other group members stayed on the periphery, watching.

'Anyone else in this scene, Preeti?' I asked. 'Only our dog, Layla.'

'Got it,' I smiled. 'We might get Layla's perspective on what's going on too, later.'

'We should,' Preeti rolled her eyes. 'She's the most sensible of us all.'

The group members laughed.

'Okay, let's start,' I said. 'So, Preeti and family at the dining table—Preeti, go ahead and say what you said that started it all off.'

Preeti took a breath and turned to Abhay. 'Cheenu, please get some juice from the flidge . . . I mean fridge.'

I invited Abhay to respond as Preeti had said he would.

Abhay was right on cue. 'Sure mom,' he said with a wicked grin, 'I'll bling it from the flidge—light away!'

That last one was his own addition, and it made the group members crack up. I smiled instinctively, but immediately noticed that Preeti looked crushed. It was as if she had become physically smaller in her chair.

'Let's pause,' I told the group. Then I asked, 'What are you experiencing right now, Preeti?'

She swallowed. 'It's a bit hard to speak.'

'I understand,' I said gently. 'We have a choice to stop now and explore what happened without the drama. Shall we do that?'

Preeti thought for a moment, 'No, actually, I'd like us to continue.'

'Alright.' I smiled and then asked her, 'What happens now?'

'They continue to make fun of me.'

I invited the group members to improvise as instructed.

Ritu spoke up as Preeti's daughter, 'Mom is just too funny when she talks like that!'

Srini added as Preeti's husband, 'This is nothing, you guys. I had thought of hiring an interpreter in the early years of our marriage.'

Everyone else in character laughed. Preeti, once again, looked overwhelmed by her emotions. The laughter died down, and now the group members sitting in the inner circle went silent. The awkwardness was palpable, and I was amazed by how quickly we had recreated the mood that Preeti had described.

'Let's pause again,' I said, and addressed her. 'Preeti— what are you getting in touch with?'

With some effort, she said, 'I feel small . . . I was the youngest kid in my family, and my brother and sister would make fun of how I spoke, and my parents would also laugh. I read a lot and picked up words from the books but pronounced them wrong, and they thought it was so funny . . .'

I nodded, imagining her as a hurt, embarrassed little girl. 'And you'd go quiet then?'

'Yes,' she said, 'I would stop speaking, and sulk for a long time.' She looked miserable. 'And now I'm thinking—I'm their *mother*, I'm the elder one now; why won't the teasing stop? Even here, I don't belong!'

'Would you like to share this with your family and see how they respond?' I said, inviting her to stay in the action and express herself authentically in the moment.

She looked at her family around the table and said, 'When you tease me like this, I feel small. Even with you all, I feel like I don't belong.'

'Would you like to hear their response to this?' I asked her. 'Yes,' she nodded.

'Who would you like to reverse with first?' I asked. To 'reverse with' was a psychodramatic term, and it meant to switch characters in-the-moment. The main protagonist, Preeti, would now play the role of her family members, and then get to hear her own words played back.

'I'll be my son first.'

She exchanged chairs with Abhay. 'Hello, Abhay,' I said, addressing Preeti, reminding her that she was now Abhay. 'What do you feel about what Mom just said?'

She rolled her eyes in the role of her son. 'Wow, here Mom goes again. It was just a little joke; I was trying to get her to laugh and be with us but now she's off! Why can't we just have fun together?'

She repeated the same exercise with the other two characters. As her husband, she said in a worried tone, 'Preeti works so hard, I wish she would just relax and have a good time with us. I know she's hurt, I feel sad for her. I don't know how to help her. I want her to belong.'

As her daughter, she said with an expression of regret, 'I know how Mom feels; the boys can be insensitive sometimes. But it *is* funny, and so I laughed—now I think Mom is mad at me for taking their side. I shouldn't have done this.'

I noticed that Preeti appeared to be going through a range of emotions—sadness, gratitude, guilt—as the group members played each of these responses back to her. On impulse, I asked her to also become Layla the dog and speak from her point of view.

'Preeti looks all smiley and happy at the beginning of the meal,' said Preeti as Layla the dog, 'but then I see when the others are getting happy as well, suddenly she becomes sad . . . and then everyone else becomes sad too. It sure is a strange family! Their food sure looks yummy though!'

I repeated her words back to her and then paused.

'I just realized,' she said with a wistful look, 'I've actually *got* the warm, welcoming family that I always wanted. I've created it.'

'You've created it,' I affirmed. 'Sounds like you can be proud of that.'

'I am proud,' she repeated. Her energy shifted. 'I want to enjoy them, and not be this hurt Child all the time. I want to be a joyful Child!'

'Would you like to experiment with that here?'

'Yes!' she said, her eyes sparkling.

'Right,' I said. 'Group, action! Shall we take it from the beginning?'

Preeti had a small smile on her face as Abhay repeated his teasing dialogue, 'Yes, Mom, I'll *bling* it light away.'

'Watch it, Cheenu,' she said in a mock-scolding tone, speaking over the laughter of the others, 'Or you might find yourself eating some flied lice, picked from your own head!'

Everyone laughed at this, and Ritu, in Preeti's daughter's role, wagged a finger, saying, 'Mom! Using an old joke poking fun at how the Chinese speak? How politically incollect!'

The group was spontaneously having a lot of fun with this, and I noted Preeti laughing along, her eyes shining. I felt hope that she might be able to show this side of herself at home—while she had chosen to respond spontaneously from her Child ego state, it was an Adult choice to do so. She was seeing reality as it was and responding appropriately instead of through the archaic lens of a hurt Child. My wish for her was that she would really enjoy the family that she'd always wanted and now realized she had. Perhaps it would help her reframe her story, and she would see her family as people who adored her—and recognize that they had been laughing *with* her and not at her.

27

Chucking the Potato

Aruna

Tasmai was in tears.

'What happened?' I asked her.

'My boss asked me to stay late and finish my work, not honouring that I was working part time. Also, she didn't give me instructions clearly. I have already put in so many extra hours because the instructions were not clear.'

'You sound angry.'

'I am.'

'And yet you are crying?'

'Yes, I don't know why I always cry.'

When children are judged for their anger or punished for it, they learn not to feel anger, and substitute it with another feeling that is allowed. In Tasmai's case, the allowed feeling was sadness, and the forbidden feeling was anger.

'Well, I am glad you know you are angry.'

'How does it help me to know I am angry?' she asked, her forehead furrowed in puzzlement.

'Do you think you would act differently when angry?'

'I think so.'

'Perhaps it might help you confront your boss about her unreasonableness?'

Tasmai considered what I had proposed, 'I can't imagine myself doing it.'

That was an opening enough for me. 'Well, why don't you practise here with me?' I nudged.

'All right,' said Tasmai. She straightened her back, closed her eyes, and gathered her thoughts.

She opened her eyes and looked at me and implored hesitantly, 'I have already worked for so many hours. The instructions were not clear. I work part time. This is not expected of me.'

'I hear you pleading with me. Would you like to bring more power into your voice?'

She nibbled on her lip, 'I know I don't sound angry.'

'So, here is the situation. This manager is not able to see or appreciate that you are doing your best and stretching yourself. The boundaries are unclear, and the manager is not acknowledging her responsibility here. Instead, she is blaming you.'

'Yes, I know, but I am unable to express my anger,' sighed Tasmai, collapsing in her chair, giving up.

I decided not to pressure her further. After a pause, I approached the issue differently.

'This seems like a familiar pattern. What or who comes to your mind when you think of an earlier experience of not being seen or appreciated?'

'My mother,' she said immediately, 'but I don't want to go there.'

'Why don't you want to go there?'

'I don't want to blame her for my not feeling good enough.'

'So, you see understanding the origin of your patterns as a way to fix blame?'

'No, but she was who she was. I am not expecting her to change. Even last night, I cleaned the kitchen. And then she went after me and cleaned it again. It doesn't matter that I am thirty-eight years old and that she is now staying with me in *my* house.' Tasmai's eyes glistened with tears.

'What are your tears saying?'

'That I am hurt,' she said, and continued reflectively, 'I remember a scene from my childhood very clearly. I was seven years old. My mum was making vegetable cutlets for guests. I was helping her mash the boiled potato. I was very excited to help her. I felt I was contributing to something important. But she was not happy. I still remember her frown when she examined the potato that I had mashed. She found it lumpy and not good enough.'

'What do you remember feeling?'

'Sad. I wasn't good enough.'

I noticed that she said, 'I wasn't good enough' and not 'my mashing wasn't good enough.' As children, we are often not able to separate our being from our doing.

'You believed you were not good enough. And what did you do?'

'I mashed the potato more diligently,' she said, tears running down her cheeks now as she recognized her pain of trying hard to please her mother. I felt love and compassion for her in my heart, and also an urge for her to get in touch with her anger.

'Shall we play with this scene a little bit?'

'Sure.'

'Imagine that your mum is five years old.'

She looked puzzled and amused at the same time. 'Have you seen a photograph of her as a little girl?'

'Yes.'

'So, you play out the scene in your own mind again. Only this time, your mum will be five years old. She is still your mum, just that she is five. It is the same scene in the kitchen. Both of you are mashing potatoes.'

Tasmai smiled. I observed that as a shift in her energy. A positive sign that she was ready to play and see what emerged.

She closed her eyes again and visualized the scene. I asked her to narrate it as though it was happening then.

'I am seven, eager to help my mum mash potatoes. I show it to her eagerly, but she is not happy. She is frowning and looks disappointed.'

'Is she five years old?' I checked. 'Yes,' she confirmed.

'So, your mum is frowning. How are you feeling?'

'I am angry,' said Tasmai, frowning, fully involved in the fantasy. It was easy to be angry when Mum was only five years old.

'What happens now?' I was curious about how the story would unfold.

'I chuck the potato on the table and say "If you are not happy with my mashing, do it yourself!"'

'Wow! Feel the energy of that anger.'

'I want to chuck something,' she said, opening her eyes.

I handed her a tennis ball. She chucked it on the floor with all her might, shouting, 'You are never happy with anything I do!' I picked up the ball and handed it to her again. She chucked it, saying, 'I have spent all my life trying to live up to your standards but nothing I do is good enough. Today, I am taking care of you but all you do is judge everything I do, from how I run the house, how I parent, how I cook . . .' And then she held her head in her hands and had a good cry.

'How are you feeling?' I asked gently.

'I am in shock. I didn't realize I was this angry. I am just so tired of trying hard to please my mom.'

'I see how much you yearned for her appreciation.'

'But it never came. And I doubt if it will ever come.'

'How do you feel when you say that?'

'Sad,' she said, tearing up again. But this time she straightened her back and said, 'It is time I saw that it hasn't come in so many years, so I might as well do what I like and stop trying to please her. Not just her, others too.'

She recognized the parallel in the situation with her boss immediately, 'My boss too is not appreciative of my efforts, and I am responding to her just the way I responded to my mum, by feeling sad and trying harder.'

'What would be the equivalent of chucking the potato on the table with this boss of yours?' I asked Tasmai.

'I should have spoken up earlier and refused to do the work when the instructions weren't clear enough.'

'If you had to express your anger now, what would you say?' I asked.

Tasmai struggled, 'I don't want to throw a tantrum like a seven-year-old.'

I realized expressing anger wasn't going to be easy for her.

I made an offer, 'How about saying "I couldn't complete the task because you missed sharing with me some crucial instructions that would have allowed me to understand it. I have already gone much beyond the contracted hours. I cannot stretch myself further tonight to finish this. I can do this by the end of the week."?'

Tasmai summarized, 'So chucking the potato on the table in this context is saying "No, I can't stretch myself."'

'Yes.'

She sighed. 'I wish I could say this to my boss. But I don't think I can.' I saw her looking very thoughtful.

I paused, waiting for what might emerge from her.

'Yet,' she added, looking straight at me.

'What does that mean?' I perked up.

'It means I want to, but I am not ready today. But one day I will chuck the potato without guilt.'

'I am sure you will,' I said confidently.

28

What's in a Hug?

Yashodhara

'Well, she's finally here,' Neetu grumbled. 'Stubborn lady!'

'How are you feeling about your mom being here?' I couldn't help but smile. 'It's been a long time since you met her—a year and a half?'

'Yes,' she said emphatically. 'Over the last few months, I told her that since the pandemic's easing up and she is fully vaccinated, she could come and stay with us. But it's taken this long for her to agree.'

I noticed she hadn't answered my question, so I pressed gently, 'So how are you feeling about it?'

'Good, good,' she said automatically and then stopped to think, concluding, 'I don't know, actually.' She looked pensive and began to absently pull at her lower lip.

'What's this?' I mirrored her expression and pulled at my own lower lip, adding, 'I've not seen you do this before?'

'I don't know, I've started doing this again for some reason!' she said. 'In fact, Mom pointed it out two days ago. I used to do it as a kid while studying, I think. Helped me concentrate—and it really used to irritate me when she kept telling me to stop.'

'And now,' I asked, 'when she said it two days ago?'

'I snapped at her and reminded her I'm a grown up now.' She rolled her eyes. 'She's a nag. Moms are supposed to drive you crazy, right?'

'Are they?'

'Well, mine always has,' she said, sounding resigned. 'It's hard for me and her to be in the same room. I mean, I guess I love her and all that. But . . . it's testing me even more right now.'

'How so?'

'I'm just . . . somehow even more bad-tempered with her around this trip. The kids are really delighted to see her, both of them are all over her. She's brought them gifts, is playing these board games and stuff with them, even reading them bedtime stories . . . but I'm just being like this *dragon-mother*—I told her the sweets she brought aren't good for them, when I see her showing them some video they like, I point out they get too much screen time as it is, their laughing at bedtime makes me walk in and scold them for staying up past their bedtime . . .'

'I wonder,' I said, 'if you are being a dragon-mother or dragon-daughter.'

This made her pause. 'Well, I suppose I am actually scolding her even though it's supposedly directed at the kids. And she becomes all quiet, doesn't argue, really, just tells the kids to stop or go away or whatever. And then I feel shitty about it.'

'Are you angry with your mother?'

'I am . . . have always been,' she said in a clipped tone, 'but have learned to live with it. She was always just so busy at work and distant and business-like at home. Really no sort of empathy or affection for me or my sister. I resolved a long time ago that it would be different for me and my kids.'

'Is it?'

'Yes,' she said, and then admitted, 'and no. I'm definitely more involved and affectionate with my kids. But I think my temper and need to have everything in order do drive them away. No wonder they run to her now that she's here! She's an old softie compared to me. Hah!' She was smiling bitterly.

'What was the "Hah!" about?'

'Just that—to think of her as an old softie. Reading stories to my kids, sweets . . . none of the stuff me or my sis got from her. Feels odd.' She suddenly looked ashamed, her cheeks flushed. 'I think I'm jealous of my own kids.'

'Good awareness,' I said soothingly. 'And it's okay to be jealous—it's maybe the little kid inside you who didn't get this kind of loving attention who is feeling this way. It's okay to talk about it.'

She gave a brief nod but looked away. We sat in silence for a while, and I sensed she didn't want to dive further into this feeling. She suddenly muttered, 'I've just never understood why she acts the way she does with me.'

I saw the deflection away from her jealousy—she was back in her usual, comfortable feeling of anger. I decided to go with the flow, respecting her unwillingness to explore her vulnerability just yet.

'You've never understood why she acts the way she does with you?' I repeated.

'Not really,' she said, shrugging.

'How would you describe it?'

'Just . . . I don't know . . . it feels either nitpicking and interfering, or cold and distant. There's no third way of being, I think, at least with me. And it's been like this from as far back as I can remember.'

'And how would you describe your own way of being with her?' I asked.

'I just get irritated . . . over the tiniest things she does. I miss her when she's not there, but when she is, I'm like a time bomb.' She paused. 'I don't think I want to be like this. I just can't figure out why we both do this, over and over.'

'Shall we do an exercise where you become your mother, and respond to my questions? So, you literally step into her shoes?' I suggested. 'Since you said you've never understood why your mom acts as she does, it might give you some insight.'

'Okay.' She sat up straighter.

'So, could you please stand up and walk around a little bit, and then when you come back into the chair, you will be your mother.'

She did just that. As she sat down, I smiled at her, 'Hello there, Neetu's mom! What's your name?'

'Hello,' said Neetu, a little stiffly. 'I'm Rina.'

'Nice to meet you, Rina,' I said warmly.

She smiled back tentatively.

'Rina, I would like to know you a little better. Could I ask you a few questions?'

'Sure.'

'Let us start with where you were born.'

'I was born in Ahmedabad sixty-five years ago.'

'What was your childhood like?'

'I was the first child . . .'

Neetu spoke haltingly at first and then got more into her mom's role. She spoke about being the little girl who had grown up in a poor family as the eldest of four siblings—her mom had been the 'good, responsible' child, taking care of everyone in the family.

'I had to help my mother out a lot at home—the other kids were small. And she was also sick a lot of the time.'

'You took care of your mom too when she was sick?'

'I had to,' she said expressionlessly. 'There was no one else to do it.'

'And who took care of you, Rina?'

She hesitated and shrugged. 'My parents did what they could, but they had enough struggles of their own. I learned to take care of myself very early. That's been a strength for me. And I decided, as a kid, that I would study well, earn my own money, and make sure that when I grew up, my family wouldn't need to give up on things. It would be different for my kids.'

I noted that Neetu had just used the exact phrase while in her mom's role that she had a while back when talking about her own kids. She went on, her face determined, 'I always worked really hard and made sure that they had the best education, and that they would do well for themselves.'

'And how are your kids doing now, Rina?'

'Kids!' She laughed. 'They are grown successful women, both of them. They are doing very well indeed. Especially Neetu, she runs her own firm!'

'You seem very proud of Neetu,' I said gently.

'Very.' She returned, immediately and confidently, with a smile. A flash of surprise appeared for a moment on her face, and I suspected that this was a new realization for Neetu.

'What are you proud of Neetu for?'

'She's . . . intelligent and determined. Once she decides something, she can make it happen! She isn't afraid of trying new things. I really admire her for these things.'

'Does Neetu know you are proud and that you admire her, Rina?'

The pride was now replaced by a look of sadness. I wasn't sure if this belonged to Neetu or her mom.

'You are looking sad. Could you tell me about your sadness right now?' I said gently.

'Neetu is just always so busy . . .' It was still Rina speaking, I realized. 'I've come to visit after a long time, but she's hardly ever around. And when she is around, she's always angry with everyone. Especially me.'

'You miss her. You would like to experience closeness with her,' I said tenderly.

'I do,' she said wistfully. Then, after a hesitant pause, she added, 'I think she's angry because I didn't do things with her—you know—just play and spend time on other things like that, when she was small. Both my husband and I struggled in our jobs for long hours; it wasn't easy. I know I could have done better—I was always tired and worried, and never knew how to be affectionate.' She paused and added, 'Neetu's the one who taught us to hug.'

'Neetu taught you to hug?' I repeated with a smile.

'When she was very small,' Neetu continued as her mom, 'she was a naturally affectionate child, and she used to love hugging her baby sister. But after her teens, she stopped hugging us properly. It's just this awkward quick thing and then she pulls away. I guess she's been angry for a long time.' Her face became very sad. 'Maybe she's punishing me.'

She went quiet. After a few moments, she began pulling at her lower lip again—I saw she had slipped back naturally into being Neetu.

'Okay,' I said, 'it looks like you've come back to being Neetu. Could you perhaps stand up and walk around again, and come back into yourself fully?'

She complied and I waited until she had settled back down again into her chair. 'What's going on for you now?' I asked.

She looked at me thoughtfully. 'I just realized I don't think I get irritated just by the gifts, the video-watching, the bedtime stories . . .' she struggled to articulate it. 'It's that my kids are hugging her or sitting close to her all the time while they do this.'

'Is there a part of you that is yearning to be close to your mother?' She bit her lip and nodded.

'And the same yearning also seems very much there in your mother,' I pointed out. Her eyes widened as this sank in. She nodded again, slowly.

'I wonder—are both of you waiting for the other person to make the first move?'

There was a very long pause this time. But when Neetu spoke, it was with a hint of a smile. 'That would be a really, really long wait. I am my mother's daughter. We are *both* very stubborn ladies.'

We had interviewed Neetu in her mother's role. She softened as she came to understand Rina's experience and her internal world at a deeper level. She was able to get in touch with the heart of the issue; underneath all the irritation and provocation and arguments, both she and her mother longed to express affection for and receive affection from each other. By the end of the session, I sensed a new warmth and a feeling of integration about her.

In the next session, Neetu reported that she had reached home after a dinner meeting that evening to see her mom cuddled up with the kids, reading them a story. Instead of scolding them all for going past bedtime, she surprised everyone by saying 'Hey, make room for one more' and scrambled right into the middle of the bed. When her son mock-protested at having been pushed to the side, she informed him 'Remember—your Nani was first my mom!' They'd laughed at this and enjoyed this moment together, and I could only imagine that Nani's laugh might have been the most delighted.

29

Three People in My Head

Aruna

'I want to come to India!' said Farhad, almost as soon as our Zoom meeting started.

It felt to me as though he wanted to jump through the screen and land in Bangalore right away. I could understand the desire to come back home to India. He lived in Armenia with his wife and child and had been away for a long time. He had also had Covid a few weeks ago. The combination of illness and isolation had increased his homesickness.

'And?' I asked him, unsure of what the problem was.

'I am unable to make a decision. I mean . . . I want to, but I'm not sure I should!'

I sensed this as a battle between his Child and Parent ego states. The Parent is the part of our personality that is introjected, or 'swallowed whole'. It means we have unconsciously identified with the beliefs, feelings, motivations, behaviours, and defences of our parent figures.

The Child ego state is the part of us where we think, feel, and act as the child we once were. We unawarely replay our childhood patterns and expectations in our current relationships. Both the Child and Parent are archaic. They carry our histories. The Adult ego state is the part of us that responds to the here-and-now, accounting for our own and others' feelings and resources.

Our Child and Parent ego states are often in conflict. The Child may have needs and wants that the Parent denies. I decided to help Farhad work through the conflict by enacting it in the form of a drama. I invited Farhad to find and set up three chairs in a C-formation to represent each of the ego states, with the Adult chair placed in the centre, almost like the mediator between Parent and Child.

'Start talking about your challenge. As you talk, see if you can recognize which ego state you are in and go to that chair. If you feel you are in Child, move into the Child ego state chair. I will also observe ego state shifts and share the same with you,' I said.

Farhad didn't even wait for me to finish the instructions. He rubbed his palms together and moved towards the Parent chair, sat on the edge and leaned forward, ready to start.

'Oh, you are starting from the Parent chair,' I observed.

He nodded and started immediately, 'Is this the best time to go to India? The third wave is imminent. Is it a wise thing to do?'

'Are you speaking from Parent?' I asked, puzzled.

'Am I not?' He looked puzzled as well.

'Why do you think you are in Parent?' I wanted to check his thought process.

'There are implied "shoulds" here. You *should* be very careful. You *should* stay in Armenia. It is not safe to go to India,' explained Farhad.

'Well, many "shoulds" are part of the Parent ego state, but not all. Do you think these are Adult statements in the here-and-now or is the Parent imposing restrictions that don't seem relevant to the here-and-now?' I was trying to help him see the difference between rigid Parent imposition and Adult reasoning.

'Perhaps it is Adult,' he said reflectively. 'This is a time where everyone should be careful.'

'I agree. It sounds like an important question to ask yourself before travelling,' I said. 'So, from where would you like to respond?'

Farhad moved to the Child chair and said wistfully, 'I really miss India. I miss my friends. I miss my food. I have really had a challenging time in the recent months with my family and friends suffering losses.'

'Are you really speaking from the Child ego state?' I challenged, again.

'Am I not?' He continued sounding puzzled. 'I am thinking about what I want. I am not thinking of logistics or other challenges.'

'Again, it is okay for you to want things as an Adult. It is a myth that the Adult ego state is only logical. We say that you are in Child when you become the child you once were, replaying the same strategies you used as a child to get your needs met.'

Farhad thought a bit and said with a glint in his eye, 'I have been telling people I will get the vaccine in India. I am using the vaccine as an excuse to go to India!'

'So, you feel the need for excuses. It looks like you need to justify your wish to go to India to someone and need approval. That does seem like the Child ego state. Speak from the Child ego state and say why you feel the need to justify your decision,' I encouraged.

'My wife is taking our daughter to spend time with her grandparents in the UK. I decided not to go with them as I wanted to spend some time by myself. But now, I am saying that I want to go to India.'

'Are you feeling guilty?'

'Yes.'

'Looks like there is a Parent voice that disapproves of this? Let us hear it,' I said, directing him to the Parent chair.

'You told your family that you wanted to spend time by yourself. How can you change your mind?' Farhad was frowning and wagging his index finger at the Child chair. These behavioural clues made it evident that he was in Parent, being critical.

I invited him back to the Child chair to respond. His tone turned a little sulky, 'I have been wanting to go to India for the longest time. I have had a lot of responsibility all my life. Now that I have this window where I can relax and enjoy myself without worrying about my responsibilities, why can't I go?'

The internal conflict was now externalized and could be worked through.

Now Farhad was in the groove and did not need much direction from me. He moved instinctively into the Parent chair. 'Don't forget that you have always been coming up with irrational, last minute, impulsive ideas. What about the expense? Once you go to India, you will have ever-expanding plans and you will blow up money. And the fact that you told your family you wanted some alone-time?'

Farhad moved to the Child chair, looked at the empty Parent chair, and said in a sharp tone, 'The commitment was not to stay in Armenia. The commitment was to give myself time and do things that I liked.'

'You sound angry,' I said.

'I am,' he said, and continued to address the Parent chair. 'You talk as if I am a kid who only brings up problems and takes no responsibility. You talk like my mother. I am a responsible man and have been working hard for fourteen years. I am successful and doing well in my office. You call me compulsive, last minute, irresponsible . . . What is the problem if I want to go to India?'

There was the heart of the conflict. Farhad had introjected his mother's criticism of him. This inner critic was now active, constantly making him second-guess his decisions. Farhad felt stuck—both the Child and the Parent were pushing against each other with equal force.

I invited Farhad to move to the Adult chair and I asked him to share what he understood about the internal conflict. He said, 'I see I have a Parent in me that is trying to keep me safe and keep my life uncomplicated. I also experience a Child in me that would love to go to India and be back home and experience what I have been missing, living outside the country for so long.'

'What are you feeling as you put this together?'

'I am still anxious, hesitant to make a decision,' he said. 'My legs are shaking.'

'So, you are now in your Child ego state. Would you like to come to the Child chair and give voice to your anxiety?'

Farhad moved to the Child chair and said nervously, 'I am scared. I don't want to make a mistake. I don't want anyone to point a finger at me and say "I told you so."'

I was moved by his vulnerability. The little Farhad had the experience of being blamed often by his mother and had to constantly defend against it. He was in touch with the fear that kept him stuck.

Little Farhad needed support. 'Let us bring in a Nurturing Parent here,' I said, inviting Farhad to bring in another chair.

'On that chair is a very nurturing part of you that hasn't been active in this decision-making so far.' I waited for him to settle into the new chair, and then asked, 'What would you like to say to the scared Farhad? What does he need to hear right now?'

Farhad took a deep breath. 'It is okay to take a risk, Farhad,' he said, addressing his younger self. The phrase 'it is OK' usually indicates what we call a *permission* in Transactional Analysis. Permissions allow us to be ourselves and access our resources and spontaneity.

Farhad continued, 'You have enough antibodies, you are safe. And you will manage your expenses. You always have. The real fear you have is that you will be blamed by others. Why are you already anticipating that things will go wrong? And even if they go wrong, so what?'

This time, I thought it important to repeat and play back these words to him. Farhad listened to himself speak.

'How do you feel?' I asked him.

Farhad moved to the Adult chair, 'I am not very convinced by the Nurturing voice. The Critical Parent is loud and impactful. I still feel guilty for wanting what I want.'

'So, what would help you right now?' I asked, wondering if we would find a way out of the impasse.

'I wish someone else would make a decision for me!'

I paused for a bit. In this moment, his Child ego state needed support. It wasn't strong enough to go against the critical voice in his head.

Intuitively, I said, 'It is okay, Farhad. Enjoy your trip to India. You deserve some time off from your responsibility.'

Farhad slumped into the chair as the tension in his body dissipated. 'That's just what I needed to hear.'

Our next meeting was in person in India. Farhad was bubbling over with stories of meeting his friends, eating *chaat* on the street, going on auto rickshaw rides to crowded bazaars, and visiting temples. I listened indulgently. I knew that we still had work to do to resolve his internal conflicts and for him to own his own agency, but at that moment, I felt very grateful for all that had come together to make this trip possible for him.

30

The Angry Young Man

Yashodhara

'It drives me crazy!' Abheek raged. 'No one in this bloody city knows how to *drive*. The other day, this guy on a motorcycle just swerved in front of my car, he almost hit me, and . . .'

Abheek's voice was getting louder and louder as he narrated the incident to me. He had trouble keeping his temper in check—it had led to a fight with his boss and had ended up getting him fired. He had been referred to me through someone known to his sister, and in our first meeting, he had been quite brash, asking me plenty of personal questions and voicing that he didn't really believe in therapy, saying that it was a last resort for him. I had a foreboding sense that he would try and test me and push my buttons—yet, there was something about him that I liked, and we had agreed to meet for six sessions.

Today was the third session, and he was ranting about all the things that had annoyed him in the last week. He complained about bad drivers, how HR managers were 'unprofessional about returning his calls', and how his sister was 'bullying' him because he 'had messed his career up during the pandemic, not that it was any of *her* business.'

He paused now and looked at me, eyes shining defiantly.

'Abheek,' I said carefully. I had decided in this session to deflect his aggression, to see if we could explore and experiment more than we had so far, 'I see you are angry about many things. Do you experience other feelings too? I wonder if there are other feelings beneath this familiar feeling of anger?'

'Why would you say that? I just feel angry—what do I do, everything and everyone just pisses me off.'

'Am I pissing you off too?'

'Not really,' he cocked his head to the side and gave me his boyish grin. 'I actually think I am beginning to like you. Maybe directing me your way was the only good thing my sister's ever done for me.'

I saw him skilfully deflecting my attempt to authentically relate with him in the here-and-now. I felt intuitively that being charming was a strategy he had learned early. Even now, Abheek had a new girlfriend every week and he seemed to enjoy narrating his escapades with them to me. I had the fleeting impression of Peter Pan—Abheek was almost forty years old, but didn't look it, and he certainly didn't behave like it—his biggest complaint with his sister was that she was always telling him to grow up, despite being older than him by only two years.

I smiled at him, staying grounded, 'I notice that you didn't answer my question. I wonder if you feel anything other than anger?'

He gave a mock sniff. 'Are you saying that you want to see me cry? That I will only "heal" if I get in touch with my long-lost trauma? What if I don't have any?'

'You lost your mother when you were eight years old, Abheek.' I took a risk here. 'That would have been very difficult.'

'I barely remember anything about that,' he snapped. 'I told you. I have like *zero* memories of my mom.'

I just sat back and waited. After a few moments, he muttered, 'Okay, yeah, so maybe you *do* piss me off too.'

I decided to walk around this and attend to the emotions that were being stirred up in him. 'What do you remember about the time when you heard she died?'

He sighed. Then he said, not looking directly at me. 'I remember Dad coming home from the hospital and sitting me and my sister down. And he was looking really sad, I guess. And he said to us something like "Mom's gone; she won't be coming home." And then my sister started to cry like this really *crazy* thing. And I saw Dad's face crumple for a second as he hugged her. Then he looked at me—and I didn't cry, and he squeezed my shoulder.'

'What did you understand about his words "Mom's gone"?'

Abheek gave a sharp laugh without a trace of humour in it. 'I was thinking "Yeah, she's been gone for a while . . . to the hospital." I think I had been missing her, she was the one who was always spoiling me.' He stopped smiling. 'Yeah, maybe I didn't actually know that he meant she will *never* come home.'

'That squeeze on your shoulder—what do you imagine that meant to you?'

He waited a few moments before speaking. 'I don't know. I felt like I was being a strong, useful person—you know, like him, like a man.'

'So, by not crying, you were being the strong, useful one—a man?' Internally, I was making a connection. Abheek's other 'racket' go-to familiar feeling was that of joy. When he wasn't angry, he was the life of the party. Sadness and fear were the ones that were hard for him to feel and express.

'I suppose,' he said, and he looked like he was getting impatient. I saw him glancing at the wall clock.

'We have half an hour left,' I said calmly. 'I saw you looking at the clock—something on your mind?'

'No, it's nothing,' he muttered. I sensed his discomfort, but he went on, 'So anyway, that's it. That's all I remember.'

'You mentioned that Mom spoilt you?' I pointed out the incongruity.

'Wow,' he rolled his eyes, 'you should be a private detective, not a therapist. So, okay, I remember a *few* things about her.'

'Tell me those few things about your mom?'

His face softened. 'She was really beautiful. She had soft white arms, and these light brown eyes. Always smelt nice, some talcum powder or whatever she used. She wouldn't let Dad shout too much at me; I was always breaking stuff and getting into trouble, but she'd just pick me up and hold me until he calmed down. She was really . . . something.' His eyes became fiery again, and he shrugged, 'Anyway, she's gone. And Dad did his best; we had a pretty happy childhood—the three of us have always been pretty close. Nothing to complain about.'

I had seen him get in touch with his sadness for just a moment there. 'I feel very moved by your description of your mom—I see that you really loved her. Do you think about your mom now?'

'No,' he said shortly. 'She comes in my dreams sometimes, but I don't remember my dreams. Before you start to analyse them!'

I ignored that too. I sensed he was contacting the sadness that he had pushed away. His anger was a coping mechanism that allowed him to blame another and take the attention away from his sadness. I asked simply, 'Is it hard for you to feel sad?'

He sighed. His voice was quieter and more tired, 'I just don't see the point. I've done what I could have in life because I decided that I wouldn't be weak.'

'Often, our childhood strategy is useful and gets us to a certain point,' I said, 'and then we may find it is not working anymore. That could be because we aren't allowing ourselves to feel the full range of feelings. The four basic ones are anger, joy, sadness, and fear. I see you having no trouble feeling and expressing the first two. What about sadness and fear?'

'Fear.' He looked thoughtful. 'I suppose that one is there.'

'Say more about your fear?' I asked gently.

'I don't know. Turning forty, whoa! Getting old, you know. How will the chicks react to being picked up by a forty-year-old . . .'

'You're afraid of growing old?' My Peter Pan hunch had been accurate.

'Growing old. Yeah.' He sobered down again. 'Not having enough money, not being a success, and never finding "the one."'

'Right.' I nodded. 'You think you want to find "the one"?'

'The *one*,' he was thoughtful. 'I don't know why I said that. Is there even such a thing? I don't know if I want to find the one. I mean, Dad had "the one", and look at how depressed he was after he lost Mom!' His face suddenly crumpled as though he was in pain. He screwed up his eyes, and after a few moments when he opened them, his eyes were bright, but the tears remained unshed.

'I see your pain right now, Abheek,' I said as gently as I could. 'It really is okay to express it.'

He shook his head vigorously, as if to clear it. Before I could say anything, he suddenly shot to his feet and bolted towards the door. 'You know what—this is bullshit.' As he left my office, I heard him say something that sounded like, 'Frickin' psychoanalytical mumbo-jumbo.'

Abheek never came back to our sessions. His sister messaged me to apologize for his decision to drop out midway. I was left to wonder for myself and in supervision whether my attempts to push him into feeling his deeper emotions were ill-timed. Was the short-term nature of our contract inappropriate in the first place, given what I knew he was dealing with? Did I give in to the pressure to get him to change in our short time together, moving into risky territory without first building a proper working alliance with him? We are often advised to meet our clients where they were, and that means allowing them to work through their racket feelings fully until they are ready to go deeper themselves.

I did recognize that Abheek's anger with me was a part of his own script—to blame others, suspect their motives, and thereby keep himself safe in his world of righteous anger—safe, but alone. Yet, I know today that I could have handled things differently—my learnings around taking things slow, seeing my clients' vulnerability behind their defences, exploring the here-and-now have all been important lessons for me. A part of me wonders about Abheek, and I find myself even hoping that I get to see him and work with him again someday. I would love to be part of Peter Pan's journey. Although, I also like to think that even if we never meet again, maybe, I have been.

31

The Mango–Eating Elf

Aruna

'I had this crazy dream last night,' said Dhruv, 'and I wonder what it meant for me.'

I enjoy working with dreams and so do my clients. As Transactional Analysts, we see dreams as communication from the unconscious Child ego state to the Adult ego state. Every element of the dream is an aspect of the dreamer. It is like the dreamer projects parts of their own self, using symbols and metaphors, onto the large canvas of the dream. This is why dreams can be so magically revealing: everything in the dream is the unconscious material placed there by the dreamer.

'Tell me about this dream? Narrate it slowly, in the present tense, as if it were happening right now,' I said. Asking the client to describe the dream in first person, present tense, and active voice allows them to 'be there' rather than report it from a distance. They are likely to then re-experience the associated emotions.

Dhruv was ready with his narration.

'*I am in this old house with an open courtyard in the centre,*' he began, '*where a patch of ragi is growing. Suddenly, there is a tornado and the ragi sways violently. I am scared that my car, which is parked on the street, will get blown away. So, I get into the car and drive up to a garage and leave it there.*' He paused, almost relieved as though he was still in the dream and had found a garage.

'Is there more?' I asked.

'Oh yes,' he continued, '*I walk towards a large multi-storied building with a glass exterior. But as I walk away, I see the car shaking because there's a little elf jumping on it. A little boy in a school uniform appears and says "He's got all your mangoes." I can smell the mangoes and see the mango juice on the elf. I feel angry. I want to kill it. So, both of us pick up some darts lying on the ground and throw them at the elf. The elf seems to enjoy the darts and starts dancing saying "I refuse to die. I have got your mangoes."*

That is what I remember,' he concluded, 'I woke up with a start.'

'And what were you feeling when you woke up?' I asked.

'Quite scared, actually.' Dhruv shuddered a little.

I was intrigued by the dream and looked forward to making meaning of it along with Dhruv.

Every dream emerges from a context. Dhruv was twenty-three years old and was leaving his home in Bangalore to do a double master's in mathematics and physics in Hong Kong. I wondered what this move meant for him emotionally and whether the dream was about that.

When I work with dreams, I follow a systematic process of exploring the significant elements in the dream using psychodrama techniques. This means I invite the client to 'become' each of the elements in the dream in sequence. They embody that element, describe themselves, and describe what's going on from that perspective. This is one of the most potent parts of dreamwork. The words they use to describe the elements are often parts of themselves that they may not allow themselves to access when they are awake because they are censored by the Critical Parent.

I invited Dhruv to become the house first and speak as the house in first person.

Dhruv sat up straight and closed his eyes, 'I am old and made of mud blocks, but I am strong. I have this open courtyard in the centre.'

'You have some ragi growing in the courtyard?' I enquired, wondering what could be significant about the ragi.

'Yes, I do. And I am also surrounded by ragi fields,' said Dhruv, as the house. 'House, could you tell me what is happening in the dream?'

'*Dhruv is relaxing and enjoying the quiet and safety when the tornado arrives. I would have liked Dhruv to just stay inside till the tornado passed, but he was worried that the tornado may blow his car away. If I could have spoken, I would have said "Let the car get blown away; you stay here and be safe."*'

Dhruv was surprised by what emerged from him in the role of the house.

We repeated the process with all the other significant elements of the dream before putting the pieces together. This is what Dhruv said for each of the elements.

As the tornado: *'I am powerful and strong and blow down everything that is in my path. Dhruv cannot leave his car on the street like that. I will just blow it away.'*

As the car: *'I am blood-red, bright, and small. I am on the street, in the open.'*

As the street: *'I am grey, dull, and rough. I get walked on. I don't think I get seen too much. Everyone looks ahead and not down.'*

As the garage: *'I am windowless. There are lots of old things dumped in me. I can be locked.'*

As the mango-eating elf: *'I am small, scrawny, springy, with pointed ears. I have magical powers. It's not easy to catch me or kill me. I may look small, but I am very powerful. I like to have fun. But I don't like to be locked up. I love mangoes. They are ripe, large, yellow, juicy, and delicious. I have juice dripping all over me and I love it. Dhruv may try to kill me or lock me up, but I will always be there. He is scared I might follow him wherever he goes.'*

As the little boy: *'I am eight years old. I am wearing a school uniform. I have come to help Dhruv kill the elf.'*

I was fascinated by the descriptive words Dhruv used. 'What connections do you make to the house?' I wondered, 'you seemed very safe in there. What or whom do you associate with safety?'

'What or whom?' Dhruv repeated, thinking deeply, 'I always felt safe with my grandmother. She would make this delicious ragi malt with cardamom in it . . . Oh wow!' he exclaimed. 'Was the old and earthy house surrounded by ragi fields my grandmother?'

'What do you think?' I said, equally fascinated. 'The imagery in dreams is symbolic.'

'I think so. I felt really safe with my grandmother. My mother couldn't force me to do anything when my grandmother was around. Grandmom died when I was just seven, but I still remember how much I looked forward to visiting her in the holidays,' he said, feeling nostalgic.

'You loved her!'

'I did. I miss her a lot. I still remember snuggling in with her and the smell of her soft, cotton sarees,' he said wistfully.

'And she protected you from mom?'

'She did.'

'Perhaps the tornado is your mom?' I asked instinctively.

'Wow, yes, that's quite likely. Very forceful. Pushing me to do things, achieve, and be responsible. She would be constantly angry with me for not doing enough.'

'How would you respond to her anger?'

'I would work hard to please her. I would take up challenges she wanted me to take up even though they didn't always make sense to me.'

'Like you went out in the tornado to put your car away in the garage?' I made connections.

'Yes, even though what I would have liked is to stay back and be with my grandma,' agreed Dhruv reflectively. 'I just remembered something else. When my grandmother died, because I was upset for a really long time, my parents bought me this big red toy car that I could drive around in our driveway. But I was very angry with them for thinking I could be cheered up with a car. I wanted to feel sad, but I was expected to cheer up and move on.'

'Were you eight years old then?' I remembered the little boy in the dream was eight. 'Yes,' he said.

'Any other significant memory around eight?' I asked.

'They changed my school. The new school was very conventional and academic. My older school had no uniforms, and we were free to play a lot. I remember being very angry with the change and also helpless that I had no choice,' said Dhruv.

'So, two significant losses at the age of eight—the old school and your grandmom.' He nodded.

We slowly pieced the dream together.

Dhruv realized he was not excited about going to Hong Kong for a course that promised to be really demanding and tough. Leaving India and his family and friends reminded him of the time when he was eight, when he had been grieving the loss of his grandmother and the comfort of the old school. With an angry and demanding mother, he'd had no space to rest or to express his anger. He felt 'walked on' and not seen, like the road in his dream. His repressed anger showed up in his using terms like 'blood-red' for the car or in wanting to kill the elf.

The elf, we decided together, was the child-like fun-loving part of Dhruv that was going to get locked away, pushed into the dark. Dhruv speculated that the Child in him was asking him to have fun again and make space for play. But he felt like he needed to walk away from this part and go into the 'large building' that was likely a metaphor for college or the world of adults. There was no room for these 'childish' activities in the new phase of his life. He was angry that he had to walk away and wanted to 'kill' that part so that it wouldn't haunt him.

'I didn't realize how much I am dreading going to Hong Kong!' he said, amazed at the meaning he made of the dream. It was not that the problem was resolved, but the emotional aspect of what was going on for him became much clearer.

'You said you woke up feeling scared?' I asked him. 'Yes,' he confirmed.

'How would you like to feel instead?' I asked.

'I know I will miss India and my life here. But I want to go to Hong Kong too. I want to look forward to going to Hong Kong. I don't want to be the scared eight-year-old.'

'Well, you can add a new ending to the dream. It's your dream and you can end it any way you like!' I said. 'So, what do you choose for it to be?'

Dhruv closed his eyes.

In a few seconds, he was smiling, and narrated the new ending, '*I tell the elf that "I am glad you have my mangoes, and I am even more glad that you refuse to die." I reach out to the mango-eating elf and make him sit next to me and we eat mangoes together! He is small enough to fit into my knapsack, and he can appear and disappear at will. So, I don't have to lock him away. I will take him with me to Hong Kong. We have fun together.*'

We discussed options for how he could feel safe and have fun in Hong Kong. We also spoke about how he could seek support when he felt vulnerable.

For hours after we closed the session, I was captivated by the creative expression of the unconscious and how his script had revealed itself. His injunctions were 'Don't Be a Child' and 'Don't Be You' and his corresponding decisions were to be a good, obedient boy and push away his feelings. In changing the ending of the dream, he made a new decision to integrate the part that he had earlier disowned.

The vivid imagery of the dream stayed with Dhruv as well. Within a few months, he sent me a photo of himself from Hong Kong—he was eating a mango! I imagined the elf in his knapsack and smiled.

32

I'm So Stupid

Yashodhara

'Again, another meeting in which I barely said anything,' Gargi spoke haltingly. 'I must have looked so stupid. My boss had to step in because I was fumbling with the numbers . . . I might end up losing this job . . .'

I listened closely to Gargi. She had come to me a few weeks ago because she was feeling very underconfident at work; in our sessions, she had recognized her strong internal Critical Parent voice that kept telling her she was stupid. I had also checked with her about where she had got this message from, and she had said it was probably her father but had seemed reluctant to discuss the same any further. Her father had passed away some years ago, and she wasn't comfortable with the idea of 'blaming' him for her issues. All I had learned was that he had been a strict person who highly valued education, and while Gargi had done exceedingly well for herself and was a graduate from a reputed engineering and management college, she still felt like an imposter.

'Gargi,' I said gently, 'you've talked about these meetings where you find it difficult to speak—what is it that specifically makes you nervous?'

'Numbers!' she said immediately. 'It's anyway tough for me to speak up in front of the CEO, but when he asks a question around numbers, my brain gets scrambled.' She swallowed hard. 'And my throat gets dry.'

'Does this remind you of anything?' I asked, 'dry throat, brain scrambled . . .'

'Hah!' she said with a smile and then went silent.

The smile had no humour in it, and I wondered if her silence was self-censure. I said gently, 'I'm curious what just came up for you—what was that "Hah!"?'

She squirmed, then seemed to gather herself. 'My father—he used to teach me math. I found it difficult, especially from Class 7 onward. And he—he didn't have much patience.' She went on hurriedly, 'He was under a lot of tension anyway with his work, so it was great that he took out time for me in the evenings. He worked really hard to provide for all of us, including the extended family . . .'

I sensed her discomfort and decided to bring it into conscious awareness. 'Gargi, are you feeling guilty as you talk about your father?'

'Yes,' she admitted softly, 'I feel I'm being ungrateful; he did his best for us . . . he was always under pressure, I don't think he had a happy life. And he's gone now. I don't want to be a . . . bad daughter.'

'As children, we tend to make meaning of what happens in a way that is self-protective but may be distorted. The idea of discussing your experience growing up is not to assign blame but to take responsibility for your own experience and update your beliefs. You're not being a bad daughter by talking about this.' She seemed to relax, and I went on, 'Are you okay to continue exploring this?'

She nodded.

'What do you remember? How old were you?'

'About twelve or thirteen. We used to sit at our dining table before dinner and he would help me revise. Mom was rushing around to get dinner ready. It usually started out okay, but then, if I couldn't figure something out, Dad would start to get angry. I mean, he didn't shout, really, but he looked impatient . . . he had this . . . *look* on his face when I didn't get a concept. It made me even more nervous. And then he would finally end up saying something like "You're just being stupid."'

'What was this "look", Gargi?'

'I don't know how to describe it . . .' she said. 'His jaw would just go tight, like . . . he was clenching his teeth, stopping himself from saying something.' The humourless smile was back. 'But then he would say it anyway. That I was slow or stupid . . .'

'It must have been hard to hear that,' I said. 'What did you feel when you heard those words?'

'I felt . . . useless,' she said, 'and that he was right. Math was the most important subject, and I struggled so much with it.'

'And where did you learn,' I enquired, 'that math was the most important subject?'

'Dad only,' she admitted. 'He was always very clever at math, and it helped him in his business also—he told us it was the only subject that really mattered. It was the only one he seemed interested in also. I don't remember him offering to help in any other subject.'

'I see. And you always struggled with math, you were saying?'

'Yes, I struggled,' she said, and then, after a pause, 'but in the end, somehow, my results were always good. As in, 80–85 per cent . . .'

'I see. And what was Dad's reaction to your results?'

'Oh,' she blinked, 'usually something like "why did you lose those five marks? You can get much higher scores in math." He was still grumpy . . .' Something seemed to strike her. 'But once I did quite well, top of my class . . . only once!'

'What happened then?'

'Hmm.' She had a puzzled frown on her face. 'I remember him being angry only . . . he just nodded when I showed him the report card, saying something like "Finally!"—but then didn't even talk to me.'

'How did you feel?'

'I felt . . . really disappointed, I suppose. But I remember thinking something else must really be troubling him . . .'

'. . . and so, you should not cause any trouble?' I guessed intuitively.

She nodded. Her eyes glistened, and she swallowed again.

'I see you are feeling sad,' I said. 'It must have been difficult to always have to try so hard to be good, to do well—and yet, never see him happy.'

A tear ran down her cheek. I leaned forward instinctively, murmuring, 'It's okay . . .'

'It's not okay,' she suddenly snapped. It took me by surprise, but I realized that her anger was not at me or about anything in the present moment. 'He told me later when I made it to engineering college that I was just lucky! He told me I would really have a bad time trying to keep up with the others unless I got serious about studying—but it was all that I was serious about!'

I recognized that this was an important moment— she was allowing herself an emotion that was difficult for her to feel. 'You are angry—you felt discounted by him.' I replayed the essence of her words back to her and also named her emotion.

'Yes,' she said, 'and for years, I've just heard the voice in my head telling me I'm stupid, that everything I do manage is only because I've been lucky, and I keep feeling scared my luck is going to run out!'

'Tell me, if you could go back to those math lessons, what would you like to say to Dad?' I was going out on a limb here. I knew Dad was a dominating figure in her head, and her own power might not yet be strong enough.

She hesitated and seemed to be struggling with this idea.

'Try imagining a younger version of him,' I suggested. 'Can you see him as maybe a kid who's around your own age? He's there at the dining table with you, and he's just said "You're stupid. If you do well, it's just because you're lucky!"'

She closed her eyes instinctively, and I could see her conjure up the scene in her mind. 'I'd say "You're wrong! I'm doing well in my studies, and one day, I'll even get into the best engineering college in India . . . and I even topped my class in math! How can that be just luck? If you believe that, you're stupid!"'

'Yes,' I encouraged, '*you're* the one who's stupid. Stop putting me down!'

'Stop putting me down,' she repeated, eyes still closed tight. 'And stop being jealous! Just because you're not the only clever one in the family!'

'He's jealous,' I nodded. I hadn't been expecting this but went with the flow. 'Go on. Tell him more.'

'Yeah, you're jealous,' she said, fresh tears rolling down from under shut eyelids. 'And maybe you feel useless if someone else in the family does well! But that doesn't mean you can make *me* feel useless!'

Gargi cried in anger and pain as she realized that she had spent decades of her life yearning for an approval from her father that had never come. It had taken her a lot of courage to overcome her guilt and get in touch with her anger at Dad. She went on to make several important breakthroughs— by acknowledging that her father's parenting hadn't been perfect, she could finally begin to give herself the validation she had sought externally, and to question her own Critical Parent voice that she had internalized from him. In subsequent sessions, she was able to see his jealousy and insecurity and need to be needed as his own Child strategies for coping; over time, she developed a new compassion for him and his complex inner world. As she made these connections and focused on updating her own beliefs about her capabilities, her confidence at work and in other spheres began to grow.

She informed me that the meetings were going better, and she was hoping to even land a leadership position in a few months. 'I've got a new mantra,' she said with a smile. 'When that inner critic gets too loud, I just tell it "Shhh . . . you're being stupid. *I'm* smart!"'

33

Permission to be Selfish

Aruna

'I have been really selfish!' blurted out Avantika. 'In what way?'

'My doctor has put me on a new diet to manage my pain. I didn't want to cook so many different items, so I asked all in the family if they were willing to adjust their diet too. Ritesh and the children were fine with the changes, but my in-laws weren't. We gave them several options—like hiring a cook just for them. Or that they stay with Ritesh's sister for a few months. Or we could order from outside. They flatly refused. I felt hurt at their indifference towards my health,' she finished, looking upset.

'So why do you call yourself selfish?'

'Because I placed an order for their food with a caterer—for a fortnight, as an experiment,' she shared.

'Why is that selfish?'

'I am feeling guilty. I did what they didn't want.'

'What does your inner Critical Parent say?' I asked. The Critical Parent shows up as a strong voice in the head that imposes rigid 'shoulds', 'oughts', and 'musts'.

Avantika was quick to reply, 'You are inconveniencing the elders. You are not being considerate to their eating habits. You must always be considerate . . . These voices are relentless!'

The inner Critical Parent emerges from a relationship with parent figures who are intrusive, controlling, and punitive. 'Do you remember your parents asking this of you?' I asked her.

'Oh, all the time!' she made the connection immediately. 'We were never to create trouble for elders.'

'Have you ever disobeyed that ask?' I wondered.

Avantika looked up, trying to remember, narrowing her eyes, thinking intensely. 'Oh my God, I can't think of a single example!'

'You look shocked!' I observed.

'I can't believe that I have never disobeyed them. Being this compliant can't be good for me,' she said.

I smiled, 'And why not?'

'What about me,' she protested, looking indignant, 'and my own needs?'

'And when you attend to your own needs, do you call yourself selfish?'

'I do. I wonder why though. I went through so much angst this week. Picking up the phone and placing the order was the hardest thing to do.'

'It seems you don't have the permission to be important enough to ask others to adjust for you,' I offered an explanation.

'I wonder why though?'

'Do you have memories of your childhood, where your wishes, views, and needs were treated as important?'

Avantika thought some more, and then shook her head from left to right glumly, 'I have memories of the opposite. I have a very vivid memory of going to a shop along with my mother and asking her to buy me a chocolate. My mother pinched me in my arms and asked me to keep quiet. I remember feeling angry. But I couldn't express that anger or negotiate my needs. I felt very small and humiliated.'

She went on, 'My mother modelled sacrifice as a way of life for me. For her, others' needs were always more important and "what others will think" took priority over what I felt as a child. When we visited our aunt's place, we were not allowed to ask for anything to eat. We were expected to fold our hands and sit in one place.'

'So, your mother modelled how to be unimportant to you,' I summarized, my tone gentle. 'Also, if you expressed a desire, you were negated or punished. How did you make meaning of these experiences for yourself?'

'I concluded that we were poor. I was to support my parents by not having any needs. My mother had to sell her jewellery when my father was out of a job. She had to do everything on her own. I made a decision early on—not to trouble her and increase the burden on her already overwhelmed life.'

'You made a decision to not be important and never inconvenience others,' I emphasized. 'Can you see why you struggled while making a call to the caterer?'

'Yes,' she sighed.

'How else does this decision to not be important show up in your life?'

'I think in all aspects of my life. I have chosen to not work and instead, to take care of everyone in the family. Like my mother, I too am sacrificing and submissive.'

'So, you have never been selfish?'

'Never!' she said violently.

'Oh my,' I was taken aback by the intensity of the response, 'you seem offended that I should even ask that question.'

'I am surprised at my own reaction,' she said, wide-eyed.

'I experience you putting enormous pressure on yourself. I can see that you have been denied the rights that every child has—to throw tantrums, argue with parents, challenge boundaries, test limits, and assert their own identity. A child must be allowed to be difficult.'

Her face began to crumple and her eyes glistened. 'I am tired of being a good girl.'

'Was there anyone who would support the "not good" part of you, if that were to show up?' I wondered if she had had any significant nurturing figure while growing up.

'No, no one. I would be judged and humiliated.'

I paused and wondered aloud, 'I wonder how it would be for you to imagine and draw an ideal nurturing parent.'

I offered Avantika some paper and crayons and invited her to create an image of the ideal nurturing parent. 'This is the parent who knows what you need and offers it to you unquestioningly. This parent always has your best interest at heart.'

Avantika drew the image of an angel with a tiara, a wand, and a flowy dress with stars on it. 'She looks radiant,' I observed. 'She has a peaceful smile.'

Avantika seemed delighted with what she had created, 'Yes. I love this image. She looks tranquil and spiritual.'

'Can you imagine yourself next to her?' Avantika closed her eyes.

'Tell me what you see in your imagination.'

'I am six years old. I am wearing the same flowy dress as her. I love flowy dresses,' she said, smiling. 'I too have a tiara and wand.'

'What are the two of you doing?'

'We are holding hands and walking around a vast grassland. There are plenty of butterflies and some big trees. After some time, I let go of her hand and chase butterflies. She is smiling. We both then lie on the grass and look at the clouds.'

I invited her to recall a stressful memory, but this time her guardian angel would be with her. She chose the one at the sweet shop.

'Imagine yourself going to the sweet shop with your mother. But your guardian angel also comes with you. What happens?' I asked curiously.

Avantika instinctively closed her eyes. 'My guardian angel asks me if I want a sweet. I reach out for one. And when my mother reaches out to pinch me in my arm, she stops my mother gently before she can pinch me. She smiles indulgently as I enjoy my chocolate,' said Avantika, smiling.

We repeated the process with many stressful memories, with the guardian angel encouraging Avantika to own and express her needs.

'Can you now imagine her next to you when you decided to call the caterer to order food for your in-laws? Tell me what happens.'

Avantika visualized the scene and said, 'She tells me that I need rest, and that this new diet is important for my health. She tells me my ideas are good, my opinion counts, I am worthy.

And she tells me "Hey, go right ahead and order, it is going to be fine."'

'She seems to have offered you a number of permissions!'

'Yes, I feel she is saying to me "You can be who you are. You don't have to be good all the time. You can be bad."'

'Wow! You can be bad!' I marvelled.

'Yes!' she grinned.

'So how could you be bad?' I offered a dare.

Avantika thought for a bit and said, 'I never order Chinese just because no one else wants it, even though I love it. Next time, I will order Chinese, even if no one else wants it.'

'Great.'

'Maybe I want some time every day to read, and a bookshelf just for me,' she said.

'Get bolder!'

Avantika took a long pause, and said, 'I might get a job and start to earn my own money.'

'Awesome! That is bold,' I said.

I saw her pause reflectively.

'What are you experiencing?' I asked. 'Another thought occurred to me right now. I don't really want to live with my in-laws, but I don't want to be *that* bad.'

'Not living with your in-laws is being really bad, is it? You don't feel ready to be that bad yet?'

'One step at a time,' she smiled.

'Do you think you might enjoy being bad?'

'I am scared that I might love it!'

I smiled at her indulgently, just as her guardian angel would have.

34

Stepping Away from the Crib

Yashodhara

'And then he took my work to Seema and just went ahead and presented it on his own!' Smitha said petulantly, 'And I thought this is just too much . . . so I went ahead and talked to him about it—but Raman is the kind of boss who just doesn't listen, *na*, so he didn't even hear me out properly, made it a rushed discussion, and said that we'd spend more time on it later. I don't know how people like him even become leaders, frankly. And last week he called for a meeting on a project I'm involved in as one of the key members, but sent me, his *own* team member, the invite at the very last minute, and . . .'

I found myself tuning out, unable to keep up with the details of her story. Smitha usually spent a lot of our session time talking about her angst with events at her workplace. I felt after all these sessions that I had heard more about her boss, Raman, than Smitha herself.

'Smitha,' I interrupted her, 'can I slow you down? You're sharing a lot of detail with me: would you like to take a moment and connect with what you would like for yourself in discussing this?'

She went quiet for a moment, and said somewhat sulkily, 'I don't know. I was just hoping to talk today. There's a lot of politics going on and I thought I'd just share it with you.'

'Just share?' I asked.

'Yes,' she looked confused.

'Could I share an observation with you?' 'Sure,' she shrugged.

'Over the last three months, you've been using the sessions to share what's going on for you. While you do seem to get some relief from this, I wonder if you are avoiding something in the process.'

'I don't know,' she repeated. 'Maybe you are seeing something and can tell me.' I recognized her defence. 'Are you feeling hurt that I interrupted your story?'

Her face was impassive now, 'I don't know about *hurt*—maybe . . . disappointed. I had a fight with my husband because he didn't want to listen to the details of my problems at work. He is being really insensitive; he doesn't understand how difficult it is for me. But I did think that my therapist at least would be okay to listen to me, but it feels like even you . . .' her voice trailed off.

'Go on,' I encouraged. 'Even I what?'

'Even *you* don't understand,' she finished. 'Why else would you cut me off?'

I nodded, and then said, 'So I also—like others in your life—don't understand you?'

She hesitated at this. 'Well, yes.' She squirmed a little in her chair. 'I suppose your point is that I'm the common factor here, and there's something wrong with me.'

'Is that how you are reading meaning into what I said—that there is something wrong with you?'

'I think so . . .' She thought for a few moments. 'I do think I would like to understand this—why do I always end up feeling like no one listens to me?' She added, in a hesitant way, 'Am I the one missing something?'

It was the first time I had heard her reach this point in our sessions—where she seemed ready to wonder what she might be missing instead of blaming others. 'What might you be missing?'

She frowned, lost in thought. 'I'm not sure. I do believe I am really sincere and mean well, in almost everything I do. So why do my interactions with others go badly?'

'Would you like to explore this latest incident with your boss and see what comes up?'

'Yes,' she nodded. 'Okay.'

'How about we re-enact that interaction where you said he rushed the discussion instead of hearing you out?' I said. 'You can say what you said in that meeting, and then I'll play it back to you and you receive it as him.'

'Okay.'

'Pretend I'm Raman,' I said. 'Go ahead. You wanted to talk about something, Smitha?'

She blinked, slumping a little in her seat, and then her eyes widened. 'See, Raman, this is something that I have noticed, and it really bothers me. I feel there is a lack of inclusivity when you go ahead and send on my work to seniors in the company without even marking me on the email. I worked really hard over the weekend and late into the nights, sacrificing my personal time with my family to get this presentation right, and all I would have wanted is a little acknowledgement and credit for the work that I've put in. And the thing is that this is actually a repeated pattern. I've seen that you go ahead and have meetings with others in the team without me, even on projects that I'm supposed to be leading, and I don't see why you keep leaving me out like this. I may not be as experienced as you, but I don't see how I'll ever get to learn if you keep taking these opportunities away from me . . .' her voice trailed off.

I was glad she paused—I had been paying close attention to not just her words but her body language too, and it was a long sentence to replay. 'Okay, you be Raman now,' I said, 'and just listen.'

I slumped my shoulders and did my best imitation of her tone, facial expression, and body language. 'See Raman . . .' I didn't get the words exactly right but managed to replay most of the content to her. I could see her draw back as I spoke, and her eyes took on a faraway look.

'. . . but I don't see how I'll get to learn if you keep taking these opportunities away from me . . .' I allowed my voice to trail off.

There was a long pause, and then she breathed out 'Oooof' and gave a wry smile.

I smiled at her. 'Tell me about that "Oooof"?'

'I found myself thinking,' she was speaking much more slowly and thoughtfully now, 'my God, how much does this girl *crib*!'

I nodded silently, waiting to see if she had more to say, but she was lost in thought. 'What's going on for you right now?'

'I'm feeling a little embarrassed,' she confessed, 'I mean . . . I knew that I was complaining, but I didn't know this is how I sounded. It's like some kid coming and whining and complaining, unable to solve her own problems.' I saw her flinch at this.

'What was that look on your face?' I asked. 'You just got in touch with something?'

'I just remembered,' she said, 'this is what I would do with Mom, and to some extent with Dad. Actually, I think I learnt it more from him—he was always complaining about things at home, and she would bend over backwards to try and please him. I didn't like that, I thought it was mean of him. But then, it definitely worked to get more attention from her—my elder brother was the boss, just had to snap his fingers and he got everything.' She wrinkled her nose. 'But I got what I wanted by complaining the loudest.'

'Right.' At this point, there was no need for me to add anything. She was in the flow of her own process.

'I even complained sometimes when there was nothing to complain about!' Her eyes widened, 'I remember thinking—if I *show* them that I'm happy, they'll stop giving me what I want!'

'If I *show* them that I'm happy, they won't give me what I want,' I replayed. It was a clinically significant statement. It revealed a Child coping strategy.

'Yes.'

'And what did you want?'

'I . . . wanted things to be fair . . . and to get attention, like my brother did.' She looked a little morose. 'My mom had it tough enough taking care of everything and everyone; I guess I made things worse by making her feel like she was being a bad mother to me. I used to tell her all the time that "You don't love me; you don't want me." And then, she would do anything she could to pacify me.' She made a face, 'Ugh!'

'Perhaps, it's not "ugh",' I said gently. 'It was just you as a child trying to get your needs met. It may have been the only way you knew back then.'

We spoke about how this coping strategy of constantly complaining had served her—and how it was coming in the way of relating with others today. She was intrigued by the idea of relating to others from her Adult ego state. 'I think I'd like to practice this—my tone and even the words. I don't want to come across as blaming or attacking.'

'How about getting in touch with your real need?' I suggested. 'What do you really want?'

'I just . . . want things to be fair!' she said, and then laughed. 'That hasn't changed from when I was six, I think!' She sobered up, 'Actually, what I'd like is to take charge and gain more ownership of the projects I'm working on. I can learn fast and am really responsible.'

'Shall we try again?' I said. 'And use a framework for communicating your real needs and feelings from Adult, without blame?'

I taught her the format of an Action Feeling statement from Claude Steiner's work on Emotional Literacy. We went back and forth a few times. It took practice, and I helped her to refer to observed behaviours in a neutral manner, to use 'I' language, to give and ask for positive strokes, and to keep the focus on her own feelings and needs. I also encouraged her to avoid Child grandiosity with words like 'always' and 'never', to weed out words of judgement, and to make a clear request.

'Okay, so the Action would be . . . Raman, when you leave me out and decide to call meetings on my projects . . .' she paused uncertainly and looked at me. 'That doesn't sound quite right?'

I nodded. 'Do you see that there is an assumption here that he is *leaving you out*? A neutral observation here might be along the lines of 'When I see that you've called a meeting on a project I'm leading . . .'

'Right,' she breathed. 'That's better. Okay, so my feeling is . . . I feel left out . . . but that's also not neutral,' she corrected herself, 'I feel uncertain and nervous about my role.'

'Good catch,' I encouraged her. 'What would your need be?'

'Fairness!' she said immediately.

'It's a subtle one, this one,' I mused. 'What do you think?'

'Even asking for more fairness is judgemental?' she asked me, looking confused.

'Think about it,' I said. 'When you want things to be "more" fair, what are you implying about how they are right now?'

'Ah.' She nodded. 'Right.'

After a few more tries, she arrived at this—'Raman,' she looked me in the eye, sitting up straight, 'firstly, thank you for the guidance in the last few months. I appreciate your involvement and it's really helped me to settle in well in this role.' She took a deep breath. 'There are times when the lines of communication and ownership aren't very clear—for example, when meetings are set up on the projects I'm leading, without discussion with me. At such times, I feel uncertain and confused. I learn and work best when I have a strong sense of ownership of my projects and can drive things independently. Is it possible for us to work out a couple of projects where I can lead things end-to-end, and discuss how best to get your inputs on an ongoing basis?'

I played this back to her as best I could. She listened carefully and grinned. Play-acting her role as Raman, she said, 'Sure, that makes sense. We can do that.'

'How do you feel?' I asked her.

'I feel good about what I said,' she said, smiling. 'I took care of myself in a straightforward way, without putting my boss down.' Her face broke into a grin. 'And this time, as

Raman, I got this thought: "*Chalo*, good, now it seems like I've got a grown-up in my team!'"

I grinned back at her. I sensed that she would be able to negotiate things better at the workplace. I also knew that, together, we would need to explore the deep sense of unfairness that she often experienced, and that it might take a lot more to uncover what had led to that, and to let her work through those Child feelings. But at least now, she had added a different Adult strategy to her repertoire and could try that out. For today, this was a great outcome.

35

Waiting for Mom

Aruna

'I am on guard all the time. I don't feel safe,' despaired Ashwin. 'I believe when I interact with people, they have an agenda, and I can never get what I want.'

'What triggered this for you right now? Did something happen recently?'

'You know I crave my mother's validation. I decided to visit her and spend a week sharing with her what is going on for me. I went to Mysore last Monday, and we had a couple of beautiful days together. It was then that we got a call that my elder brother was down with dengue, and we had to rush to Delhi!' He rolled his eyes.

'You rolled your eyes!' I observed.

'Yes,' he said, 'I thought "there he goes again." He always manages to come up with a need that takes Mum away from me!'

'Right. So, you rushed to Delhi with Mum. What happened then?'

'Mum spent all her time attending to him.' He threw his hands up and sighed, 'Well, I suppose that was okay because he was ill and in hospital. While I was there, his wife, Anagha, asked me to help her get confident with her driving. So, I would go for a short drive with her every morning. She gained confidence rapidly. One morning, my mum asked me to drive her to the grocery store and I asked Anagha if she would like to drive. Mum looked horrified and said "I can't handle one more thing going wrong. Your brother is already sick."'

Ashwin went pale as he said it. I noted that his breathing was becoming laboured. 'What meaning did you make of her saying that?' I asked compassionately.

He struggled to speak, 'Where I am concerned, she always expects things to go wrong. She cannot trust me even though I have taken care of myself well. Actually, I have learnt to take care of myself because she has never been there for me! And now, she assumes that there will be an accident, it will be my fault, and she will not be able to take care because my brother is already sick. All her life, she never found time to accommodate me or to spend time with me.'

'She hasn't been there for you,' I said softly, attuning to his inner world. He shook his head, lowering his eyes, 'I have always been alone.'

I felt the moment was right for a dialogue with his mother in the therapy room. I checked if he was willing and he nodded, taking off his glasses again to wipe his tears. After a sip of water, he got up, on my request, to get another chair and placed it to face his own. He had a zoned-out look about him. I sensed his body was resisting the surge of emotions. I hoped the chair work would stir up the repressed emotions and he could profoundly experience them, leading to the possibility of a new meaning emerging.

I asked him to imagine his mother on the other chair and asked if he could see her. He nodded mechanically. I asked him her name, and he replied that it was Rukmini. I asked him what he wanted to express to her. He stared at the empty chair with glum energy.

'Let me be your mum for a moment,' I said. Stepping into the mum's chair, I said, mimicking the panicked tone he had used, 'I can't handle one more thing going wrong.'

I saw him wince. I repeated, 'I can't handle one more thing going wrong!'

He exploded, 'If you can't handle anything related to me, then why did you . . .' He stopped midway through the sentence. His lips were quivering.

'Finish the sentence,' I said, coming back to my chair.

He gathered himself and said, 'Why did you have me?'

We both paused as we took in the significance of that question.

I asked him to respond from his mother's chair. Literally stepping into another's role can give us a visceral experience of them and bring to awareness newer thoughts and feelings. It can allow us to get to the heart of the conflict.

He moved and sat on the chair with a glazed look.

'Say whatever comes up for you,' I encouraged. 'Don't hold back. Let it flow.'

'Ved has Dengue,' he said as his mom, sounding tired. 'I was just exhausted. That sentence didn't mean anything. I am there for you.'

I asked him to switch chairs again.

'But you are not,' he cried out. 'It is always about Ved! This was supposed to be my week with you. He is thirty-five years old. His family, including Anagha's parents, are with him. Why did you need to come all the way from Mysore and be in charge of everything? And when has he ever taken responsibility for himself? Even today, you take water for him when he sits down for a meal. I have always had to look out for myself. Have you ever brought me water?' He put his head in his hands and began to sob.

After a few moments, he went quiet. I asked him to switch chairs again.

He came back to his mother's chair and his body slumped. 'I don't know what to say,' he said as Rukmini. 'I am feeling helpless. I can only say sorry.'

He shifted to his chair and responded with anger, 'Don't say sorry when you don't mean it. Do you know the only time I get your attention is when I get into a deep mess? Do you recognize how often I get into messes because of that?'

Back in his mother's chair, he had a slumped posture and the same glazed look. 'I am worried for you; you shouldn't get into trouble to just get my attention. Let us discuss this.'

As himself, he said, 'Don't talk to me like I am one of your employees. Can't you see I am lashing out at you?

What more do you want to discuss? Do you know anything about me at all?' he screamed, his body shaking with rage.

I pulled out a rolled mattress, placed it in front of him, and handed him a *bataka*, a foam padded stick. 'Go ahead,' I nodded. 'It's okay. Let it out.'

He screamed and thrashed the mattress for a few minutes after which he flopped down, exhausted.

'How are you feeling?' I asked after a few minutes.

He got up slowly and sat back on the chair, 'I can't believe how angry I was.'

I could see his body was more relaxed and his breath was steady. 'Do you want to continue the dialogue with your mother now?'

'No, it is not going anywhere. In her chair, I only experience helplessness. I find myself saying "I am sorry, I don't know what to do."'

We had reached what in Transactional Analysis, we call an *impasse*. An impasse is a point where two equal and opposing forces meet—a stuck place. An impasse is used to describe conflicts between the Parent and Child parts of the client's ego state structure. In the client's internal dialogue, the Parent repeats a script message. In this case, while socially the message from the Parent was 'I feel helpless; I don't know what to do', I intuited that the ulterior message was 'Don't feel safe, because I can't be there for you the way you want me to'. The Child responds with an autonomous desire for change, in this instance, 'I want to feel safe, be there for me'. Each side in the internal conflict pushes with equal force with the result that the client expends a lot of energy but stays stuck.

'If this is Mum's response, what would you like to do?'

He shrugged his shoulders, with a quizzical look on his face. Breaking out of an impasse involves stepping into the unknown. It is often not easy. It was especially difficult for Ashwin in the moment as he was coming to terms with his grief.

'I am feeling very sad,' he said. 'I can see now why I believe I will never get what I want in relationships because I believe I will never get what I want from my mum.'

'And you believed that if you got into a deep mess and felt sad enough, then she might finally really be there for you,' I highlighted the coping strategy that had emerged in the two-chair dialogue.

'I do believe that,' he said, his lips drooping.

'I see your sadness,' I said gently. 'I see there is a very wounded part of you that is feeling very let down by Mum.'

'Yes,' he said.

'Can you visualize that part of you?' I wondered. Ashwin closed his eyes.

'I see a young boy, six or seven years of age, waiting by the phone for his mother to call. He waits and waits, but Mum never calls.'

'What do you feel as you look at that boy?'

'I feel very sad for him,' he said, tears falling from under his closed eyelids.

'Is there anything you can offer him?' I asked.

He shook his head, confused and overwhelmed with sadness.

'Breathe,' I soothed him gently. 'The little Ashwin is there waiting by the phone. Perhaps he needs some support and some nurturing.'

'I want to tell him "Enough waiting. Go out and play."'

This was a pivotal moment in his work. He was letting go of waiting for Mum to change and taking charge of his life.

'Enough waiting, go out and play,' I repeated.

'Go out and run. Your friends are waiting for you,' he continued talking to his younger self.

'What does he do?' I asked curiously.

'He is still looking at me, unsure.'

'What happens now?'

'I put my hand out, reach out to him, and he takes my hand. We go out and play.'

'What are you playing?'

'Cricket,' he says smiling. 'It is his favourite game. He is really good at it.' I observed the shift in his energy, 'Who are you playing with?'

'There are six of us. They are all friends from school.'

'Describe what you see, hear, or feel.'

'The sun is setting. The breeze is cool. The field looks golden. I can hear our laughter as we run around. The field is very dusty, and I can see our running raising the dust.'

'How is little Ashwin?'

'Ashwin is happy, engrossed in play.'

'How do you feel?'

'I am happy too. I give him a hug.'

'Soak in that image of you and little Ashwin hugging each other. What do you say to him?'

'Stop waiting for Mom. I am here. You are free to play.'

This was a here-and-now dialogue between Ashwin's Adult ego state and Child ego state. The Adult as the grown up was a powerful resource for the protection and permission for the Child, while the Child was a source of playfulness and spontaneity for the grown-up. The Adult Ashwin could say 'I am here for you' with absolute integrity, and the Child could trust that. I knew that from the blissful smile on Ashwin's face.

36

Divorced, but Not Quite

Yashodhara

'And now that woman's gone and got herself a *boyfriend*!' Krishnan declared. 'Can you believe it?'

'That woman' was how Krishnan referred to his ex-wife. His question to me was not one that I could have easily answered without offending him, so I chose to ask him one of my own.

'Tell me more about how you're feeling about this?'

'I don't feel anything,' he returned immediately. 'I mean, it doesn't affect me now, right? I'm just thinking about the girls.' They had two daughters together, and the arrangement was for them to spend a week with him, and a week with their mother. 'It's been bad enough for them having to see the divorce, to adjust to living in two homes. It's only been a year since we split up . . . they might not be ready for this, that's all.'

'You found out about the new boyfriend from them, right?' I asked. 'How did they seem to be reacting?'

'Anya told me about it last night,' he said, a frown on his face. 'She didn't say much, except that "Mom's seeing someone; he came over for dinner and seems like a decent guy." But she's a kid; what will she say? That woman wouldn't think about the kids though. Or anyone in the family. That was always the problem.' His frown deepened, and he leaned forward. 'Did I tell you how she almost burned the house down in our first year of marriage?'

I had heard this story many times over the last six months. I acknowledged, 'You have mentioned it often— where she accidentally left the gas stove on and left the house?'

'Accidentally!' He looked affronted. 'You are sounding almost sympathetic to her.'

'Was it not accidental?' I enquired. 'Do you believe it was on purpose?'

'Maybe not exactly on purpose,' he grumbled. 'But it sometimes sure felt like she was deliberately irresponsible.'

I asked gently, 'What does the idea of my being sympathetic to her mean to you?'

He paused. 'I mean. I feel you're then taking *her* side, not mine.'

'Taking her side?'

'Well, that woman is to blame for everything falling apart! I always tried to make it work.'

I nodded and waited to hear more. After a few moments of silence, he muttered. 'It's like, sometimes it feels like I've only got Mum, and I'm so grateful to her for being there. But she's getting old now. In a way, I'm glad to be able to spend time with her, now that I've moved in with her, and this way the kids also get to see her each week, but she's never been in the best of health—and the separation has also caused her so much stress. That woman could never understand that Mum needs my attention. We were supposed to partner and look after her, but there was always just some unpleasantness or the other, she didn't know how to adjust and . . .'

He launched into another tirade I had heard before, narrating incidents that highlighted how his ex-wife had mistreated his ageing, well-meaning, sickly mother for the year that they had lived in the same house. I went into a reverie of sorts even as I listened to his words, and the image that came up for me was that of a poor old woman being attacked by her nasty daughter-in-law, with her good son stepping in between to defend her. It was the classic *drama triangle* with the three positions of Victim, Persecutor, and Rescuer—all three of which represented unhealthy, compulsive ways of relating to each other, even as the players occasionally shifted their positions around the triangle. I was interested in Krishnan's inner experience and noticed how easily he shifted from the exploration of his inner world by getting into the narrative. It was as if he was just stuck in the past, and for some reason, deeply invested in maintaining the same story.

'Krishnan,' I said as he paused for breath. 'You started by talking about your ex's new relationship, and then we got into how it might affect your daughters, how it's been hard for them, and your mom—how is it affecting *you*?'

I was deliberate about emphasizing the last word, and it seemed to be making him reflect. He was a little quieter as he spoke. 'I am not sure. I mean, she's free to do what she wants with her life, right? The only thing we said is that we will try to co-parent the girls properly and amicably. But it just gets tough, our views on parenting differ so much. It's more like, I'm the only one with a view on parenting. She just wants to wing everything. You can't just *wing* everything.'

'I wonder if it is her dating again that is really bothering you.'

He winced. 'Dating! She's over forty years old, it sounds strange—but then, she's never known how to act her age. Still needs someone to take care of her, I guess. I used to do everything for her, practically.'

I remained silent. I half-suspected he would go into another story about her selfish and irresponsible behaviour, and I saw that my questions were being deflected. After a few seconds, he just muttered in a disgusted tone, 'Anyway. It's not like we're still married.'

'Yes,' I said, adding instinctively, 'I wonder if there's a part of you that hasn't accepted that yet?'

He froze at this. When he spoke, it was in a cold voice. 'Look, *she* was the one who asked for the divorce, with loony, childish reasons like not feeling understood, not being given enough attention . . . I accepted it because I could see she was unhappy and seemed to want her freedom. I had a responsibility to look after her, and I would have, but she walked out. I knew she needed me more than I needed her, so accepting her decision has never been an issue for me.'

His coldness almost caused me to backtrack, but I felt we were on the verge of something and hence went on, keeping my voice tentative, 'And yet, it seems that she still plays a leading role in the story that keeps playing in your head.'

This really seemed to touch a nerve. At first, I sensed that he felt cornered and was about to deflect or attack me. But then his expression softened—it was perhaps the first time I saw Krishnan look vulnerable. He looked away, said 'Hmmm', and then, a small, twisted smile appeared on his lips.

'What's going on for you?' I asked gently.

'Leading role,' he looked at me, and I saw what looked like a combination of affection and pain in his eyes. 'She was always this drama queen. She had this way of taking centre stage. I thought of her as this heroine, actually. And now, she's the villain in my story.'

'There was something special about her heroine-like qualities?' I guessed. 'Something that appealed to you?'

'The day I saw her,' he was looking at me, but apparently seeing something else, given the faraway look in his eyes. 'I remember thinking, I've never seen anyone *so* full of life and vitality. Funny and loud and carefree. Maybe all the things I could never be.' His lips tightened. 'I guess I stopped seeing her that way though, especially after we had Anya almost right after getting married. And then I got so involved in being a dad, not giving any attention to her . . .' He cocked his head, and I saw that he was wondering. 'So, maybe she *was* right.'

Those four words—'*maybe she was right*'—were the beginning of an entirely new phase in the therapy. Krishnan was able to move from a rigid position of seeing her as the 'villain'. We processed that the dynamic between them for fifteen years had been that of he Rescuing her from her child-like irresponsible way of being, while also seeing her as the Persecutor to his mother. In both cases, he had played Rescuer, and had not been in touch with his own needs, exhausting himself in taking care of everyone else. He resented his wife for not sharing the load but had staunchly denied her the opportunity to take care of him in any way.

By not seeing her as the villain of the piece anymore, he was able to acknowledge his feelings for her that included affection and a sense of loss; he could fully feel and thereby process the sadness and regret he had been suppressing about the ending of the relationship, and therefore, could finally accept it was over and grieve it fully. He also began to examine his relationship with his mother, realizing the complexity and co-dependency involved there as well as the suppressed resentment he felt for having to always take care of her.

We worked on creating a new vision for what it would mean for him and his ex-wife to cordially co-parent the children, and in time, a far more conflict-free arrangement was created, wherein the girls primarily stayed with the mom (I learned her name was Rimi, as the term 'that woman' faded away) and came over to stay with him on weekends. Things improved as he began to see his ex-wife as a capable adult and trust her with the care of their children—he remarked about it to me months later, with humorous irony, 'It's a better partnership now than when we were married!'

37

The Hot Potato

Aruna

'Urmi did not get into the final round in the badminton tournament,' scowled Akhila. Urmi was her eight-year-old daughter. 'I yelled at her so much that she shut herself up in her room for a whole day. I knew she was crying.'

'What does it mean to you that she did not get in?' I asked, curious about the intensity of her disappointment.

'Urmi has so much potential. She just doesn't care. She is just too lazy!' Akhila spat the words out angrily, not listening to my question.

'You sound really angry,' I said.

'Yes, if she had no talent, I wouldn't mind her having a relaxed attitude to life. But with so much talent, when I see her just chilling or playing video games, it kills me.'

'It kills you?' I repeated so that she could hear herself. But she was in her own world and continued, 'I don't care about whether she wins or not. That is not in her hands.

What is in her control is her commitment to practice. Urmi is just not worried about anything!'

'Do you want her to be worried?'

'Yes. Then she will make an effort. With no worries, she has no motivation to act.'

I decided to highlight her unconscious pattern boldly, 'If she worries, you can relax.'

'Yes,' she said instantly, but slowed down and became thoughtful as she thought about it again. 'If she is worried, then I can trust that she herself wants to do well. I can take my hands off.'

'So, if she worries, you can relax.'

She became more reflective. 'Do I want her to worry?' she hesitated. 'I think I want her to perform.'

'You said you don't care whether she wins or not.'

'I did say that. And that is true. Winning is less important to me than trying. If she cares, she might win. And if she didn't win, it would be okay. She cared enough to try.'

'And how would you know she cares?'

'She would need to put in effort. She should plan backwards. She should think about competition. She should consider the long-term impact of her actions. This kind of cool confidence that she has scares me.'

'Her confidence scares you.'

Akhila became quiet.

'What are you experiencing?' I enquired.

'I am seeing the same pattern at work. I cannot bear to see my team members chatting or being casual. That makes me tense. Then I turn on the heat, by setting up meetings, yelling at them, warning them that we won't be in business if they continue to relax. I need them to mirror my tension for me to know that they understand.'

'This reminds me of a hot potato game,' I said. She straightened up and listened curiously.

'It is like "passing the parcel". Music is played while children toss what is supposedly a hot potato back and forth between them. When the music stops, the child who is holding the hot potato either gets out of the game or does something that is asked for, say hop around the room on one leg. This game has become a metaphor for passing on something that is uncomfortable to another.'

'How come you thought about this game? Am I passing on something that is uncomfortable?'

'Think about it. What is happening between you and your daughter is like a seesaw. Either you can relax, or she can relax, but not both.'

Akhila contemplated what I said, 'I have heard people say I worry too much, I am highly strung, and that I make everybody around me worried and tense. Am I passing on my worry?'

'Why don't you answer that?'

'Hmmm,' she was reflective, 'I am worried all the time. Maybe I am passing it on.'

'Tell me a little more about why you worry so much.'

As we explored her history, we saw that behind her aggressive nagging of her daughter and her team members was her own unrecognized sense of worthlessness and unlovability. Her highly critical mother would often humiliate her, leading her to believe that there was something fundamentally wrong with her. She experienced shame at who she was. She compensated by setting high standards for herself and being perfect. She had internalized her mother's exacting perfectionist standards and imposed them on Urmi. When Urmi didn't match up to these standards, Akhila experienced the same shame as she had experienced as a little girl—the unbearable hot potato. She then switched from her normally affectionate stance towards Urmi to becoming so critical of her that she (Urmi) experienced shame and worry. Thus, the hot potato was passed on. When Urmi was worried and stressed, Akhila could then focus her energies on managing her schedule, encouraging her, and staying up with her at night. All of these gave her a purpose that allowed her to forget her own shame.

In life, the passing of the 'hot potato' is far from playful. It is typically passed on from a more powerful 'donor', often the parent, to a more vulnerable recipient, often the child.

'I have got the hot potato of shame from my mother,' said Akhila glumly.

'Very likely. Her criticism of you possibly came from her own unresolved shame of feeling not good enough.'

'And with my constant worry of my daughter's future, I am inviting her into feeling not good enough,' she flopped down in her chair. After a pause, she said, 'I wonder for how many generations this hot potato has been transmitted. Can I do something to stop it right here?'

I smiled.

'How come you are smiling?' she asked curiously.

'What does it mean to you if Urmi doesn't win the badminton tournament? And don't tell me about her potential. Tell me what it means to *you*?'

I saw the colour drain from her cheeks as she had an insight. 'I did tell you a few minutes ago that I don't care if Urmi wins or loses. But I do. I want her to win. I sometimes cry like a little child when she does badly in school. It is like I have failed.' She held her head in her hands. 'I feel horrible. I am making my eight-year-old compensate for my shame. She needs to perform so that I can feel good about myself!'

She took this in for a while, and then wondered out loud, 'How do I begin to trust that I am okay as I am, and she is okay as she is? I wonder if I will get there. I worry about things going wrong all the time.'

'Then you bring those to the therapy room and work through them here with me,' I said. 'This includes your unresolved issues with your mother. Otherwise, you may unawarely recruit your eight-year-old to take care of you by taking on your worries.'

Akhila went back from this session feeling more relaxed. We continued our work with her acceptance of herself in the forthcoming sessions. I saw her steadily drop her worries about several issues and move into a state of relaxed confidence.

'When I travelled to London last, I discovered jacket potatoes. They were in little carts in the farmer's market and were served with huge dollops of butter,' she shared with me one day. 'I thought to myself: I want to eat these hot pōtatoes by myself, not pass them on.'

'Do you mean you want to resolve your own shame and not pass it on to Urmi?'

'That, of course. Those are the painful ones, easy to pass to another. But the ones I saw in London were the delicious ones, not easy to share. Some hot potatoes are meant to be enjoyed!'

'Oh yes!' I said, salivating.

38

I'll Leave Before You Do

Yashodhara

'How have I been?' Avinash's smile widened and he boomed. 'Very good actually! Things at work have been super busy. Dad's been off my case. And no women-related issues to worry about. So, not much to report this week!' He cleared his throat. 'Actually, I was thinking—it's our eighth session, and given that there isn't that much to talk about, maybe we could take a break.'

I reminded myself that I had sensed this coming. Avinash moved quickly from subject to subject, and I suspected that his increasing vulnerability with me was making him uncomfortable. My role here was to give him the space to be himself. And yet, I had to say what I felt honestly.

'I hear you, Avinash,' I said, 'and I must say, my first response is that I feel a little sad, but let's talk more about this. Could you tell me more about your decision here?'

'It's not a decision as such,' he said quickly. 'I was just thinking—these sessions have helped me so much and I've got a lot of clarity on what I really need to focus on and that's my career. And things are so crazy on the work front, I think I can't even do the homework exercises that you've asked me to, so it's not really productive for me to come in unprepared. Today, in fact, I was really struggling to think about any problem to bring in, and so I thought it would be good to just stop. For a while.'

I realized that although Avinash had initially come into therapy to address his feelings of anxiety, we had fallen into the pattern of his bringing in a new issue week on week, trying out a new behaviour and then bringing back evidence of change back to me.

'Avinash, do you remember the initial goal you stated for yourself? Exploring your fear and increasing confidence and clarity at work and home? To what extent has this been met?'

'Well, there's been a lot of progress on many fronts, right?' He sounded defensive. 'And we did sign up in blocks of eight—and if there's nothing to discuss, it's okay for me to move out, isn't it?'

'That's right,' I kept my tone even. 'And while people may move out after eight sessions, there is no compulsion either way—to stop or continue is an individual decision. I've been especially curious about the last session where you were speaking about your break-up—I did feel there was something unfinished there.'

'Unfinished?' he repeated, and then he smiled. 'This whole thing about "closure" we always hear about? I don't actually subscribe to that.' I was getting familiar with this dynamic of his 'knowing' things. He went on, 'I move on very, very fast. This whole dating business, it's really become like a game. With the apps, it's anyway hard to find someone you can even consider a serious relationship with. I'm done with that scene now anyway.'

I remained silent—I found myself debating about whether I should open up anything given that he seemed to want to move out of therapy.

'Well, see—I'm not sure what to talk about now,' Avinash said. He then added, 'It's not like me to be unsure, right? Ha ha. I suppose today I could just summarize and reflect on the various insights and progress I've made in the sessions so far? What do you suggest?'

I opened my mouth to respond and then shut it again. For some reason, I felt uncertain about how to proceed in the moment. I was very aware of the conflicting emotions within me, and I found myself saying, 'I don't really have any suggestions.'

This seemed to throw him off a little. He was quiet for a long time and looked thoughtful. I decided to sit back and wait. After some more time he spoke, a little frustrated, 'I really don't know what you want me to say.'

'Are you feeling pressured into saying something?' I asked gently.

Another few seconds passed, and I noticed his cheeks were flushing. He said flatly, 'I don't know.'

I just nodded, watching him attentively. For the first time so far, I saw that he looked really uncomfortable. I waited.

'I feel like you're angry with me,' he finally burst out, with a dark scowl on his usually smiling face.

'I am wondering if *you* are angry right now?' I commented.

He looked like he was struggling to maintain control, and his words came through clenched teeth now, 'Well, yeah.'

'Could you tell me about it?'

He seemed hesitant and there was a long silence. Then he blurted out, 'See, I primarily came to you about conflicts at work making me nervous. But then, as we spoke, I just feel like we went into these other areas—how I'm afraid of Dad, of being in groups, of letting my guard down, and of the issues with women. It makes it seem like . . . it's like I'm afraid of *everything*. That's not who I want to be. It feels pathetic.'

'And you're angry with me because I see this fearful part of you?' I asked gently.

'Maybe.' He wasn't looking directly at me as he said this, but then his eyes met mine, and I saw something in him relax. 'I mean, it feels weird to have someone know so much about what's actually going on inside me. But . . . maybe I'm angry with myself because *I* think it's pathetic.'

'Does this feel familiar to you—what's going on between us?'

'I've never been in therapy before,' he said, and then, after a few moments of thought, he added, 'but most of my break-ups happen after I feel like I've slipped, shown some . . . vulnerability, feels like weakness to me. I can't stand the feeling that someone is pitying me. So, I feel the need to get out in a hurry.'

This was something I had been wondering about bringing up, and now seemed the time. 'Could this also be the reason your problems get magically resolved in a single session here?'

He shrugged and responded in a quiet voice, 'Maybe.'

'How might you describe your pattern in relationships?'

He smiled wryly and looked off into space. Then he looked back at me, 'Easy one, right? *I'll leave you before you leave me.*'

I sensed his pain and loneliness, and realized it likely stemmed from an underlying fear of abandonment, which ironically kept him from finding and keeping romantic relationships. It perhaps stemmed from the original pain that we had not yet touched—I knew his mother had walked out on the family when he was a small child, and we hadn't yet explored what that had meant to him. He had always waved it off as being too long ago, saying he had already come to terms with it. But there was something new that he was able to get in touch with today.

We continued to speak about his fear of intimacy and vulnerability, and how it showed up across relationships and how he still felt deeply sad after his last break-up. At the end of the session, he said he would like to continue the therapy, joking that this was maybe going to be his first 'long-term relationship'.

I smiled and expressed my gladness at his decision to continue and internally resolved to keep reminding myself that we could go deep but also step lightly.

We didn't need to rush anything. Hopefully, we would have plenty of time together.

39

I Need You; You Don't Need Me

Aruna

'I can't meet you on weekdays; I have long days at work. Give me a slot for Sundays.' Rachna's brusque ask felt like an order more than a request.

'Well, I don't work on Sundays,' I said, piqued at her tone. She was not yet a client. Today was our first meeting where we were arriving at how we would work together.

'It is just one hour,' said Rachna shrugging her shoulders, frowning disapprovingly. 'Don't you have other clients who work full-time?'

'I am sorry, Rachna,' I said firmly, while noting my increasing annoyance. 'I have set aside my Sundays as personal time. I can share my weekday slots. We can find a weekly slot that works for both.'

'That is another thing I wanted to bring up. I don't think we need to meet weekly,' she declared.

I was mighty irritated by now, 'Well, you may work better with another, more flexible therapist.'

Rachna looked intensely at me.

'You are telling me to get lost,' she said, picking up the ulterior message from my tone, much to my embarrassment. 'You are leaving me with no choice then but to go to somebody else. Well, it is easy for you to push me away. I need you; you don't need me.'

I was struck by that statement. It brought me back into my Adult. I had, without awareness, gotten entangled in a game that I can now name 'You can't control me'. Rachna was a smart and sharp client. While I was irritated, I knew there was some truth to the statement, 'I need you; you don't need me.' From the very first day of training in psychotherapy, I had been instructed to pay attention to the balance of power between therapists and clients and to never exploit vulnerable clients.

On the face of it, Rachna was no weak client whom I could exploit. But I knew her aggression was self-protective for her in some way. She was not aware of how she was using shaming as a way to get me to comply with her. Bringing that into her awareness would be one of my tasks if we got to work together. Underneath aggression is always vulnerability.

I softened and responded, 'I understand you need a therapist to work with right now. Setting and agreeing to clear boundaries contributes to the effectiveness of our work together. Would you be willing to make time on weekdays? I could give you the first slot in the day or the last if it makes it easier.'

She softened too and we started work. But as time went by, she continued to challenge boundaries repeatedly, showing up a few minutes late every time, cancelling at the last minute, and continuing to ask me for slots on a Sunday.

'What would it mean for you if I were to give you a slot for Sunday?'

'Hmmm,' she said, pausing to consider my question, and then looked straight into my eyes when she had found an answer, 'that you cared enough for me to make an exception.'

'If I created a slot for you on Sunday that would mean that I cared *enough* for you,' I repeated, quite fascinated with her fantasy.

She recognized her unconscious relational pattern. 'I do this all the time. I push people to do something extra for me.'

'If they went out of their way to do something for you, that would mean, you are . . .'

'Special.'

And that led to a series of discoveries she made for herself about her need to feel special.

Rachna had been adopted by her parents when she was just four months old. She had a heart condition at birth and had required surgery at the age of four. Her doting mother, Kusum, had indulged her by setting no limits and doing too much for her. Kusum had gone through depression at being unable to conceive for ten years and needed Rachna to be happy to feel good about herself. In the process, she denied Rachna the opportunity for important life lessons like patience, tolerance for disappointment, reciprocity, and responsibility. Her father, Ayan, had been the high-profile CEO of a software company. He made it his personal mission to showcase the child as a superlative achiever and to ensure that she would be 'no less than any biological child' they might have had. So, Rachna could never be herself or trust that she was wonderful as she was. It was not enough that she did her best—she needed to be visibly extraordinary. She did that by being precocious. It made both parents happy and more indulgent. Her father proudly showcased his wonder-child to his colleagues. He even went on to finance her venture as she set up her own company at a very young age.

The whole experience of being treated as special made Rachna believe that she was entitled to a certain type of treatment and a separate set of rules from other people. Her external stance of 'I'm OK-You're not OK' defended her from feeling the pain of her internal experience of 'I'm not OK-You're OK.'

What she denied and pushed away was the deep fear of abandonment that came from her earlier experience of being given away for adoption. She realized that in her formative years, she had experienced little emotional attention from her needy mother or overachieving father, so her own needs for unconditional love, understanding, and security were left unmet. The unique combination of emotional neglect and overindulgence had made her substitute achievement and material success for intimate connection. But even the most enormous material success could never compensate for the hollow, empty feeling within her.

She had come to therapy because she felt that 'everyone' in her 200-member company hated her even though she 'gave her life to make the company a success'. The irony was that even though she desperately wanted to feel loved, what she did was push people to the exacting standards she subjected herself to, held idealized expectations of them, and, in the process, invited them to reject her. Her pattern showed up in her work with me as well. The therapy room became another place for showing off, being right, comparing, and winning.

'Why are you asking me about the past? What good will come of it? I came here to feel good, not to go back with more pain.'

She labelled anger, sadness, grief, fear, shame as dark emotions and said staunchly, 'I don't want to go there. I want to rise above these dark emotions.' She would launch off into tangential storytelling to avoid contact with any emotions. I was barricaded from entry into her feelings.

'We are not making progress,' she announced one day, after several weeks of meeting me.

'Well, I feel stuck,' I said. 'I do not know of a way to feel better unless we visit emotional experiences that have not been processed. I don't recommend "rising above" emotions as a way to ignore or suppress what you are feeling. I would recommend "sinking into" emotions and exploring the meaning they hold for you.'

'But what is the point in feeling painful emotions?' she challenged me as usual, but I sensed she might actually listen this time.

'There is a point,' I said, explaining to her the role of emotions in our lives. 'Unaddressed emotions can show up as the need to excessively control others. I wonder how it would be for you to trust me to be able to hold you as you sink into painful feelings?'

Something shifted for her, and her resistance reduced. I sensed her softening and felt a sense of hope.

She took back a homework assignment of observing her emotions and naming them without judging herself for having them and writing down her accompanying thoughts. My first goal for her was to simply increase awareness of her thoughts and feelings.

'I am angry, frustrated, irritated, and disgusted with others all the time,' she said, showing me the log of her feelings. 'The accompanying thoughts are "How long will I suffer this fool? How do I fire him?"' She paused, reflectively.

'I see I am being judgemental,' she went on, 'but I do believe what I am asking for is so reasonable.'

I could see her reflective capacity increasing.

'What do you do when you have these feelings and thoughts?'

'I yell at people. I am sarcastic. I punish my employees by not sharing information with them, shifting their roles.'

'What fantasy do you have of how they are experiencing you?'

'I am not really sure what could be going on in their heads. But I know people go quiet in front of me. They also do what I want.'

'But if you were to think of what might be going on within them, what would you say?'

'I don't like what is coming up for me. But I will say it, what the heck. I imagine them calling me a mean bitch.'

'And how do you feel as you imagine that?'

'I rationalize it, saying it is envy. I am so much more than all of them put together. No one has the sense of ownership that I have. This is my company. If I do not call a spade a spade, who will?'

'But my question was, how do you feel when you imagine them calling you a mean bitch?'

She was silent.

'I imagine you are sad,' I named the feeling.

'I am,' she acknowledged, looking sad for just a moment and then stiffening again, 'but what's the point?'

'Would you be willing to sink into your sadness?' I said, ignoring her protest. She went silent again, but I sensed her readiness.

'Close your eyes, and just feel this sadness. Attend to what is happening in your body.'

She closed her eyes and then I saw her body transform.

Her shoulders slumped, colour drained from her cheeks, the corners of her mouth drooped downwards, and tears began to pool around her closed eyelids. 'Everyone hates me!' she said despairingly, with tears streaming through her shut eyelids. Her body started to shake, her voice became hoarse, and her nose started to run, but she didn't stop, 'However hard I work, it is never enough. What is the point of working so hard and killing myself if nobody is going to love me anyway?'

She pulled the cushion next to her, buried her face in it, and bawled away for several minutes.

'I am sorry you had to see this,' she said, after she had had a good cry and gathered herself.

'I am not sorry,' I said, smiling kindly.

'Well, you won,' she said, smiling. I recognized this smile as a healthy one, indicating that she recognized the irony of her coping strategy.

In the next few conversations, I brought to her attention her words *'giving my life to the company'*, and *'working hard and killing myself'*. We wondered together about the significance of these words.

'I imagine myself dropping dead while working,' Rachna said. 'I have never really paid attention to this fantasy though I now realize I have it.'

We connected the dots. Having been given away for adoption, Rachna had experienced the trauma of being unwanted. At a deep level she believed that her very being was a burden to others. Rachna's despair was that no one would ever love her. To cope, she unconsciously decided that she would be 'special' to get love. These defiant coping decisions often have an *'I'll show you'* quality. The intense anger masks deep pain.

'You have spent your entire life working hard to get love,' I offered an interpretation. 'Yes, and ironically, I believe I will die without it,' she said, sadly.

'Do you want to continue believing that?'

'No. I am tired now. I am ready to give up being special. And I don't want to die alone.'

We crafted a few behavioural experiments together to allow her to manifest her new intent. For example, she started thanking people for their efforts. She challenged her own grandiosity of being 'special' by acknowledging that she was an ordinary mortal, capable of mistakes and poor behaviour. She decided to just listen in meetings, without making them all about herself. She started reaching out to friends from college with whom she had no work agendas— so she could experience being valued for her being.

'I am not as bad as I thought I was,' she laughed with me after a few months of working together, 'and I am sorry that I pushed you so much initially. I am amazed that you didn't stop working with me. And that brings me to the topic of the end of our work. Will you get bored of me and stop working with me?'

I could see that she had developed an attachment to me and was feeling scared as it was unfamiliar. She didn't trust that it would last. But it was very significant that she had dropped her defences to allow herself to get attached in the first place.

'So, you believe I might leave you?' I said aloud, starting a new chapter in our work.

40

The Tombstone

Yashodhara

'They're talking about shutting offices down again,' Abhijit scoffed. 'Just like last year. This stupid pandemic . . . just when you think it's over!'

'What are you feeling right now?' He seemed annoyed but I guessed he was anxious under the surface. He had mentioned in passing that the previous year's pandemic and the lockdown had been difficult for him—he had become more aware of his tendency for overthinking and that was what had brought him into therapy with me.

'I'm . . . a little concerned,' Abhijit said, and then added 'okay, *quite* concerned. Ours is the kind of business that really centres on travel and retailer visits—the last time offices shut, things eased up for me like anything. It was terrible.'

'Things eased up for you . . . and that was *terrible*,' I repeated, curiosity in my voice.

'Yes,' he laughed ironically. 'Because that's when my mind goes into overdrive, right? I suddenly found myself with *hours* free in the day, and then I was like—okay, *now* what am I supposed to do!'

I nodded. 'Tell me more about your thoughts and feelings when you have free time?'

'Thoughts . . . there are like a million of them. It's crazy, like I'm talking to myself in my head about what next, what next—okay, let me think about what to eat, should I just call someone, watch something but that will waste time but what the heck, why not . . . at its worst, I even found myself puzzling for hours on what to order for dinner from Swiggy!' He shook his head from side to side vigorously as if to shake off the memory.

'And what do you feel?'

'Feel? I don't know.' He frowned. 'I try *not* to feel it, but there is this . . . constant anxiety, I suppose.'

'What are you anxious about?'

'Oh . . . everything!' The same ironic laugh. 'About losing my job, family pressures around finding a partner, or finding a partner and then it not working out, or what if Mom gets the virus and I'm stuck here away from her, or my cholesterol issue getting out of control again . . . all of it!'

'Is there something else going on underneath all these thoughts and feelings?'

He became quiet for a few moments. When he spoke, it was more slowly than before, 'Well, sometimes I think, at least these thoughts mean I'm not thinking about . . .' he hesitated.

I leaned forward and nodded, silently encouraging him to continue.

'It's just . . .' he swallowed. 'Last year, there was so much news of people dying. I think I just developed this sort of panic. And not just for my mom. I was thinking, I'm alone in a different city, away from family, no one around. What might happen if I get sick. What if I, I don't know, get sick and have no one, or even random stuff, what if I get a heart attack or something . . . like Dad did, but at least Mom was with him when it happened. What if they just find me like that . . .' his voice trailed off. He shrugged. 'I know it's silly, I just don't want to go through that phase again.'

'It's not silly,' I said softly. 'It is natural to feel this way. The pandemic did a lot to get us in touch with our own mortality. And you've lost your dad to a heart attack, and you do live alone and manage everything by yourself. It's okay to feel worried.'

'Yeah, well . . .' he said, 'I somehow pulled myself out of it last time, forced myself to think about other things, got busy with some stupid new projects, created work for myself . . . and then offices opened up again. It was so uncomfortable though . . . what if I can't handle it this time?'

I looked at him thoughtfully. Death anxiety was something that didn't come up often in my work with clients. I had read about it as an underlying anxiety that was universal, but I hadn't experienced it getting talked about. And yet, here it was right now.

'You know, Abhijit,' I began tentatively, 'I hear you say you forced yourself to think of other things . . . and yet, there is a saying we have in therapy. It is that "You can never really leave a place unless you have visited it fully." What meaning do you make of that?'

He shifted around in his chair. 'I guess you're saying— let's visit my fear? I'm not sure about that.'

'I get that. But any feeling has some underlying positive intent,' I said. 'Processing it properly means giving it space to be experienced. Do you feel safe right now in exploring your fear of death?' I was deliberate about naming the fear, which often served to take the edge off it.

He thought about it for a couple of seconds before saying, 'Okay. Let's do it.'

'Okay. Why don't we first take a couple of deep breaths to centre ourselves?' I did that as well, along with him. 'Now, just plant your feet firmly on the floor. Ground yourself. Let your body relax.' I guided him. 'If you're comfortable, close your eyes. You can open them whenever you feel like. Whenever you're ready, go ahead and make contact with your fear. Do you feel it in your body?'

'I feel this lump in my throat,' he said, swallowing hard. 'And a . . . heaviness in my chest.'

'Right,' I acknowledged. 'Can you describe them to me? This lump, this heaviness . . .'

'The lump is—it's stuck . . . and something in my chest, it's so heavy, it's not letting me move . . .' He seemed to be getting restless already. 'I feel like I need to open my eyes, move around, or something . . .'

Seeing his increasing discomfort, I invited him, 'Go ahead and open your eyes.'

His eyes snapped open, and he shifted around in his chair, wriggling uncomfortably and then settled down again. I noticed he was now staring into space in front of him.

'What's going on for you now, Abhijit?' I enquired gently.

'Huh.' He looked bemused. 'I'm just seeing this picture, some visual coming up in my head—my own funeral.'

'Could you tell me more about what you are seeing?' It seemed that visualization was working better for him, it was possibly less scary for him to imagine a scene with his eyes open.

'It's a sort of burial,' he said, still looking off into space. 'Even though we're not Christian. My mom and brother are there, some of my friends and family. It's a beautiful green cemetery, and I can see this—what's it called—there's a grey slab, a tombstone . . .'

'Your tombstone?' I went along with him.

'Yes.'

'Can you see if something is written on it?'

He paused and then said, '*Here lies the most hard-working soul on earth—he worked till the last moment . . .*'

'How do you feel about this?

'I don't think I like it. And there are other things I'm seeing that I don't like, like my mom crying . . .' He went quiet and I watched him attentively. Suddenly, I noticed he was cringing. I drew my chair close, intuitively putting my hand on his, and asked, 'What are you seeing now?'

His hand was clammy. He said, 'I see myself in the coffin—I'm just *lying there* . . . and people are looking at me.' His face contorted. 'I don't want them seeing me just . . . not moving like that. Why didn't we just have a cremation?'

His voice was getting louder, and he was writhing in discomfort. I said soothingly, 'Okay, how about this—let's come back to this space and talk about what meaning this has for you?'

It took him a few seconds to reorient himself, and then he looked at me with a tight, humourless smile.

'What is that smile about?' I asked.

'I just saw the irony,' he said, with a short hollow laugh. 'Even when I'm *dead*, I'm thinking about how people are seeing me—it's always about what they will think!' He threw his head back and looked at the ceiling.

'Hmmm,' I said thoughtfully, 'I noticed that both times in what we just went through, there was something about *not moving* that made you uncomfortable.'

He paused. 'Well, I do hate not moving. If I'm not working or doing something, my mind goes into overdrive, it's like . . . okay, at least there's *mental* activity.'

'What was it like for you as a kid if you weren't moving?' I asked. 'What would your parents say?'

'Hah!' he said. 'That wasn't allowed! Mom was always hyper, always saying "Look how hard your dad works; even though he's sick, he's killing himself for your education. And what about you, just sitting there!" She was really worried all the time, about money, studies, whatever . . .

and she kept telling me we had no back-up plan for me and my brother, so I better work hard . . .'

'What about your brother?'

'He's seven years younger—it was as if I needed to set a good example for him and the younger cousins.'

'What would happen if you didn't?'

'I don't know. It's not like my parents would punish me or anything. But it did make her calm down—she was only happy if she saw me doing well in school or helping around the house. She got sick quite often, still is that way.' He frowned. 'Always been the type to become very anxious and upset easily. Dad always told us we needed to behave well or something might happen to her.'

'*Something* might happen to her?'

He just shrugged. 'It wasn't ever spelled out. Just that "something" that would be really bad. It is ironic that *he* was the one who died of a heart attack. Maybe she was right—maybe he actually killed himself working too hard. I think there was just too much stress on him.'

'I wonder if, for you, *working* and *moving*—as opposed to not doing anything—felt like a matter of life and death?'

He said nothing, but his lips tightened again. Then he said, 'I guess it's more like—*feels*.'

I stayed silent. After a few seconds he said, 'In a way, being dead would mean finally being able to stop and rest, right? But that thought is so uncomfortable.'

I nodded, and then offered, 'You know, I read something that stayed with me—"*our anxiety about death is proportional to the unlived life in our bodies.*"' I paused. 'What might this mean to you?' I was curious what the idea of an 'unlived life' might open up for him.

He was quiet for almost a minute and seemed to be turning this over in his mind. 'Maybe a large part of my fear of death stems from the fact that I'm missing something important as I live?' This seemed to be significant for him and he thought for a long while about this. I waited.

Then he looked me straight in the eye. 'That tombstone. I don't want it to read that stuff—about working so hard till the end . . .'

'What would you like it to read?'

'I want it to say . . .' he looked off into space and then back at me, a little smile forming on his lips. 'I want it to read—*he loved it here.*'

His shoulders relaxed, and I noticed he was still, his breathing even and smooth. It was as if some physical tension was leaving his body.

Over the subsequent sessions, Abhijit would get in touch with the feelings beneath his fear, especially his anger towards his parents for having denied him the permissions to relax and to play; as time passed, he would work through those feelings too and learn to give those permissions to himself. It would take a lot of practice to learn to be okay with enjoying himself without feeling guilty and practising just *being* versus constantly *doing*. He would learn about how stillness was not just okay but an important part of living well. His brave exploration into his fear of death would give him a new meaning to life.

All this would follow, it wouldn't be easy or without setbacks. But today, he had made a major breakthrough in deciding he didn't have to follow in his father's footsteps or pursue a predetermined plan set in his childhood. We took it in as we both sat still.

41

A World Where Farts Are Welcome

Aruna

'Could you write a fairy tale about an animal or a bird? You have fifteen minutes.'

This was a task I gave to four teens who were attending a teen therapy group with me. My experience with creative exercises like these was that themes of their own stories, which in Transactional Analysis we call 'life scripts', would show up in surprising ways in the stories they wrote.

Agastya volunteered to read out his story first.

Once upon a time, far, far away in the North Pole, lived Zoey the polar bear. He was big and white with a cute little black nose. When he was born, everyone around him said that he was meant for great things. But as he grew up, Zoey showed no signs of greatness. He seemed slower than the others. He was teased by the other polar bears. He also had very smelly farts that he was ashamed of, so he preferred to be by himself. He wandered away from the pack often. He quite enjoyed diving through the ice on his own and coming up with juicy fish, caught with one clean sweep of his large paw.

One day, he saw some unusual activity in the otherwise tranquil North Pole. Humans! They had huge machines that made horrible noises. It looked like they were going to dig the ground searching for something. Zoey couldn't bear to see the serene white vastness destroyed. He crawled closer to the men, being careful so that he would not be seen. And then he let out a huge silent fart with all the strength that he could gather. The stink filled the North Pole. The men looked around, but Zoey blended perfectly into the white background and was invisible. Unable to bear the stink, the men packed up and left. One of them, however, saw Zoey's black nose and recognized he was there. He pulled out a gun, but he was so flustered that he shot himself in the foot instead, leaving a red line on the white snow as he ran away. Later that day, other polar bears came and saw the red line and asked one another, 'There were humans here. Why did they leave?' A wise old polar bear said, 'Someone great is protecting us.' Zoey kept quiet. This was his secret. He wandered off again to enjoy fishing on his own.

Everyone spontaneously applauded at the end of this delightful story. Farts still amused them. 'Shall we see what this story could tell us about your life script, Agastya?' I said.

'Ooooooh,' said the other kids; they had not been expecting this.

'Oh no!' Agastya protested. 'If I had known we would analyse it, I wouldn't have written a story about farts.'

'It is okay to have smelly farts,' announced Mythili, bursting into giggles. Since our session on permissions, they had been giving each other hilarious permissions such as this one.

'Remember our contract of relating to each other in an OK-OK manner?' I gently nudged. 'I am going to make meaning of this story with Agastya. If anyone wants to add, they can raise their hand and offer their observations or interpretations to Agastya for consideration.'

They acknowledged my request and became reflective.

'Agastya, I wonder if you often feel you don't belong?' I inquired.

'That's right!' said Agastya, bewildered. 'I feel like the odd one out in my family and in school. I have twin sisters, and everybody is always saying "Oh, they are so cute; oh, they are so pretty." So, the attention is always on them. But how did you figure that out?'

'Well, Zoey always wandered off and he never told the other polar bears that he was the one who scared the humans away.'

'Because they would laugh at him! Better for him to be quiet and on his own.' There it was, I thought—Agastya's coping strategy!

'Is that what you believe, Agastya? That you are better off by yourself?'

'I do. I am like Zoey in that way. I prefer to be alone.'

The children got very interested and began contributing excitedly. 'But the fart was actually a strength. It scared the humans away,' said Kanishka. 'The other bears could not appreciate that it could be a strength, and Zoey felt ashamed and moved away.'

'Wonderful observation, Kanishka!' I cheered. 'What is conventionally seen as a flaw could be a strength!'

Kanishka looked pleased with her contribution, and I was enjoying the group's involvement.

'Shall I challenge you all here?' I said, wondering if they could see other elements in the story too as a symbolic representation of Agastya's inner world.

They leaned forward eagerly.

'What do you think the other story elements might represent? The guy with the gun shot himself and left a tell-tale red line that allowed the other polar bears to figure out something had happened . . .'

'Yes,' said Agastya. 'I could imagine a bright red line on perfectly white snow. The visual was very striking.'

'I think Zoey wanted the other bears to find out that he had done something wonderful—that is why he left that line as a clue!' said Mythili.

'I think Zoey was angry. Blood and red mean anger to me,' offered Anish. They all looked at me in anticipation, waiting for me to validate them.

I smiled, 'All of these are possible. And there is no right answer! We are all sharing our intuition with Agastya, helping him to make connections to himself.'

'How are you all coming up with all this? It feels so right. It is spooky,' said Agastya, 'I do have a fantasy that all those who are mean to me will one day know that I am a good person, and then they will be sorry.' He went on to share how he was bullied in school for his weight and his slow walk. 'And I often imagine the bully stumbling down the stairs or hitting his head against a tree branch,' he admitted bravely.

'Are you angry with the bullies, Agastya?' I asked.

'No, I don't want to waste my energy being angry with them,' he said in a resigned manner. 'I would rather read an interesting book.'

'Have you ever been angry?'

'I don't think so.'

He had no permission to own his anger though I could see that he experienced it. 'Do you feel hurt?'

'I do. I feel judged and not understood. But it is okay,' shrugged Agastya, and I saw he was dismissing his pain.

'Is it, Agastya?' I confronted him tenderly.

'Well, it isn't,' he said, beginning to look sad, 'but I don't know what to do.'

Seeing him access his vulnerability, I ventured, 'Have you, like Zoey, decided to show your anger by never letting people know who you are?' I was hoping to raise awareness of a coping strategy often used by people who don't have permission to be angry. They punish others by never sharing themselves with them.

'Maybe I have,' he was reflective, 'when I am angry, I stop meeting people and I stop talking to them. I can't believe this!' He seemed fascinated by what was emerging, 'I thought I wrote some nonsense, and it turned out to be the story of my life!'

A key feature about working with art experientially— whether through stories or drama or drawings—is that the discoveries are often unexpected. Clients find that they have, in a sense, confronted themselves with their own defences. We had uncovered some of Agastya's *script beliefs* already: he didn't belong, he didn't trust that anybody would appreciate him, and it was not okay for him to be angry. His coping strategy was to avoid pain by being alone and keeping his world private.

The next task was to challenge these decisions using the story as a metaphor. 'So, what permissions does Zoey need?' I asked.

All of them rattled off several permissions together, creating a cacophony: 'It is okay to be who you are!'; 'It is okay to be angry'; 'It is okay to be close'; 'It is okay to be important'; and 'It is okay to be seen.'

'Shall we give Zoey these permissions and rewrite the story?' I encouraged. 'How would the story be now if Zoey was offered these permissions? I will read the story line by line, and you can stop me and make suggestions. Agastya can choose the suggestions he likes.'

I started reading: '*Once upon a time, far, far away in the North Pole, lived Zoey the polar bear. He was big and white with a cute little black nose.*'

I paused, 'Do you folks want to change anything?'

'So far, so good,' said Anish.

'*When he was born, everyone around him said that he would be a great polar bear.*'

'Objection!' Mythili chimed in. 'That is too much pressure. Why does he have to be great! He can be himself.'

'I like that,' said Agastya.

'Great work!' I beamed and continued reading.

'But as he grew up, Zoey showed no signs of greatness. He seemed slower than the others. He was teased by the other polar bears. He also had very smelly farts that he was ashamed of, so he preferred to be by himself.'

'Objection,' said Anish. 'Zoey should tell the polar bears that he didn't like being teased. It is okay for him to be angry.'

'But they won't listen to Zoey,' protested Agastya.

'Then maybe the wise old bear should say it. In the story the wise old bear only showed up at the end. Where was he earlier when Zoey wandered off?' said Kanishka indignantly.

'But why is the wise old bear a "he", anyway?' challenged Mythili. 'She could be a "she".'

'Of course, she is a "she". What is wrong with me!' chuckled Kanishka, 'but my point is—should she not stop these bears from teasing Zoey?'

'She should have,' I affirmed, 'because the elders didn't stand up for Zoey or have guidelines on how the bears treated each other, Zoey believed he needed to take care of himself and wandered off.' Often in stories, as in life, it is the adults who need to change, not the children.

Agastya listened to me attentively. I could see that what I said felt supportive to him.

'Let us say that the grand old wise bear had this rule for their community that farts and belches are good,' pronounced Anish.

'Better out than in!' laughed Agastya.

'So, Zoey could fit in and fart happily along with the other bears,' said Anish. Agastya nodded in agreement.

'And then, the humans came with their drilling machines,' I said.

'Zoey need not deal with it alone now,' said Mythili. 'He is with everybody else since he didn't have the need to wander off in the first place.'

'So, what happens now?' I turned to Agastya, curious about the possibilities he was seeing now.

Agastya began to flow with the story, 'Zoey is angry. How could humans destroy their habitat! He tells the other bears that "Let us all growl and fart together and scare them off." A hundred of them gather and walk towards the men, growling and farting, with Zoey right in the front. The humans are alarmed. The sound, sight, and smell are terrifying. They flee for their lives.'

'Did a man shoot himself?' I asked.

'We need the red-line man. That is important to the story,' said Anish.

'That was important to the earlier story,' said Agastya, 'when Zoey wanted to be discovered for his greatness. But now he is leading the pack. There is no need for the secret.'

'So, there is no mysterious superhero in the new story?' asked Kanishka.

'No!' confirmed Agastya.

'How does the story end?' I asked.

'The story ends with all of them congratulating Zoey and then having a nice meal of fish together!' said Agastya.

All of them took a minute to ponder over the new story that they had created.

'You know,' said Kanishka, 'I liked the old story better. It had more drama—it had injustice, tragedy, mystery . . .'

'It was great for the listeners, but it was sad for Zoey,' said Anish.

'I agree,' said Agastya. 'The second story has all the right elements—there is a wise elder, bears can be who they are, and they solve problems together. But it doesn't make for a dramatic story.'

'So, what would you choose for yourself—drama or peace of mind?' I challenged.

They went quiet. It is a tough choice. We all love dramas. They make us feel alive even though they are painful.

'There is so much of Zoey in me,' said Agastya finally. 'I think while I would like to watch a movie where the hero dies unsung after doing great things, I don't want to be like that in real life.'

'I think you are the wise old bear, and not Zoey,' said Kanishka admiringly.

'Whatever!' said Agastya, rolling his eyes. But I could see how much he liked that idea.

42

It's Alright, I Understand

Yashodhara

'I'm really sorry about forgetting to call you back a few days ago,' I said to Prithvi. 'It was a crazy week. Apologies for that.' I had seen Prithvi's missed call; I had messaged him saying I would call him back—and then I had forgotten.

'It's alright,' he said with his usual polite smile. 'I understand. It doesn't matter, it was nothing that couldn't wait, really.'

'I see. So, what's been going on for you?'

'Mostly work stuff for me. Otherwise, it's been okay, I guess . . .'

As we spoke further and he went on to talk about upcoming transitions at work, I became aware that the conversation seemed stilted. Prithvi was a quiet, unassuming young man, who had taken a few weeks to open up to me, but of late, our conversations had been warm and rich in insight. I had seen a change in him—from the depressed and hopeless air that he had in the beginning to a more active and engaged way of being. But today felt strange—it was turning into a sort of question-and-answer session. I had the feeling of being walled out by him.

There was a pause in the conversation as I wondered how to ask him what might be going on between us. He filled it by saying nonchalantly, 'By the way, I got promoted.'

'You got promoted!' I exclaimed in surprise and delight. 'Congratulations!'

'Yeah.' He allowed himself just a small smile before looking away. 'Thanks.'

I hovered uncertainly for a moment, feeling deflated by his reaction. And then it hit me. 'Prithvi, are you upset with me?'

'Upset?' he repeated, and then said dismissively. 'No, no. I'm not upset.' And then there was silence again.

'I'm picking up a sense that something is different today,' I said gently. 'Why would you wait till almost midway into the session to tell me something so important?'

'It's not *that* important.' His air was scoffing. 'It was long overdue anyway. No big deal.'

As I heard his words, I realized what had happened—or at least, I thought I could make a good guess.

Prithvi had an uncomfortable relationship with his family and had talked about how he often felt left out in the dynamic with his father, mother, and elder brother. His brother was the dominating one and an achiever who had blazed a trail ahead of him, and Prithvi had always felt like he was expected to catch up. Because he hadn't had the same grades nor the larger-than-life personality, he felt unseen and small. He also had to hear often that he was 'the shy one' in the family, and so he had shrunk into his own world, spending his time reading and daydreaming. As a grown-up now, he displayed the same tendency to feel like the odd one out—whether in his circle of friends or his team at work. He had come into therapy because he was worried about not being able to do well and frustrated at being constantly passed over by his boss for a promotion. With me, he had acknowledged his trouble with speaking up for himself and his work and asking for what was due to him, and now he was casually tossing in a mention of the promotion to me as though it was nothing.

'Prithvi,' I ventured, 'that call you made to me last week that I didn't answer and get back on—it was to tell me about your promotion, right?'

After a second, he just gave a small nod, and then shrugged, his face expressionless.

I realized the feeling of deflation that I had experienced about his reaction was his unconscious communication to me about his own feelings. In not answering that call and, more significantly, in forgetting to get back to him, I had unconsciously reinforced his belief about himself—when he had said dismissively 'It's not important', what he was really saying was 'I'm not important'.

I felt a pull to apologize to him immediately, but first, it was important to bring the unconscious dynamic between us into the realm of the conscious.

'Prithvi, can I ask what did my not calling back mean to you?'

'I don't know,' he said with a little frown. 'As in, initially, I was excited about the news and wanted to tell you—I was afraid of calling home and hearing Dad say something like "It's about time" or give some other dismissive reaction. But when you didn't answer, I told myself that "It's okay, not a big deal; she's probably busy". It was nothing very extraordinary.'

I nodded, and ventured, 'So, because I didn't see you, you dismissed yourself?' I realized I had unconsciously taken on the role of his dad. My 'forgetting' was clinically significant.

He was silent for a long time, and then admitted, 'Yes. I suppose I did that. That's why it's easier for me to not get excited about things.'

'Then you won't be disappointed.'

'Yes,' he said, looking sad.

'Prithvi,' I said, 'I am sorry that I didn't call you back. I feel sad that I missed the opportunity to celebrate with you. You are important, and this promotion is an important event. Can you believe that I am really excited for you?'

Prithvi's face had remained impassive as I spoke, but his eyes had softened. He gave a small smile, 'Thank you.'

'May I ask how you're feeling about my apology?'

He took a while to respond. 'Actually, I don't think I really know how to respond to an apology. Maybe I haven't been apologized to very much.'

'Can you tell me more about that?'

'I'm thinking of Dad right now,' he mused. 'he's *never* apologized to me in my whole life. He's somewhat—almost—afraid of Bhaiyya. Me, he barely seems to notice.'

'And what was his actual reaction when you called home with news of the promotion?'

He looked a little uncomfortable. 'Well, I . . . haven't told them yet. I thought I'd tell them in person when I visit home next week for a couple of days.'

'What has stopped you from sharing this with your father?'

'It's partly my fear of his dismissive reaction,' he said, 'but also, I don't like to tell Dad stuff nowadays. He keeps asking, but I prefer to talk to Mom.'

'You said *he* barely seems to notice you?' I gently pointed out the incongruity.

He was quiet. 'Maybe that's more . . . in my head. It's how I felt when I was a kid. Now, I think he does try and reach out to me a lot more.'

'I wonder if you are angry with him, and it makes you not want to share your good news? Just as you were angry with me and withheld the news of the promotion.'

He was quiet as he reflected on this. He was able to acknowledge his pattern of repressing his anger and turning it into withdrawal. That also protected him from feeling the disappointment of not being seen or celebrated.

I realized later, while reflecting on my work with Prithvi in supervision that I had gotten pulled into the role of Prithvi's dad; his 'I'm not important' was playing out with my becoming 'the busy one' that was 'forgetting' him and Prithvi's becoming the accommodating one, who was 'okay with always being forgotten'. My supervisor stroked me for being authentic with him with my apology and my meaning-making of the forgetting. We also discussed that such moments in the therapeutic relationship provided for valuable corrective experiences for our clients: in receiving a warm and sincere apology from me, Prithvi could acknowledge wanting to feel important, and going forward, would perhaps learn to ask for it in direct ways, rather than shutting out people.

For me, this experience was a reminder that the most potent therapeutic instrument is often a therapist's own self. Learning to be authentic, present, owning our mistakes, and starting over afresh in the relationship with our clients is a part of the healing process. And like many aspects of a relationship, you can't learn that from a book. You have to practise, fall over, get up, and try again. Much like most really important things in life.

43

To Heal, We Must Feel

Aruna

It was a beautiful September morning and nine of us sat in a circle outdoors, under a magnificent Gulmohar tree. We had hired a farmhouse for our group therapy session. The air was fresh and cool. The silence was interrupted only by birds. It was a perfect setting for all group members to connect with their inner worlds.

'Let us talk about "unfinished business" today,' I said to the group.

'*Unfinished business*' in the world of therapy refers to experiences that haven't been processed because the feelings around them are too painful and overwhelming. But the challenge is that repressed feelings don't stay quietly repressed. They show up in seemingly unrelated ways, as chronic body pain or habitual anger or inexplicable tears. As a result, people feel cut off from themselves.

To help the group members get in touch with what their unfinished business might be, I asked, 'What people or circumstances in your life do you have resentment towards? What did you do or fail to do that you regret?'

In a moment, Aditi began to squirm in her chair. I noticed and looked invitingly towards her.

'No, no, I am not ready yet,' she said, resisting the attention.

I waited. My intuition said that she was ready.

After a few moments, Aditi spoke. 'I have never shared this with anyone before,' she said with quivering lips. 'I never even think about this. But your question brought it flooding back.'

'How do you feel about sharing what is alive for you right now, with us?' I asked.

Aditi looked around and experienced the loving encouragement in the eyes and body language of the group around her. She instinctively reached her hand out and Meera, who was sitting next to her, held it supportively. Aditi told us her story.

'This is the first time I am gathering the courage to talk about this. When I was six, my parents left me at home with a sixteen-year-old cousin for caretaking. He undressed in front of me. I was terrified, and I locked myself up in my room with my three-year-old brother for hours, till my parents came back. I was terrified every time they called him to babysit us. It meant I would be locked up in the room or face abuse. The creep would even try knocking on the door, asking me to come out. I somehow never told my parents any of this. They kept calling

him. He would come with a smirk on his face and try to get me to see him. This stopped only when I was around thirteen. Even today, when I see this cousin of mine, he has the same smirk on his face. This incident scarred me so much. I became a tomboy. I would wear boys' clothes all the time. I learnt martial arts. Now that I am married and I have a son, I fiercely protect him. I have taught him about good and bad touch and told him that he can share anything with me. I work with an NGO that educates people on how to protect children from sexual abuse. It fills me with purpose.'

I saw that she shared the story in a stoic way, fighting her emotions. Her energy only perked when she spoke about her work with her NGO. She had sublimated her painful feelings into a sense of purpose.

'How do you feel having shared this with all of us?' I asked.

'Actually, I feel relieved. I thought I wouldn't be able to share it. But now that I have, it doesn't feel so bad,' said Aditi.

'*It* doesn't feel so bad?' I challenged her. Using the word 'it' is a way of distancing ourselves from our feelings.

'I don't want to think more about it.' Aditi's face hardened.

'I sense your sadness,' I said, naming the feeling, 'and I'm feeling sad too. This shouldn't have happened.'

'I feel numb. I think I have learnt to not feel anything around this,' she said.

'Would you like to explore your feelings around this, taking the help of the group?' I encouraged her gently.

Aditi nodded, relieved that the group would get involved. I knew she felt held by the other group members. They had worked together on very personal issues for eight months. Trust had built up.

I invited Aditi to sit next to me. I placed a chair about ten feet in front of us and invited a volunteer to sit on the chair and retell Aditi's story in first person, mirroring her tone, expressions, and body language. Aditi heard her story played back to her. I noticed that her eyes began to glisten.

I then gave the group the following instructions, 'We are now going to help Aditi explore the emotional landscape of her story. Don't change the facts but offer different possible emotional responses to the same situation. For instance, if you feel there is a potential for anger, come and sit on this chair. Speak as Aditi in first person. Express your anger and your reasoning for it. Embody the anger. Use your tone, facial expressions, and gestures powerfully. Say "I am angry that . . ." or "how dare he . . ."'

I turned to Aditi, 'As each member steps in and retells the story offering a possible emotional interpretation for consideration, just listen. You have the right to take only those offers that make sense to you. No explanations are needed. You are free to disagree with, modify, or expand what is presented to you.'

Group members stepped in one by one, offering various emotions that Aditi could have experienced. These were some of the offers they made.

Anger

I am furious with my parents for not protecting me. How could they let this happen? Were they blind?
I am angry with this jerk for traumatizing me when I was only six. I hate this fucking bastard. I want to kill him.
I am angry with myself for not saying anything about it.

Fear

I was terrified all the time that something worse could happen. I feel unsafe all the time.
I feel scared for my son's safety.
I was scared that if I shared it with my parents, they might blame me.

Sadness

I feel sad that I decided that to be a woman was unsafe.
I feel sad that I could never explore or enjoy my sexuality. I feel sad that no one was there for me.
I feel sad that I have lost my capacity to trust.

Disgust

I feel disgusted by what I saw.
I feel disgusted with a culture that allows men to do this and get away with this.

Guilt/Shame

I felt ashamed of being a woman. I feel I have let my parents down. I feel in some way responsible for what happened. I feel guilty for not telling anybody about this.

Curiosity

How come my parents couldn't see the scumbag that this cousin was?
I wonder how they would have reacted had I shared what happened with them.

Pride

I was resourceful enough to lock the door. I took care of my little brother too.
I took charge of myself.
I learnt to protect myself.

Gratitude

It could have been worse.
It allowed me to find a purpose.
I feel grateful that this incident didn't block my capacity to love.

Aditi cried profusely as she listened while holding on tightly to Meera's hand. The process offered her a powerful permission to feel. I had observed her listening carefully to all the offers. Many appeared to be significant to her.

I asked Aditi, 'Would you like to tell your story again?' No other instruction was needed. Aditi wiped her tears, got up and sat on the chair in front of us, and narrated this story.

'I am sad that when I was six, I had to go through sexual abuse the way that I did. I am angry that I had to deal with it alone. I was left alone with someone who was clearly not deserving of that trust. I am angry with myself for protecting my parents instead of protecting me. But I was afraid that they would not believe me. And I thought being beautiful would harm me. I was scared of being attractive. I feel sad that, as a young girl, I could never fully explore what it meant to grow into a young woman. All these years, I believed I was not lovable. It was only after my son was born that I realized how much love one human being can have for another. I could be looking most ridiculous, and he would still have so much love for me.'

Her voice broke and her tears began to flow again, but she went on.

'I know I had the same love for my parents—then why did my parents not protect me like I protect my son? Why were they not here for me? There were so many signs. I was an introvert. I had no friends. I was bedwetting till the age of eleven; no amount of medication was working. Why did they not see the signs? Why did they leave me alone again and again? I wish this was the only guy, but it wasn't. I had cousins who lived in my house forever. I wonder why my parents allowed that. What were they thinking? I feel a deep sense of loss. I lost my childhood.'

This was a very different story from the one that she had narrated a few minutes earlier. She had accessed her anger and sadness. The group had allowed her to recognize and voice many internal feelings and thoughts that she had felt but never expressed. The permission to offer these interpretations as gifts for considerations, and not 'the truth', allowed group members to be bold and empathic improvisers. Their genuine interest also offered a form of compassionate holding. Several group members cried along with Aditi during her second narration.

When she finished, they gathered around her and shared their own experiences with abuse, body shaming, and lack of protection. Aditi felt seen and validated. She also recognized she was not alone. Her guilt and shame transformed to anger and sadness. The experience was painful but not as terrifying as she had imagined it would be.

In therapy, we say '*the only way out is through*'. Facing and accepting her pain offered her a relief that was better than the angst she experienced when avoiding it. In shutting off painful feelings, she had shut off feeling altogether. Today was a day for celebration for she had allowed herself to feel again!

44

Black or White?

Yashodhara

'I am so *clear* about this: I am going to one day be screaming from the rooftops about who I am—a proud gay man!'

'Right. Got it,' I marvelled at Sahil's courage and confidence. 'How do you feel when you think about this?'

'Oh, you have no idea,' he said, a glint in his eyes. 'I'm an activist at heart, and I want to be an advocate for gay rights—it's the purpose of my life. I know how different things would have been for me when I was a kid and when I discovered I was gay—if only I'd had a role model to look up to then, things would have been so much easier for me.'

'What made it the hardest?' I knew the stigma for someone born in the nineties to come out as being gay in India was hard enough, but this fire in Sahil made me curious about his story. Right from the moment he had walked in for his first session, I had been struck by his energy and enthusiasm. He mentioned he struggled with anxiety, had been recommended long-term therapy by his psychiatrist who had diagnosed him with Generalized Anxiety Disorder, and that he 'mostly had it under control and was determined never to take pills.'

'My *parents* made it super hard,' he replied now, his face darkening a little. 'The day I came out to them . . . it had taken me months to work up the courage to tell them, and I chose to do it on my nineteenth birthday. Mom absolutely lost it, went hysterical, all the "why me, why my son", chest-beating and all, tried to talk me out of it! And Dad—it was like he didn't even hear it. He just chose to walk out of the room—he hasn't acknowledged it or talked directly with me about it since.'

'I can see you were very hurt by their reaction,' I said gently.

'Yeah, well.' He looked vulnerable for a split second before shrugging. 'Let's just say it wasn't much of a party on that particular birthday of mine.'

'Right,' I said softly and waited to see if he would say more. But he changed track.

'So, anyway,' he said, straightening up, 'it has served me in finding my purpose. No kid should have to go through what I did—so I'm very clear about my five-year vision: I'll be working full-time towards gay rights advocacy. It's the only thing making my life worth living.'

I paused for a second. 'The "only" thing?'

The question seemed to surprise him. 'Well, in the past, I've been almost suicidal, feeling so worthless about not being able to be open about who I am. This idea brings meaning into my life—that there is a point to what I've been through and that is to educate the world and help other kids through it.'

I nodded, 'Could you tell me more your experience— you mentioned you were almost suicidal?'

'I've had tough times, but I've made sense of it all over the last ten years.' I could see from his blithe tone that even though he spoke about his feelings, it was from the head-level. 'I know I've lacked being understood and accepted; it's taken a lot from me to conquer my sense of worthlessness, but I've fought through it. This is why I get so upset when my friends don't stand up for themselves. I might even end up losing some of my oldest friends at this rate.'

'Why?'

'Well, I have these two friends—both are gay and have known it for years since we were all teens. One hasn't come out to his parents yet, and now it's getting awkward because we are at the typical Indian "why don't you get married" age. The second told his parents recently but has agreed to keep it a secret—from their own relatives!'

'Hmm.' I nodded, indicating that he should go on.

'It drives me crazy!' he said, his voice getting louder. 'I mean, highly educated, well-to-do people in the twenty-first century—if they aren't going to speak up about who they are, what hope do others have?'

'You seem really angry with them,' I commented.

'I *am*—I think they are being cowards,' he emphasized. 'I mean, they keep telling me that I don't get their personal situation, but I can't get how *they* can't take an actual stand—for the gay community, for kids discovering their sexuality . . . I get so mad that eventually, I just have to completely shut up about it.'

I noticed a pattern and decided to share it.

'Sahil,' I began, 'could I play back what I am hearing? You think either your friends should be completely open or they are cowards; you can either tell them exactly what you think or shut up; you can either be a gay rights activist or life isn't worth it . . . do you see a pattern?'

'Well . . . maybe,' he said, a tad defensively. 'My friends say I'm stubborn once I've decided something, and so have folks at work. But I think it's helped me be very clear about my decisions.' He leaned back, arms crossed. 'I need to take clear stands—anything else would be fence-sitting, and I hate that.'

I waited for a few moments, wondering whether and how to help him see that even what he had just said was an example of thinking in extremes; it proved unnecessary. With a sheepish smile, he admitted, 'Okay, I heard how that sounded. Yes. It's quite black and white.'

'That is exactly what it is called! It is a form of grandiosity; sometimes called "All or Nothing" thinking as well,' I told him.

'All or nothing! That describes me quite well.'

'Say more about that?'

He went silent.

'I do get worked up and upset about the way things are. I can be really intense about everything.'

'Being intense about *everything*,' I said gently, noting a sense of tiredness coming over him with that last sentence, 'does that get draining?'

'Yes,' he said, sighing. 'I'm often all fired up, working myself to the bone, full throttle types . . . but then, I crash. My high and low states—like, my anxiety followed by my depression—they seem correlated to this.' He paused for a long while. 'I don't know. I want to change this . . . but I feel really uncomfortable at the idea too.'

'What about it makes you uncomfortable?'

He shrugged. 'My intense feelings about my sexuality, my issues with my parents, my trauma . . . they are all related to my higher purpose. I don't want to lose my fire.'

'Do you know, you tend to use "*my* trauma", "*my* anxiety", "*my* purpose",' I pointed out. 'What do you make of this?'

After a long pause, he spoke with a new sense of recognition. 'I think—all these things, they all make up my identity.' He looked at me, his face vulnerable. 'Maybe I'm scared. If I let go or even loosen my grip on what I believe, will I even know who I am?'

I felt deep empathy for him. He was scared that if he didn't have his purpose and his anger, he would have nothing to hold on to. It seemed superfluous to add anything to his understanding. I just nodded, trusting that my silent presence and acceptance spoke for itself and conveying he was okay right now, and would be, no matter who he discovered himself to be.

In subsequent sessions, we were able to go beneath his anger at society and his friends and uncovered the deep shame he felt at not being accepted by his parents. This shame was what was unbearable and had been substituted by his anger and urgency to change the world.

He realized that his father's disappointment was even more painful for him than his mother's loud reactiveness. As he allowed himself to re-experience the pain of what he had perceived as total rejection, he also got in touch with a deep yearning for closeness to his father. Over the course of a few months, he started initiating more conversations with his dad—which he reported as being reciprocated far more warmly than he had expected.

'Maybe it's not really about screaming loudly from the rooftops,' he said to me reflectively. 'I still want to advocate for gay rights and mentor young people, but there are other things which are also important. I've cut myself off from everything remotely traditional, just because I've been so mad at my parents—whatever they've been interested in, like religion or having a family . . . I've always said "Please! No way! None of that for me!" Well, what if I *do* want to figure out my own faith someday? And maybe I *do* want a long-term relationship and a family of my own. What if I want to adopt someday, even if it means moving out of the country? Maybe living on my own terms in a different place won't be so bad?'

Berne had coined a term called *Anti-script* to describe the pattern of choosing to do the opposite of what one is 'supposed' to do, in a way defying the script. It is a child's way to break away from parental control and domination. However, even though it masquerades as freedom, it is not. The Rebellious Child in us, in violent opposition to parental demands, loses spontaneity, and is as script-bound as the compliant one.

I saw that Sahil was now exploring for himself the various shades of grey in between the extremes of black and white. His fiery air and intensity had indeed come down over the months, but his curiosity and vitality were intact. He seemed okay with not having all the answers, but with exploring new possibilities.

So, I smiled and agreed. 'Maybe.'

45

A New Normal

Aruna

'I've become a celebrity's wife,' wailed Simran. Her husband was a very popular corporate leader. 'He is the most sought-after mentor these days. He has these "Evenings with Indranil" sessions at home, and we have a dozen people coming home every day to seek his advice,' she said with her left eyebrow raised and a twisted smile on her lips.

'What does this mean for you?' I was curious about her disgust.

'This means he has no time for me. And I have to watch these twenty-something college girls come to him for advice and throw themselves at him. They are so starstruck. Uggh!' she shuddered, shaking the disgust off.

'How does he respond to them?'

'He is restrained and dignified, though I know he enjoys the adulation. I don't worry about him leaving me, but . . .'

'But?'

'He is really not attracted to me anymore,' she said as her shoulders drooped. The contempt morphed into sadness.

'Are you missing him?'

'Am I missing him?' she wondered, tilting her head to the side, looking beyond me.

I waited.

'This is very strange. I don't miss him. While I know we don't love each other like we did when we got married, I can't bear the idea of him loving somebody else.'

'Why is this strange?'

'I don't know. It just feels strange,' she looked around as if trying to search for answers.

'Perhaps you are confused by what you are feeling.'

'You are right. I am confused. Do I want us to get back to the way we were? Why else would I feel angry when I see others drooling over him?' She shook her head.

'So, you are angry?'

'I am . . .' her voice trailed off. 'I know our relationship is dead. We have been married almost thirty years now. I know for sure that he can't give me what I want. So why am I holding on to the anger?'

'Your relationship is dead?'

'Yes,' she sighed. 'For many years now, he has had no interest in my life. As long as I was starstruck with him, like the girls who come home these days, we had a relationship. He was in love with how much I loved him. But when my "starstruckness" wore off, our relationship rapidly deteriorated. I think I am a star too. But when he is around, there can be only one star. It is always about how great he is and all the wonderful things he is doing. Well, he is great in many ways, there is no doubt. But there can be two great people. He discounts my feelings, my needs. He is disdainful of my choices, my friends, my family. My need to feel important or safe has never been met with him. So, I created my own world, outside of his. In that world, I am a star.'

'You created your own world?' I was intrigued.

'Yes, I am very proud of it. I have the organization that I built, my friends, and my own support systems of various kinds, from the staff at home, to my doctor, to plumbers, to my financial planner . . . everything. Indranil and I even go on separate holidays.'

'But you have stayed with him for thirty years. How come?'

'I am too chicken to do anything else. I often wonder if I am living a half-life,' she said, her eyes brimming. 'He doesn't see me or cherish me. But he is a responsible partner. He shares parenting responsibilities and helps in managing the house. So, if I don't make any demands on him and tolerate his judgements of me, I can be who I want.'

'What do you mean when you say you are too chicken to do anything else?'

'I feel scared of what the change could look like. I like where we are—socially, that is. We get invited as a couple for dinner with other couples. My life feels normal.'

'Are you happy, Simran?' I was puzzled.

'That is not easy to answer. I am happy that I built my own parallel life. That life is just what I want. I am thrilled with it. Indranil is often disdainful of my "career focus". How dare he?' She raised her chin defiantly. 'It is through my work that I express myself, grow, and make a difference. I have a sense of freedom. And I have a really healthy income that offers security.'

'I can see how proud and fulfilled you are about this,' I affirmed.

'But I am very sad that I can't share this life with my partner,' she ignored my acknowledgement of her. 'Sometimes, I second guess myself. What does all that I have achieved mean if I don't have a partner to share it with? I feel lonely and empty sometimes.'

'Hmmm,' I sighed along with her, 'what would you like for yourself, Simran?'

'I don't like this feeling of emptiness and loneliness. But I don't know what I can do.'

'You have a full, flourishing life on one side, and at the same time, you feel empty because your husband is unwilling to share it with you?'

'Yes. I wonder why?' she sighed. 'I suppose there is a part of me that secretly does hold the expectation that our marriage will come back to normal—though there is enough that tells me it won't.'

'I wonder what you define as normal.'

'Ha ha, good question!' She became reflective for a few seconds, 'I think I am holding on to the image of our very early days in marriage, when we were in love.' Her laughter indicated to me that she recognized the absurdity of an unconsciously adopted image of 'normal' influencing her feelings and choices.

'I thought so. This romantic ideal is popularized in our culture,' I said. 'There is an image of what falling in love looks like and that marriages should be that way throughout. I often think that these ideas of how things "should be" create more harm than we can imagine. They determine our self-worth and how we interact in relationships.'

'I can see what you are saying. We fell in love in college. We were physically attracted to each other back then. We had a vision for the life we would have together. But often, I have felt that was a fleeting period where both of us were delusional. We ignored each other's flaws.'

'The idea of "happily ever after" makes people deeply hopeful about marriage.'

'I did believe then that that excitement and euphoria of being in love would last a lifetime. And Indranil would cherish me and there would be no loneliness.'

'But are you really lonely? Don't you have many friends?'

'I do. I am very proud of my deep friendships. But can these replace being close to your husband?'

'That is a cultural expectation, isn't it? That the relationship with the husband is *the* most special? Is it possible you are discounting the joy that comes to you from other relationships, and maximizing the sadness of this not working?'

'But is this not the most significant relationship for me?'

'Who says that?'

'Well, everybody. Aaaah, that is what you are saying! It is a cultural expectation.'

'Well, the template of a perfect marriage is one where partners are soulmates. They understand each other intuitively. They are attracted only to each other. The attraction doesn't diminish in intensity even after children are born. They have no secrets and want to spend all their time together.'

'Ha ha. You missed saying that they are both good looking and have passionate sex as well,' she laughed.

She became aware that she had taken in some of these cultural beliefs to be the truth. This is what in TA we call a *contamination* of our Adult. Parental demands (*you must have a soulmate for a partner*), and corresponding Child conclusions (*I don't have one, so my life is empty*) are mistaken for the here-and-now reality.

Simran sighed, 'Well, mine is far from that ideal. We have a practical marriage. We have been responsible parents. We take care of each other when sick. Otherwise, we pursue our own lives. We are like roommates who aren't really great friends but are non-intrusive and responsible.'

'The way you described it just now is different from how you described it earlier. The idea of loneliness does not dominate this.' I observed that she was challenging the contamination.

Simran pondered over what I said.

'I know your marriage is not what you would like,' I said gently, 'yet you are not choosing to walk away.'

'No, I am not. I love my independent life too much. I am not motivated to search for love again. I worry about losing this independence. And everyone has flaws. I may end up feeling lonely again.'

'So, you are *choosing* to be in this relationship because something is working for you. Then why the sadness?'

'I guess I do have a picture of how I should see my marriage, and I agree this is very cultural. And when I judge my life against these standards that I have adopted, I feel I have failed, I feel ashamed and small.'

'So, you are sad because your life is not picture-perfect.'

'Yes! Am I delusional? Expecting every aspect to work perfectly?'

'What do you think?'

'Rationally I agree. But I cannot get rid of the ideal expectation—that I come home to a partner who is interested in my endless rambling about my day. Now that the children are grown up, I keep asking "Who am I coming home to?"'

'How is holding on to this expectation serving you?'

'It makes me miserable. I need to do something about it. Either I open myself to the idea of leaving him or accept that this will be a practical relationship where we will just be sharing an apartment, not really our lives.'

'Do you have no hope at all that you could revive the intimacy?'

'No, none. Years of hurt have accumulated. We want very different things in life. I cannot tolerate taking second place to him anymore.'

We both paused and took in the significance of all that had emerged. 'So, Simran, where are you at the end of this session?'

'I can now see that my marriage cannot fulfil all my expectations. The love and romance is gone—I need to accept that. It is a practical arrangement that feels like the best among available options. So, what has really changed is that I am choosing to not see it as a calamity. I have my independent life, and I am going to enjoy it. Giving up my sadness around this can free my energy up for newer experiences. I want to accept my marriage without comparing it to any ideal standard.'

Norms such as 'A marriage without love is a disaster' or 'One must always be happy' or even that 'One will eventually find true love' can be tenacious. These culturally inherited ideologies are enemies of satisfaction and acceptance. I was moved by Simran's courage to challenge these contaminations and find her own normal.

'So, Simran, you asked yourself "Who am I coming home to", and what is your answer?'

She took a deep breath and said with conviction, 'I am coming home to myself.'

'That sounds like a modern fairy tale ending—coming home to self!' I said admiringly.

'I love it! Definitely more realistic than the "happily ever after" idea! And it doesn't set me up for disappointment. I can come back to whoever I am without judgement,' she said, her eyes shining.

46

They Don't Really Want Me

Yashodhara

'Well, they offered me the job,' Brinda said, a sheepish smile on her face.

'Really? Congrats!' I was delighted but couldn't keep the surprise out of my voice—Brinda had lamented in the last session how she had 'screwed up' the final interview for the new company. We had spent the hour processing her disappointment and learnings from the experience. Even though I had offered the possibility that it might not have been as bad as she thought, she had been adamant in 'knowing it wasn't going to happen'.

Her smile widened for an instant but still didn't quite reach her eyes. I asked, 'How are you feeling about this?'

'Good.' Her reply was automatic. Then she paused and said, 'I don't know.'

I had learned by now that Brinda's '*I don't know*' was a qualifier to almost everything she said. So, I just waited.

'It's just that . . .' she seemed uncomfortable, 'I genuinely wasn't expecting them to make me the offer. And it came out of the blue, so I'm not sure I've fully registered it yet.'

'I see. When did you hear from them?'

'Five days ago.'

'So, it's been five days—and it hasn't sunk in?' I was trying to understand her experience.

'I know it seems weird,' she said, 'but . . . I don't know. It's like, the first two days, I couldn't even believe I had made it.'

'It is a significant achievement,' I said. 'You mentioned it's been eight rounds of interviews!' She shrugged. I noted that my stroke didn't seem to land but went on, 'So, the first two days you couldn't believe it . . . and then, in the last three days?'

'Oh,' she let out a sarcastic laugh. 'I guess this thought came to me—the HR Head there had mentioned they have a strong focus on diversity. So . . .' Her voice trailed off and she looked away.

'You think they chose you because they had to fill a quota?'

'It's hard to get women at a senior level, right?' Brinda answered my question with a question, still avoiding my eye.

I said gently, 'What's going on inside you right now?'

'Oh, I don't know,' she said. 'I guess I've also been worrying about it in terms of . . . it's an important role, reporting directly to the CEO. They've chosen me, but what if I just conveyed something in the interviews that isn't really *me* . . . and then I end up letting them down?'

'So, you got the news of being selected,' I said slowly, 'and your reactions have been—first, surprise. Then, doubt about whether you got in just because you're a woman. And finally, a fear you'll let them down?'

She took this summary in, and then sighed. 'I don't know. I mean, it's weird. But I just have this feeling that they don't really want me.'

'They don't really want you.' It sounded familiar to me, and then I remembered. 'Three months ago when you decided you would apply outside your current organization, you used this phrase about your team here—"They don't really want me."'

This seemed to strike her. 'Yeah. I guess that's true. I think—I guess—I often feel that.' Her mouth twisted into an ironic smile. 'I'm even feeling it in advance in this case!'

'Have you at all celebrated the news of the job?'

'Not really,' she squirmed. 'I mean, my husband has been telling me we should go out and celebrate. He's been acting all happy, and says he is proud of me. But it's just making me more uncomfortable—like he doesn't really understand what my work is like. Anyway, it's more like . . . he's always my biggest cheerleader. That's his job!'

'He has been acting all happy? Says he is proud of you?' I repeated. 'Could it be possible that he may actually *be* happy for you and proud of you?'

She looked impassive and didn't respond, but I could sense her internal agitation.

'So, Brinda,' I began again after a pause, 'when I said congratulations to you, what did that mean for you?'

She looked even more uncomfortable now, 'I don't know. It was like . . . I mean, you were being nice and happy for me, but I felt like maybe you also were just saying that. Like . . . you're my therapist, after all.'

'Do you see how you are discounting the strokes coming your way?' I asked gently, 'The job is yours, but that's *just because* you're a woman or gave the wrong picture about your capabilities; your husband is proud of you, but that's *just because* it's his job; I'm delighted for you, but that's *just because* I'm your therapist . . .'

She smiled sheepishly again, 'Yeah, I guess I'm just one of those people who can't take a compliment.'

'Even though plenty of compliments come your way!' I emphasized. 'What do you imagine could be going on for you?'

'I don't know. I just find it difficult to believe them.'

'I imagine a kind of wall around you,' I shared the imagery coming up for me.

'Yes, nothing can get to me. The compliments just hit the wall and fall off.'

'That is a solid stroke filter. No way a stroke could impact you.'

'That is right.'

'So, the wall protects you from strokes?' Brinda looked surprised, 'Maybe.'

'Do strokes remind you of some pain?'

'I am not sure.' She was frowning with concentration. 'I mean, I know that I find it difficult to believe anything good anyone says about me. But when you say it gets tossed back . . .' Her brow cleared. 'Actually, most people do seem a little taken aback by how awkward I am about deflecting compliments. Then they don't offer them anymore. Except my husband. He's quite relentless.'

'He sounds like he really loves you,' I mused. Her face looked vulnerable, but she didn't react to this at all, apart from a tiny shrug.

'Did you just think,' I went with my intuition, *that's his job?*' She laughed out loud. 'Yeah, that's what went through my head.'

'Tell me about the strokes you received as a child, Brinda?' I asked, 'What do you remember your parents or other significant people praising you for?'

'I don't know!' she said automatically, and then, 'I did well in school—I wasn't as pretty or ladylike as my sisters. The eldest one was the real beauty, and the one older than me was charming and cute too. I was the awkward, ugly one.' She laughed in a scoffing way. 'Nothing much has changed.'

I noticed how the question about strokes had resulted in an enumeration of her negative qualities. I felt a wave of sadness and hopelessness at how severe her inability to see good in herself was. I wondered suddenly where all this had really begun for her. Instinct propelled me to ask, 'What do you know about your birth?'

'Not much,' she said in a deadpan way. 'I was quite small at the time.'

I had to smile. Her flashes of humour were a defence that came through sometimes, but I didn't want to get sidetracked, 'Tell me what you have heard about your birth story?'

'Not much. Well, I was a pain even before I was born apparently,' she said with a sigh. 'I've heard Mom saying it so many times—that it was the most difficult of her three pregnancies. She was sick and exhausted throughout, had complications all through her third term, and finally, labour had to be induced. Then, the procedure went wrong because I had my feet down or whatever, and then there was a surgery—and there I was. Small and sickly, apparently, but finally out.'

'And how do you believe you were received?'

'You're kidding me?' She rolled her eyes. 'I was the third girl and not even healthy.'

'You know they wanted a boy?' I asked.

'It's like that in my family,' she said, without expression. 'My uncle once told me some distant relative who couldn't have kids of their own had asked my mom if they could have me since I was the third girl, and then my parents might try for a boy instead!'

'How old were you when your uncle told you this?'

'About six, I think.'

'Did you talk to your parents about it?'

'Maybe I did ask mom once,' she said. 'She just said it was all hogwash.'

'Did you believe her?'

She remained silent, but I saw the hurt on her face. I was struck by the similarity between her birth story and current experience—'I'll struggle to get there, but then find no one really wants me.' She believed she was unwanted as a child. In being who she was, she felt as though she had let down her parents. In her fantasy, they might have been better off without her.

I could now see how Brinda's working hard and constantly struggling to achieve was her way of achieving a 'conditional OK-ness'—which was 'I'm OK, as long as I'm trying hard'; but she was unable to enjoy the fruits of her work, because at a deep level, she believed she had no place in the world and that she would need to earn it by always trying hard. I could now see why she protected herself from praise—it didn't fit with her view about herself being fundamentally unwanted. In any case, strokes for 'doing' could never replace strokes for 'being'.

'You believed they didn't really want you,' I said, compassionately. The colour drained from her face.

For the rest of the session, I held space for her to explore the pain and hopelessness that she felt deep inside. These were feelings based on an underlying idea that she had now allowed herself to acknowledge: that she had no right to exist and would always have to try—in vain—to earn that right.

Carl Rogers would call *unconditional positive regard* from a therapist a key contributor of the healing process. In this space, and in relating to the therapist, clients can begin to take in that they are OK, that they matter and that their feelings are important.

Today, I could offer Brinda my silent compassionate presence, as she started to finally acknowledge—and grieve for—her unhappy little child-self. The one that didn't know yet, but hopefully would learn with time and more work inside and outside of therapy, that she *did* belong and that she had a right to *be*—just as she was.

47

The Drama of Life

Aruna

'I have thoughts that I don't like,' said Mihira, scrunching her nose. 'I feel guilty for having them.'

'What are these?' I enquired.

'I have spent the last year with my parents. I came here for the summer vacation with my children and got stuck here because of the lockdown. I am now seeing how difficult it is for my parents to manage by themselves. My being here has been a great help to them but catch them acknowledging that! Now I am in a dilemma. They won't come back with me to Coimbatore. Nor will they allow me to appoint a caregiver for them here. They are paranoid about anybody else living with them.' She snorted, slapping her hand on her forehead, 'They have delusions about being murdered in the middle of the night! They just love drama!'

I was all too familiar with the challenges of caring for the elderly and dealing with an ailing but excessively stubborn mother. I remembered my mother double locking three doors every night. I instantly found myself over-identifying with Mihira.

'They hate allopathic medicine,' she went on. 'I have to struggle with them for weeks for them to agree to consult a doctor!'

'And do they refuse to have the medicines they have prescribed, after you have bought them?' I asked, dipping into my own experience.

'Yes!'

'And do they groan and moan about their pain and discomfort, while not supporting any effort to get them any relief?'

'Yes!' She threw her hands up in the air. 'Exactly!'

We both laughed. It was a moment of connection. I bet both of us were thinking at that moment, 'Here is one person who understands my pain.' I visualized us huddling together, commiserating with each other over our shared stories.

'You mentioned you were having thoughts that you did not like,' I said, pulling myself into the present. I attended to my breath and reminded myself of my role. In some moments, the boundaries between therapist and client come across as unwanted barriers that limit spontaneous expression. But the boundaries are protective. My awareness and training reminded me that I was there in service of the client, not to look for new friendships. And it was important for me to separate my feelings from hers. 'So, what are these thoughts?'

'I am sometimes so angry, that I say to myself "Serves them right!" They make it really difficult for me to help them.'

I smiled kindly, 'And you feel guilty for having these thoughts?'

'Oh, terribly.' She held her head in her hands. 'They are old now. Even though I am angry, I don't want to punish them for their behaviour.'

'Murderous thoughts don't make a person a murderer,' I invited her to be kind to herself.

'I know,' she let out a sigh.

'What do you think feels like punishment here?'

'My leaving them alone here, to suffer like this in their old age.'

'Are you leaving them? I thought they were refusing to come with you?' I highlighted the incongruence.

'Well, yes, they are refusing to come. But a part of me says that I must not heed their protests and take them with me somehow.'

'How would that work out for them? And for you?'

'It would actually be miserable for all. They have been in this village house for over fifty years. Living in an apartment in the city without their social circle will be a nightmare for them. And I will have to tolerate their incessant complaints the whole day and I will turn into a mean, horrid bitch.'

'If it is going to be this miserable, why would you want to do this?'

'I can't leave them to die here!' She looked indignant.

I paused.

'And you said *they* loved drama?' I smiled gently.

'Oh.' A grin appeared on her face as she heard me, '*I* am the drama queen.'

'My sister stays out of all the drama,' she continued, 'She is in Singapore. She calls often and chats with them but has not moved her butt to India to do anything for them. They seem to have no complaints about her; in fact, they are always praising her—but they have tons of complaints about me trying to help them.'

'She doesn't help; she gets praised. You help; your help is not valued,' I summarized. 'You feel angry and frustrated.'

'That is my story! To them, I am a pain in the ass because I want to help.'

'What if you don't help?'

'My dad had a mild stroke six months ago. If I had not been here, he would have died. My mother didn't have the resources to call an ambulance or get him to the hospital in time.'

'Caring for elders is tough. People often understand the challenges of the elders. But the challenges of caregivers are rarely understood.'

'I find it so difficult to be compassionate. Worse, I have become unkind and judgemental. I find that they are just not able to see reality and accept it. They love their own groaning and moaning.'

'What would they see as help?'

Mihira paused for a long time.

'What is going on for you?' I asked.

'I don't like the answer that is coming up. What they want is that I listen to them and sympathize with their groaning and moaning. That is just what my sister does.'

'Why don't you like it?'

'Because that is not what they need. And it is easy for her to be the good one. If I spoke to them for thirty minutes, once a week, even I could be all sugar and honey.'

'Are you angry with her? Is there an old wound there?'

'Yes, she always chooses the easy way out. And yet, she is the one they love more,' she slumped into her chair.

She then went on to speak about her fury at the injustice, her sadness at always being the second choice for her parents, and her long-standing envy of her sister. 'I have always done so much more for them than she has. I don't know what else to do to get them to see me,' she choked, beginning to cry. She was still the little girl trying hard to get her parents to love her as much as they loved her sister.

She reached out for a glass of water, blew hard into a tissue, and then looked up.

'I see how exhausting it has been for you, working hard to get their love,' I said gently. 'I see your bewilderment, your grief, and your loneliness.'

She welled up again, 'Maybe I am so caught up in trying to prove my worth, that I am unable to see what they really need.'

I was moved by her vulnerability and authenticity as she said that. These moments of poignant insight are what make therapy such a fulfilling experience for me.

'I don't want to struggle like this with them any longer. I am tired.'

'So how will you be with them instead?'

'I must remember that they love drama. And that their life will always have drama. I don't have to get pulled in. I wish I could laugh about it rather than get all worked up.'

'So, you want to be an observer of their drama without getting pulled into it?'

'Yes. But I am unable to differentiate when it is drama and when there is something more serious. Like when my dad says "I want to die, and I am tired of living."'

'You are wondering whether he really wants to die or whether he wants your sympathy?'

'Yes, and I get angry because he doesn't realize how panicky that makes me. I shout at him for not taking care of his health.'

'So you get pulled in.'

'Yes, I do.'

'What if he wants to die—would that be okay?'

'Both of them say that so often. They say they want to die in the Kerala house, nowhere else,' she said, accessing her vulnerability again. 'Maybe I should accept that they don't want to leave.' She was twisting her fingers in her lap.

'You love them and can't bear the thought of their dying.'

She shook her head silently, looking down, tears pouring down her cheeks.

'And because they don't visit doctors or take their medication, you feel helpless.' She nodded wordlessly, still looking down.

I went on gently, 'And they say that they want to die. And that makes you panic.'

She sighed and then said, 'Maybe it is okay that they want to die. It is okay for me to respect what they want, even though it makes me sad. Perhaps they are just saying it to create some drama. Perhaps they really want to. Whatever the reason, it is what they are saying they want.'

She had cut to the heart of the matter.

I experienced her as calm and open to contact, even though she was immensely sad. The calm from facing and accepting the idea that her parents might die prevailed over the painful content of it.

'Stay with the significance of what you said just now,' I said.

Mihira closed her eyes. Her face was calm, and her breath was steady. 'I need to give up trying to control what I can't. Whatever is meant to happen will happen.'

'So, what are you thinking now?' I enquired. 'About going back to Coimbatore without them?'

'I think I will go back. And trust that the universe will keep them safe. I am not too far away. I can reach them in a few hours if they need me.' I could see that Mihira was giving up the illusion of a perfect solution.

'And if they want to die . . .' She bit her lip.

'Finish the sentence,' I encouraged.

'I will honour that.'

It is a myth that psychotherapy offers solutions. Often it is about giving up illusions of who you, others, or life 'should' be. It is a tender-hearted and bitterness-free acceptance of the idea that we will travel through agony as an inevitable part of life.

48

The Golden Boy

Yashodhara

'Is this a new painting? It's quite lovely. You always pick up unusual colourful things,' said Aarav as he settled into his seat across from me.

I smiled with pleasure. Aarav always had something nice to say. He was a very likeable young man, well-turned-out and well-mannered. It was our third session, and we had not yet arrived at a contract or explicit agreement on our main goal together. He had come into therapy because he said he had heard from many of his friends that it benefited them and was curious about what he might be missing about himself.

'How has your week been, Aarav?'

'Very well, thank you,' he answered, adding graciously. 'And yours?'

'It was good.' I smiled and asked, 'What might you like to talk about today?'

'You know,' he said, leaning forward, 'I still can't put my finger on this "what might be missing" feeling. I'm getting recognized at work already for my contributions and may get to the next level quicker than anyone else—unheard of pace, really; things with the girlfriend are great; Mom and Dad are happy I'm back to finally living with them after those years abroad. I mean, let's face it, they're getting older—it's important I'm around. So, I don't know. I'm wondering . . . am I just looking to "fix what ain't broke"?'

'How do you feel right now as you say that, Aarav?'

'I'm feeling I may be a little self-indulgent in this whole quest.'

'That's what you are thinking,' I said gently. 'Can you describe what you are feeling?'

'Oh, yes, of course,' he said smoothly, and then paused. 'Guilty maybe? A little confused?' After another moment's hesitation, he added, 'Am I just creating problems where none exist?'

I did a mental run through of our conversation last week; and realized that he was discounting something. 'Aarav, when we spoke last week, you said your work hours have increased so much that it's hard for you to get more than four hours sleep a night; that your girlfriend is under pressure for marriage and you're much younger, only twenty-six, and not thinking about it; and that your parents still having fights after all these years has taken you by surprise. So, what do you think? Are you really "creating problems where none exist"?'

'I mean, if you put it that way . . .' he laughed, 'I guess what I'm saying is these are all niggling little things that are always there. Overall, I feel I should be grateful. You know, look at the bright side.'

I went with my instinct, 'Tell me about your ability to look at the dark side, Aarav?'

'Hahaha.' He said, 'I suppose I am not in that habit. I've just been so lucky growing up.'

'You mentioned you're an only child and your parents had you quite late,' I said curiously, 'What was it like for you growing up?'

'Oh, I had everything I ever wanted,' he said with a smile. 'I'm so grateful to both of them. They'd worked so many years building their business together but always wanted a child. They were so happy to finally have me. Mom was almost forty—very late, especially for those days. They've always given me the best of everything, I've never lacked a thing—their time, attention, money. All of it.'

'So, you've been quite the apple of their eye?' I asked.

'*Apple*, I don't know . . . if at all, maybe one of those Golden apples,' he said, flashing me a smile. 'I guess I've been a bit of the golden boy.'

'The golden boy?' I repeated. Something about that phrase fit quite well. He was quite princely and had a perfect, polished shine about him.

'It's funny,' he said, his smile a little tight now. 'I actually was voted the Golden Boy in school. I was that kid who did everything—topped school, best at sports, debates, music, drama, art, you name it. I had tutors and classes for almost everything and my parents were always so encouraging of all my talents.' He sighed as if a little tired. 'My teachers loved me too.'

'What was that sigh about?'

'I'm not sure. Well, I was just thinking—not everyone loved me. Some of the students gave me a hard time,' his face darkened slightly. 'I tend to invite jealousy a lot.'

'So, there *are* people who don't like you?'

'Of course,' he laughed and then stopped abruptly. 'There are always a few such wherever I go—usually my peers. Competition, I guess.'

'How do you feel about their not liking you?' I noticed a new steely look in his eyes.

'I don't enjoy it.' His tone was distinctly less warm now. 'I do tend to make extra effort to get them to like me, but it doesn't work. Feels unfair. But then, I feel lucky that those who count always like me.'

'Those who *count*?'

'Yes. Bosses. My parents. Teachers. Girlfriend.' He cocked his head and grinned. 'The people with the power.'

'The people with power,' I mused. 'I notice these folks are all usually senior—much older than you? Even your girlfriend?'

He considered this. 'Yes . . . I sort of gravitate towards older people. Feel a natural connection with them.'

'And how do you feel about your connection with me?' I asked.

'Oh, I have been very comfortable, from day one,' he said immediately. He hesitated for a moment. 'I didn't tell you this, but when my friends talked about their therapists, one of the first criteria I had in my mind was *I* wouldn't go for anyone around my age, or even in their thirties. When my aunt recommended you, I guess I knew I'd benefit from interacting with someone mature.'

It was a well-chosen word, and I saw again his natural ability to say the right thing. I was beginning to make some connections—he gravitated towards people older than him and seemed to then make it very easy for those people to like him too. I fell into a reverie thinking about how I had been charmed by him even from the sound of his voice when he had first called to speak to me.

I was still thinking about this and formulating my next question, when I noticed he looked uncomfortable. He blurted out, 'Everything okay?'

I wondered where his question was coming from and asked, 'Why would you ask?'

'Oh, nothing,' he said, with a little frown on his face. 'You just went quiet. I mean . . . well, I thought maybe I said something wrong. I am rambling on and on a bit, aren't I? I thought I offended you by talking about your age.'

I nodded. 'When I went silent, you wondered if you had done something wrong?' This seemed to open up something in him and he became reflective.

'I think . . .' he said with the air of one making a confession. 'Silence can be . . . difficult for me. Even with my girlfriend, I find, when she goes all quiet and sulky, it's much tougher for me than if she's openly mad at me.'

'What do you remember about dealing with silence when growing up?'

He paused for a second. 'Mom was usually very cheerful and bubbly, but she and Dad would fight, and then she'd become very quiet. Well, so would he! The whole house would go silent.'

'What was it like for you if they went quiet?'

'Well, Dad would disappear and do his work in his study or go to the office or whatever, so I don't know if that affected me much. But Mom—I guess I'd feel I should do something to just cheer her up. Draw something or show or tell her something I thought she might like.'

'And then?'

'Usually, it would work. She'd cheer up, and call me her little sunshine, or the joy of her life . . .' his voice trailed off.

'You were her Golden Boy?' I offered softly. He nodded, looking rueful.

I went on, 'So it seems you often saw Dad being angry and Mom being sad—what was it like when *you* were feeling those things?'

His frown was deeper this time. 'Actually, I don't recall being upset too often. I had everything, right?' He crossed and uncrossed his legs, foot tapping against the desk lightly. 'I think the only time I'd be upset was if *they* were unhappy, especially if it was with me.'

'If they did get unhappy with you, what did it mean to you?'

'I felt super guilty. I've always heard about how long they waited for me to come along and then, I've seen them not really . . . get along, you know. I suppose I've always had the feeling they stuck together just for me.'

I nodded slowly. Perhaps this was where his desire to look on the bright side and be grateful came from, as well as guilt for feeling anything negative—it seemed to be a long-standing idea that he perhaps owed everything to the older, powerful people in his life and so, felt the pressure of having to keep them happy.

'You know, you came into therapy asking what you might be missing,' I said. 'And I hear you now questioning whether asking this question is self-indulgent, that you should be grateful, that you should look on the bright side. How about we talk about what you *actually* feel? Is it possible that what is missing is the permission for you to look at your own dark side? The part that is less than ideal?'

I saw the flash of vulnerability on his face; it was perhaps the first time the mask had dropped.

The Golden Child Syndrome is a term used to describe what happens when a child is loved with 'troubling intensity'; the pressure that Aarav had felt from a very early age was from messages about being long-awaited and special and destined for greatness and to hold his family together by pleasing his parents constantly—it was natural that his main driver was 'Be Perfect'. What ended up missing for him was the ability to be in touch with his own feelings, to please himself, to know what he wanted for himself, and most importantly, to make mistakes and be imperfect. In pushing away any emotions other than gratitude and joy, and in not acknowledging that he—like everyone else—had a side to him that was less than glorious, he was unable to experience wholeness. He was now able to describe and make sense of a hitherto inexplicable sense of hollowness. With this recognition, our work could finally begin.

And as it often happens in therapy, I could thank a seemingly innocuous event—a few seconds of silence on my part—that led to our discovering so much.

49

Texting 'I Love You'

Aruna

'I miss Emma,' sighed Zubair, and then looked confused. 'Should I tell her?'

Zubair had travelled to India from Australia when Covid struck. His company had subsequently shut down and he lost his job. Emma had been his colleague in Australia.

'I was there for six years, and never realized how significant she was for me. She doesn't even know how I feel about her!'

'What stops you from telling her that you miss her now?'

'Will I come across as weak?'

We discussed the difference between being weak and being vulnerable. I shared with Zubair that vulnerability was the capacity to reveal one's own feelings and needs, even when there was a risk of attack or rejection. So vulnerability required courage. It wasn't weak.

'Why don't you imagine Emma to be here on this chair, and say what you want to say to her? Experience for yourself what vulnerability feels like.'

Zubair gathered himself, closed his eyes for a moment and opened them again, and then addressed the empty chair across from him, 'I really want to come to Australia to see you, but COVID makes it impossible. There is no point waiting . . .' He stopped, turned his head to the side and said, 'This sounds vague. I don't even know that she is waiting.'

'Remember you are practising being vulnerable.'

Zubair straightened his back and said, 'Emma, I miss you.'

He smiled with relief after he heard himself. 'That is it. That is all I want to say to her.' I smiled, 'How do you feel as you say this?'

'I was scared. But I relaxed the moment I said it. I am not asking her to say yes or no to anything,' Zubair said brightly.

When we met the next week, he announced, 'I told her I missed her!'

'How did she respond?' I asked.

'She smiled and said she missed me too. And then we chatted for an hour about life in general. I felt thrilled.'

'Great, then!' I cheered.

'No, no. You haven't heard the whole story,' he continued. 'In the evening, I don't know what came over me. I sent her a text message saying "I love you. But I know there is no possibility for us to meet in the future, so goodbye."'

'Oh!' I exclaimed, quite puzzled by the message.

'She replied by text. "We are in different places right now. I can't give you what you deserve. I hope this doesn't make our relationship weird."'

'And how did you make sense of this?' I asked curiously.

He said darkly, 'I have blown this. I was stupid. I am not even sure that I love her. I just know I miss her. I sent such a confusing message. She probably thinks I should grow up. I have made it weird for both of us!' His voice cracked.

'How are you feeling?' I asked, sensing shame.

However, he was too agitated to hear what I said, 'Should I write to her again? Should I tell her that my "I love you" message was sent in haste, and I don't really "love" her?' His hands flew to his head, and he was all but pulling his hair now. 'Should I lie low for a while? I don't know what to do next!'

I noticed the strong urge in me to respond with advice. However, I stayed grounded, containing his anxiety in silence. I slowed down my breathing and invited him to trust his own thinking. 'How would you know what to do next?'

However, Zubair responded tangentially, 'I asked many friends.'

'You want others to think for you?' I confronted gently.

Zubair ignored what I said. 'I just need someone to tell me what to do.' I waited.

Zubair continued, 'She might never want to talk to me again!'

'Are you assuming the worst?' I asked.

'Yes, because at the end of the day, I have to deal with the worst.'

'What does that mean?'

'Finally, I am the one who will end up sad.'

'Is that what you believe? That finally, you will be sad?'

Zubair continued to ignore my questions, and pulled out his phone, 'What does this line from her mean: "I cannot give you what you deserve?"'

'Who can answer that?'

'Well, I know only she can. But I don't want to ask her.'

'Why not?'

Zubair buried his head in his hands and didn't answer my questions. The session ended inconclusively. I found myself worrying about him throughout the week.

To my surprise, he came to the next session with a smile.

'I must say I am relieved to see you smiling. So, what happened?'

'I thought about it. I was kicking myself for saying "I love you." I thought I had misread the situation. I have always been attacked for doing something wrong. But here, I did nothing wrong, but I was still attacked.'

'Attacked? Who attacked you?'

'Emma.'

'In what way?'

'She made me feel like my message came out of the blue. But there was something between us. She had led me on. She never acknowledged that. I felt like a fool.'

'I see something has shifted about how you are seeing the situation. You are angry with her.'

'Yes, I wasn't all wrong. She is also partly to blame.'

'I see that you are able to be reflective today. Shall we look at what made you send the "I love you" message in haste?'

'I have been wondering too. When things were going well, I blew it.'

'Be kind to yourself. This is an unconscious process. Outwardly, it feels like self-sabotage, but internally, it does protect you in some way. Let us unravel it.'

Zubair leaned forward in anticipation.

I asked him, 'What did you conclude when she said "I can't give you what you deserve"?' The outcome of a psychological game can give us clues about the players' unconscious motivations.

Zubair looked sad and mumbled, 'I thought I wasn't good enough for her.' I took a risk, 'I wonder if you think you will be good enough for anybody.' Zubair nodded, and I noticed the colour draining from his face.

'What's going on for you, Zubair?'

He paused and then began, 'All the people I've loved were taken away from me.'

He went on to share that he was raised by his grandmother, as his parents had moved to another town to set up a business. His parents would come to see him on weekends. Every time they left, he would cry. His mother would say, 'If we don't go, where will the money come from?' His mother's younger sister and her husband also

lived with the grandmother. But they had some differences
with her and decided to leave. Zubair was six then. When
he asked his grandmother why they were leaving, she had
said, 'Everything you love will eventually go away from
you.' Perhaps she was angry with them. She didn't let them
say goodbye to Zubair and called him selfish when he said
he missed them.

'So, you felt attacked or judged when you expressed
your feelings and needs.'

'Yes, I was always put down for it. I expected that I
would be attacked.'

'What did you conclude from these experiences?'

'My parents cared about money more than they cared
about me. If my aunt loved me, she would have known
how unsafe I felt without her. She would not have left.'

'You concluded that they didn't love you.'

'I did,' he said thoughtfully.

'The adults around you did not show up as they should
have. You have had to deal with frightening feelings on
your own.'

Zubair nodded, looking sad.

'What would you have liked your aunt to have done?'

'She should not have left. Or at least she should have
told me why she was leaving.'

'She should have done that. She should have hugged
you and said goodbye. The adults were caught up in their
own issues and you were ignored in the process.'

'As you say this, I am feeling angry. Neither my mother,
nor my aunt directly confronted my grandmother.'

'Tell me more about your anger.' I observed his feelings transforming.

'Nobody cared about the impact of all this on me. They were just caught up in their own fights. Nobody got along with my grandmother. They all left to find their own spaces but left me with her. I am feeling so mad. And all the while I was thinking that there was something wrong with me!'

That was a very important moment in our work. I waited to let the significance of that insight sink in.

'I often imagined they left because they didn't love me.' He went silent.

'How are you feeling now?'

'I am scared,' he looked up at me, 'about whether I will be able to love myself or another.'

'I can see how scary the feeling of love can be for you. It feels unfamiliar, unpredictable, carrying the risk of abandonment.'

'Is that why I sent Emma that "I love you" message in a rush?'

I paused. 'Could be. There is certainly some process there. What did you believe the outcome of the message would be?'

'It was bound to fail,' he admitted with a sigh, 'The message was ill-timed. I was unsure. The medium of communication was wrong. And it was confusing.'

'So, this act of sending a message that is likely to fail— how does it serve you?'

Zubair was silent.

'Am I proving to myself that I am not lovable?'

'Stay with the question and see what answer comes up for you!' I said. 'Getting close to people feels unfamiliar to you. Being unloved is more familiar and therefore, safe and predictable.'

Zubair nodded. 'I see the connection. With Emma too, I believed that if she cared about me, she would know how vulnerable I was.'

'That is similar to "if my aunt knew how scared I was, she wouldn't have left."'

'Exactly, but my aunt had her own challenges. She did love me. Emma has her own challenges too.'

'And perhaps she does love you, but not in the way you would like.'

'I was actually really happy with what we had. What I see now is that, perhaps, I believed it was too good to be true and acted in ways that the outcome felt more true to me.'

'I couldn't have expressed it better!'

'I need to learn to love myself,' sighed Zubair.

'And that's our work for the forthcoming sessions,' I said kindly.

We were moving towards the heart of healing work—loving and accepting ourselves.

50

Addicted to Therapy

Yashodhara

'I don't know where to begin! Such a long gap; you have no idea how much has happened over the holidays,' Komal said in a rushed manner. 'Let me start with what's going on with Rajiv, and then I'll come to the work scene—major developments there too . . .'

I could see that this was going to go the usual way. Despite a whole year of work with Komal, it was always just one crisis after the other, and I felt I needed to intervene.

'Just a minute, Komal,' I said, 'do you remember we agreed before the holidays that we would relook at how we are working together as we start our second year? Today's the first session, so I was hoping we could first pull back a little and review where we're going.'

'Where we're going!' She laughed a little nervously, running a well-manicured hand through her straight black hair. 'You sound like every boyfriend of mine ever—just before a break-up. I hope you're not breaking up with me?'

Komal had no idea how unwittingly close she had come to something that I had actually been thinking about. I'd been frustrated with her focus on her problems without taking action, and her constant reaching out to me between sessions—there was always one crisis or the other in her life; I had taken her case to my supervisor for discussion, and recognized it was really important for me to talk to her about what was going on in our relationship. With my supervisor's help, I recognized that our dynamic had become this: she was the damsel-in-distress, and I was the Rescuer—and I was increasingly angry with her for not valuing my time. We needed a new, authentic way of relating. And the first corrective action that we needed was going back to our contract and starting to work in a way that respected boundaries.

'It's interesting that you use the word break-up,' I said. 'Tell me what you're imagining right now?'

'Oh, you know already,' she didn't miss a beat, 'my abandonment issues or whatever. I'm now so used to meeting you every week, it's become an anchor for me— and I've been making progress too. But there is so much that I'm dealing with right now. Over the holidays, I got a call from the big boss, and . . .'

'I'm sorry to interrupt you again, Komal,' I cut in. '*Abandonment issues or whatever?* I wonder what is going on for you?'

'Yash,' she was practically pouting now, 'why are you being like this? Now I feel like you're my boss, not just the boyfriend! So formal . . . why can't we just talk like we always do?'

'Komal, can I share with you what I see when we "always talk"?' I could see she was taken aback at my changed response to her today. I was still being pulled in by her tangents but was inviting her back into her feelings. But after a moment, she nodded.

'I have been wondering,' I went on, 'if always talking about some or the other current problem might be protecting you from dealing with issues that are painful—what might you be avoiding?'

Komal took a deep breath and sighed, 'I don't think there's a mystery here. I told you when I first met you that I have this underlying, constant fear that I'm going to end up alone, which I've been trying to get rid of from day one. Almost everything that I talk to you about stems from that.'

I nodded thoughtfully. In my supervision session, I had processed my own way of being with Komal—overly tolerant, making exceptions, and allowing boundary violations. I had justified it with the fact that she was going through difficult times, and additionally, that she had become a long-standing client. I had felt obligated to make the exceptions—extra sessions, longer sessions, and unpaid-for 'catch ups' during her times of crisis. I had been seeing my actions as 'supportive'. With my supervisor's help, I had been able to see that the difficult times never stopped, and that supporting people also included appropriately challenging them. I needed to hold boundaries and confront her, and not just accommodate her needs. If I didn't, it was likely that the tension would escalate into a game—over time, I would get fed up and find a way to terminate our work, and then I would have unconsciously colluded with her in reinforcing her story: that she would be rejected and would end up all alone.

'I remember that, Komal,' I said gently. 'And do you also remember what you wanted for yourself?'

'We discuss a lot of things. I do remember, of course . . . it was . . .' She looked like a sulky teenager who was resenting being given a surprise quiz. She racked her brain and then her expression turned beseeching. 'You'll have to help me out here, Yash. What was it?'

I couldn't help but smile because of the irony. 'You said, Komal, that ultimately you want to become more self-reliant.'

The irony didn't escape her either. She shrugged her shoulders and gave me a sheepish grin. I was genuinely fond of her and was glad that she seemed okay with slowing down right now.

'What is going on for you right now, Komal?' I asked, observing that she had become reflective.

She stayed in the silence for a while, looking down at her hands as she thought about it. 'You know,' she finally said, 'one of the most helpful things over the last year has been that I have *reduced* my reliance on so many external things— things I've just been addicted to for years, whether it's been relationships or work or sugar or shopping or Instagram or

Netflix. I really have begun to spend more time by myself, thinking about my patterns, and what I really want.'

'Right,' I said. A thought hit me, and I remembered my resolve to surface things more boldly with her. I ventured, 'I'm wondering—is there something you're addicted to in our relationship?'

Her eyes widened as if to argue, but then she froze. It looked like the dawn of a new recognition. 'Whoa,' she breathed, '*maybe*. I definitely feel like I depend on our time together. And it's distressing to me when you don't respond or when you interrupt me when I am talking in a flow. I really do worry sometimes that maybe you will not want to see me anymore.'

'Would you share more about how you depend on our time together?' I wondered about her fantasy of how she saw our work. 'What would you say feels like an addiction?'

She went into deep thought and then finally, murmured, 'It's something to look forward to. It feels good in the moment, keeps me busy, keeps me going.' She looked at me. 'But . . .'

'But?' I encouraged her to go on.

'I am not really sure how it is helping me. I usually just unload stuff onto you and experience some relief,' she shrugged. 'At least there's no harmful side effect here.'

'So, you see no harmful side effect?'

She looked puzzled, 'I have been thinking lately. The more I complain, the more things there seem to be to complain about.'

'Wonderful awareness. It *is* like an addiction. Complaining distracts you from pain. The more you complain, the more you need to. So, do you see the harm in avoiding dealing with pain that is much deeper? That feels unbearable perhaps?'

She bit her lip and nodded. And then said, slowly, 'In the last eight years, I've had a string of relationships. Each time I think "this is the one", and I lose myself in it, investing so deeply and passionately—and then something happens, things blow up, and eventually, they end up walking away. It's . . . too painful and scary. What if I never find the one?'

She became quiet and I noted that this wasn't the usual rushed, rambling energy that she brought in.

'You are really scared of ending up alone,' I said emphatically.

'I am.'

'So, you invest very deeply and passionately, but things blow up.'

'Yes. I become clingy and desperate. Others get fed up with me.'

'Is that what you think might happen between us too?' I asked gently. 'Go back to the moment I asked you about what you meant when you thought I was "breaking up" with you? What would that really mean to you?'

She took a deep breath.

And then, we began to really talk.

Our relationship was finally moving to a more authentic level, and we were starting to address issues that had been avoided and skirted around. She expressed her fear and how painful it would be to lose my support. I heard her, reassured her of my commitment, and then shared with her how I felt taken for granted by her and consequently, drained in the relationship. She received what I said with grace and even gratitude. We were letting each other into our inner worlds and re-contracted as to how we would work together as we went forward.

I recognized this refreshing of our relationship as a key benefit of long-term work with a client. The next phase in therapy would likely be far deeper and more beneficial for her. Our realization that therapy had become an addictive crutch for her was an important step towards changing how we were with each other. And I looked forward to discovering where we might go from here.

Acknowledgements

The two of us began writing these stories as an experiment last year, driven by a desire to demystify psychotherapy. We had no clue where it would lead us, but we enjoyed the process and decided to trust in the universe. Over the months, our collection began to develop into an actual manuscript.

Luckily, our book proposal landed on the desk of one editor passionate about the subject of mental health; she was so enthused by the idea and the sample stories that we experienced renewed enthusiasm in the possibility of this book. For enabling this book to see the light of day and for all the work done on shaping it, we thank you, Shreya Punj.

Tarini, who took the project over and got the book into its final form, was a delightful editorial partner and instrumental in creating the go-to-market plan. Thank you, Tarini, for your belief in this book's potential!

Gunjan, thank you for helping us get to a cover design we absolutely love. And Shaoni, for your painstaking and thorough copy editing.

To the marketing and sales teams, many thanks to you for your role in getting this book to the right places.

To two senior practitioners who guided us on the process—Annie Rogers and Suriyaprakash—we'd like to say a special thanks, and let you know that your encouragement on the stories that we shared with you for supervision made a huge impact on our confidence around this book. And to Meghna Singhee and Sanjay Deshpande, friends who believed so wholeheartedly in our work.

To our families—thank you for letting us be ourselves and giving us the space we needed to write and rewrite and edit for months on end.

And last but not least, to our clients—for letting us be part of the wonderful journey of exploring your inner worlds.